CALDERÓN
DE LA BARCA

Four Great Plays
of the Golden Age

Smith and Kraus *Books for Actors*
GREAT TRANSLATIONS FOR ACTORS SERIES

Aeschylus: The Complete Plays Vol. I Tr. Carl R. Mueller and Hugh Denard *The Oresteia Triology: Agamemnon, Libation Bearers, and Eumenides*

Aeschylus: The Complete Plays Vol. II Tr. Carl R. Mueller and Hugh Denard *Persians, Seven Against Thebes, Suppliants, and Promêtheus Bound*

Chekhov's Early Plays Tr. Carol Rocamora *Platonov, Ivanov, and The Wood Demon*

Chekhov Volume I: Four Plays Tr. Carol Rocamora *The Seagull, Uncle Vanya, The Three Sisters, and The Cherry Orchard*

Chekhov's Vaudevilles Tr. Carol Rocamora *On the High Road, On the Harmful Effects of Tobacco, Swan Song, The Bear, The Proposal, Tatyana Repina, The Tragedian in Spite of Himself, The Wedding, The Jubilee, The Night Before the Trial, and In Moscow (A Moscow Hamlet)*

Euripides: The Complete Plays Vol. I Tr. Carl R. Mueller *Alkêstis, Mêdeia, Children of Heraklês, Hippolytos*

Euripides: The Complete Plays Vol. II Tr. Carl R. Mueller *Andromachê, Hêkabê, Suppliant Women, Êlektra, The Madness of Heraklês*

Euripides: The Complete Plays Vol. III Tr. Carl R. Mueller *Trojan Women, Iphigeneia in Tauris, Ion, Helen, Cyclops*

Euripides: The Complete Plays Vol. IV Tr. Carl R. Mueller *Phoenician Women, Orestês, Bakkhai, Iphigeneia in Aulis, Rhesos*

Eduardo de Filipo: Four Plays Tr. Maria Tucci *Filumena — A Marriage Italian Style (Filumena Marturano), Christmas in Naples (Natale in Casa Cupiello), Those Damned Ghosts (Questi Fantasmi), and Naples Gets Rich (Napoli Milionaria)*

Faust Part I Johann Wolfgang von Goethe, Tr. Carl R. Mueller

Faust Parts I and II Johann Wolfgang von Goethe, Tr. Carl R. Mueller

The Villeggiatura Trilogy Carlo Goldoni, Tr. Robert Cornthwaite *Crazes, Adventures, and Returns*

Vaclav Havel: The Short Plays Tr. Rocamora and Rychetsky

Henrik Ibsen: Emperor and Galilean Tr. Brian Johnston

Henrik Ibsen: Four Major Plays Vol. I Tr. Rick Davis & Brian Johnston *A Doll House, Ghosts, An Enemy of the People, and Hedda Gabler*

Henrik Ibsen: Four Plays Vol. II Tr. Brian Johnston *Pillars of Society, The Wild Duck, Rosmersholm, and The Master Builder*

Henrik Ibsen: Four Plays Vol. III Tr. Brian Johnston *The Lady of the Sea, Little Eyolf, John Gabriel Borkman, and When We Dead Awaken*

Heinrich von Kleist: Three Major Plays Tr. Carl R. Mueller *The Prince of Homburg, The Broken Jug, and Amphitryon*

Peirre de Marivaux: Three Plays Tr. Stephen Wadsworth *Changes of the Heart (The Double Inconstancy), The Game of Love and Chance, and The Triumph of Love*

Boulevard Comedies Molière, Becque, Feydeau, Tr. Charles Marowitz *Georges Feydeau's Stark Naked, Henry Becque's La Parisienne, and Quack, based on Molière's The Physician in Spite of Himself*

Luigi Pirandello: Three Major Plays Tr. Carl R. Mueller *Right You Are (If You Think You Are), Six Characters in Search of an Author, and Henry IV*

Felipe Santander: Three Full-Length Plays Tr. Lynn Alvarez *The Agronomist, The Unwritten Law, and Mexico, U.S.A.*

Arthur Schnitzler: Four Major Plays Tr. Carl R. Mueller *La Ronde (Reigen), Anatol, The Green Cockatoo (Der Grüne Kakadu), and Flirtation (Liebelei)*

Sophokles: The Complete Plays Tr. Carl R. Mueller

August Strindberg: Five Major Plays Tr. Carl R. Mueller *The Father, Miss Julie, The Stronger, A Dream Play, and The Ghost Sonata*

August Strindberg: Five Major Plays Volume II Tr. Carl R. Mueller *Playing with Fire, Creditors, The Dance of Death Part I, The Dance of Death Part II, and Storm*

Frank Wedekind: Four Major Plays Tr. Carl R. Mueller *Spring's Awakening: A Children's Tragedy, Lulu, The Tenor: A Farce in One Act, and The Marquis of Keith*

Frank Wedekind: Four Major Plays Volume II Tr. Carl R. Mueller *Earth Spirit, Pandora's Box, Death and Devil, and The Solar Spectrum*

If you require pre-publication information about upcoming Smith and Kraus books, e-mail us at publicity@smithandkraus.com or send your name and address to Smith and Kraus Catalogue, P.O. Box 127, Lyme, NH 03768. To order books call us at (888) 282-2881 or visit smithandkraus.com.

CALDERÓN
DE LA BARCA

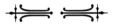

Four Great Plays
of the Golden Age

translated by Rick Davis

Great Translations for Actors

SMITH AND KRAUS, INC.
Hanover, New Hampshire

A Smith and Kraus Book

Hanover, New Hampshire 03755

smithandkraus.com

Cover photo: Nate Jedrzejewski as Muley in *The Constant Prince.*
Unseam'd Shakespeare Company, Pittsburgh, PA, 2007. Directed by Rick Davis.
Scenery and Lighting by Gordon R. Phetteplace. Costumes by Marissa Miskanin. Photo by Rick Davis.

First Edition: November 2008

9 8 7 6 5 4 3 2 1

ISBN-13 978-1-57525-596-5 / ISBN-10 1-57525-596-0

Library of Congress Control Number: 2008939883

CONTENTS

ACKNOWLEDGMENTS

Many people must share credit for this volume's existence. First, and indispensably, my early Spanish teachers: Marta Gonzalez, Rosa Oliveras, Luis Ramírez, Mrs. Myers (whose first name I never learned), Randi Brye. At Lawrence University, Professors John Alfieri and Hugo Martinez-Serra (Spanish); Fred Gaines and Richard France (Theater); Bertrand Goldgar, Mark Dintenfass and Herbert Tjossem (English). At the Yale School of Drama, Leon Katz, Michael Cadden, Stanley Kauffmann and Richard Gilman, librarian Pam Jordan, and much later, Mark Bly, Jim Leverett, and Gordon Rogoff. A special thanks to Prof. Marion Peter Holt, emeritus of CUNY and distinguished translator, who read large portions of this work as a member of my Yale doctoral committee and has been a source of encouragement and advice since then.

The ambitious young professionals of the Bowman Ensemble in Baltimore got me started by commissioning and producing *The Phantom Lady*. My students at George Mason University made possible *The Great Theater of the World*, and I also benefited from a subsequent production at Belhaven College, directed by Hector Ramírez of Madrid. *The Constant Prince* first saw the stage thanks to the vision of Laura Smiley and her Unseam'd Shakespeare Company in Pittsburgh, including an old friend and talented designer, Gordon Phetteplace, who made it happen. The genesis of *Life Is a Dream* was a commission from Voice and Vision Theater in New York in the summer of 2003 to create a "literal" translation on which the company based an original, free adaptation by Jean Wagner and Wendy Weckwerth. I am grateful to Jean and Wendy for the initial excuse (and support) to tackle the play, and for their gracious permission to go forward with a completed translation of my own after Rachel Katz Carey of Seattle, directing a production for the University of Minnesota at Duluth, requested me to do so. Without all three of them (and their respective institutional partners) this text would never have seen the light of day. It was a joy to collaborate with Rachel and her talented colleagues and student-artists in rehearsal, and they helped shape the text profoundly.

My colleagues at George Mason University, especially Provost Peter Stearns and Dean Bill Reeder of the College of Visual and Performing Arts, have been supportive and even indulgent of this effort. And to my wife Julie Thompson, constant collaborator in all things, the largest debt and deepest thanks.

INTRODUCTION

All the Universe a Stage:
Calderón de la Barca and the Modern World

Calderón de la Barca, by most accounts the greatest playwright of a great age—the luminous *Siglo de oro,* or Spanish Golden Age, which embraces Cervantes, Lope de Vega, and Tirso de Molina among others—has remained largely a subject of specialized interest in the United States. Despite his soaring language, his profound inquiry into the nature of things, and his comic gifts, all of which place his greatest work on a level with Shakespeare, Calderón has not fully entered the consciousness of the American theater or academy, to the impoverishment of both.

Here is a playwright whose voice ranges effortlessly from matters of the highest seriousness to situations of low comedy; whose subjects include statecraft, theology, warfare, illusion, and his persistent trio of obsessions: love, honor, and power. His long life (1600–1681) and large output (some estimates run to two hundred works, of which one hundred and twenty are full-length plays) allowed him to explore a vast terrain of the human condition in multiple genres.[1] Yet only one of his plays, *Life Is a Dream,* is widely anthologized, studied, and produced by American college theater departments and professional companies.

There are many reasons for this invisibility, of course, from theatrical economics to the way in which we teach drama and cultivate artistic leadership in the United States. A major playwright's place in the general theatrical consciousness seldom rests so squarely on the shoulders of one play as Calderón's does on *Life Is a Dream.* Rather, an impression of greatness builds up through multiple exposures to a satisfying body of work. We value Shakespeare more highly because we know him as the genre-spanning author of *King Lear* and *Twelfth Night,* of *Richard II* and *The Tempest.* Ibsen's stature grows when we acknowledge *Brand* and *Peer Gynt* along with *Hedda Gabler* and *The Master Builder* (not to mention *Love's Comedy*). Our sense of Brecht's artistry must

1

include the voices represented by *The Measures Taken, Threepenny Opera,* and *The Caucasian Chalk Circle.*

Duality and Greatness

One possible marker of greatness in an author is the ability to embrace duality. Sometimes that duality finds form as dialectic, in the Ibsenian/Hegelian mode (consider the opposition of the pagan and Christian worlds in plays such as *A Doll House, Ghosts,* and *Hedda Gabler*),[2] or in a Shavian argument built on relentless antitheses (unbridled militaristic capitalism vs. romantic altruism in *Major Barbara,* the paradoxical visions of heaven and hell in *Man and Superman*), or as a conversation within a single author between genres, the pattern for which is set by the Homeric epics. An artist who sees the world through both "Iliadic" and "Odyssean" eyes—whose imagination includes the tragic and the comic—arguably demonstrates the capability to contain more complexity, reveal more paradox, and (in the best instances) give voice to a broader range of human experience, whether in a single work or, more to the present point, throughout an *oeuvre.*[3]

Duality was, of course, part of the intellectual and cultural landscape in which Calderón found himself. The complex racial and religious history of the Iberian peninsula—more diverse than the majority of Europe, and either significantly more or spectacularly less tolerant of this diversity than elsewhere, depending on the moment—encouraged thinkers and artists (and rulers) to hold both sides of a duality constantly before them. At the turn of the seventeenth century another duality emerged in the widening distance between national ambition and accomplishment, as historian J. H. Elliott notes, describing the period of Calderón's youth:

> [Castilian society was] based on paradox and contrast. The contrasts were everywhere: Moorish and Christian; devoutness and hypocrisy; fervent professions of faith and exceptional laxity of manners; vast wealth and abject poverty. There was no moderation here, no sense of proportion.[4]

In the yawning gaps between these opposites Calderón finds not only material for his craft but also, I would suggest, an entire habit of mind. His embrace of duality, the enormous variety and energy of his work, and the humane understanding that he extends to all levels of society are conditioned by the radically paradoxical world in which he finds himself. Like his immediate literary ancestors Cervantes and Lope de Vega, his response as an artist is to meet that world in full—a response that takes many forms and speaks in many voices throughout a career that spans six decades.

Calderón's body of work runs the genre gamut of the Golden Age, a list that conjures images of Polonius advertising the talents of the traveling players: the cape-and-sword play, the philosophical drama, the religious play, the honor play, the honor-and-jealousy play, the historical play, the sacramental one-act play, the palace play, the novelesque play, the mythological drama, the zarzuela.[5] To most people in the American theater and academy, however, Calderón remains a one-trick pony, though that one trick—*Life Is a Dream*—is sublime.

If Calderón is to emerge here as a writer of more than passing interest (and of more than one play), a case will have to be made both for the range and substance of his interests and the theatrical viability of a larger number of his plays. The four plays in this volume, which span a wide range of his available tonalities, genres, and themes, and are offered here in production-tested new translations, should help make the case for this great writer both on the stage and in the study.

Calderón in the World Today

Here is a challenging question about Calderón that deserves to be asked regarding any classic body of work: If we are indeed able to see him more often on our stages, will we be adding any value to the world beyond the worthy exercise of keeping a classic author alive? In the spirit of Eric Bentley's deliciously argumentative essay "The Universality of the Comedia," I have tried to claim that Calderón's stage is all the universe, and that his greatest works should find a ready audience on stages in the twenty-first century. Bentley addresses the most frequently asserted objections to a broad acceptance of the Comedia: its location in an exotic place and time, and its specifically Catholic background:

> It is always a matter of equivalences. A great deal changes, and it is the business of historians to say what, but the same sentiment endures, though attached later to another object. Unless things—within us as well as without—were to be turned quite topsy-turvy, there would always be equivalences between one historical situation and another. One does not need to be a Catholic to enter into a great Catholic poem. One only needs to be able to enter into the sentiment of faith. The Jewish faith would do, as would the Moslem or the Hindu. One does not even need to pos-

sess faith in any of these theologies. One only need be able, in Coleridge's phrase, to suspend disbelief, to enter, emotionally and for the moment, into the believing attitude.[6]

Perhaps Bentley's "equivalences" are not so hard to find after all. Writing in 1991, Michael McGaha draws some suggestive parallels—which more than a decade's passage has, if anything, intensified—between Spain's Golden Age and our own (so far unnamed) era:

> Like the Spaniards of the seventeenth century, we live among the ruins of vanishing or vanished empires. We have experienced the bitterness of high ideals gone sour, crushed hopes, economic chaos, pointless and unpopular wars, and government by cynical, self-serving bureaucrats. We are living through a crisis in values, unable any longer to live by our fathers' creed, and uncertain of what to teach our children. Our age is marked by a world-weary *desengaño* [disillusionment] just as Lope's was.[7]

Finally, of course, a body of work from the past will speak to the audience of the future if and only if it meets the essential test of universality. Beyond the "suspension of disbelief," beyond the compelling sociopolitical resonances that connect the two eras, Calderón offers us what great drama always does: a clarifying lens through which to view the human spirit. We come away from a successful encounter with our repertoire of askable questions expanded, our sense of possibility enhanced, our perceptions sharpened, our being enlarged. When that transaction between the work of art and the audience occurs, the test of universality has been more than met. The possibility alone makes the journey worth attempting.

Assessing Calderón's Range

The title of this essay makes certain claims for Calderón's range of reference, and the plays in this volume do indeed provide a sense of his breadth of style and theme. In *The Phantom Lady* his subject is romance, set against a social backdrop of honor and *desengaño*. In *The Constant Prince*, he takes up the honor question again—and its corollary, constancy—in political and theological terms, amid a highly charged setting of religious warfare. *Life Is a Dream* sets honor, metaphysics, power, and romance before us in a profound journey into the nature of human consciousness. And in *The Great Theater of the World*, he takes on perhaps the largest subject of all, albeit in a parable form that is deliberately simple and accessible, and full of delicious metatheatricality: the proper role for humankind in the play of life.

An Aside about Honor

The Spanish honor code, rooted in a system of racial and social classification by which the standing of one's family depended in part on *limpieza de sangre*, or purity of blood, was designed to protect the stratified Castilian society from "pollution" by Moorish, Jewish, or foreign influences.[8] A family's honor, therefore, depended on guarding the chastity of women with a fanaticism that could lead to tragic consequences. Yet this very concept was known to be at least somewhat illusory—Spanish "blood" had for so many centuries been a composite entity that it was impossible to guarantee or even trace the kind of "purity" that was defended with such ferocity by the code's mandates. Honor could also consist in reputation: one's honor was compromised if someone else *perceived* a blemish. The restoration of honor all too frequently involved fatalities, either through duels or through less public means, especially when reputation was at stake.

A code that so clearly insists on unverifiable external valuations of internal qualities, and whose enforcement is both individualistic and absolute, cannot ultimately be sustained, though its exterior form can linger much longer than its actual practice. Thus the honor code itself came to be a subtle source of *engaño* in society, an illusion of an illusion, making it an irresistible subject for drama. A full discussion of honor in Calderón or the Golden Age is beyond the scope of this volume, but it is important to note that the code informs the action of three of the plays in this volume in different ways: *Life Is a Dream, The Constant Prince,* and *The Phantom Lady.*[9]

Life Is a Dream: or, a *Desengaño* Primer

Nearly equal in importance to honor as a governing trope for Spanish life and letters of the period, *desengaño* emerged as a powerful theme in Spanish culture of the seventeenth century as the nation saw its quest for world empire coupled with peace and prosperity at home begin to slip away. Historians associate the term with the period beginning in the 1590s, after a series of reverses (the defeat of the Armada, the death of Philip II, an outbreak of plague, unsuccessful wars in the Netherlands, loss of income from the Americas) began to erode the previous century's sense of confidence. J. H. Elliott sees the erosion exemplified in Spain's most characteristic work of literature:

> In was in this atmosphere of *desengaño*, of national disillusionment, that Cervantes wrote his Don Quixote, of which the first part appeared in 1605 and the second in 1614. Here, among many other parables, was the parable of a nation which had set out on its crusade only to learn that it was tilting at windmills. In the end was the *desengaño*, for ultimately the reality would always break in on the illusion. The events of the 1590s had suddenly brought home to more thoughtful Castilians the harsh truth about their native land—its poverty in the midst of riches, its power that had shown itself impotent.[10]

Don Quixote and *Life Is a Dream's* central figure, Segismundo, experience two distinct kinds of *desengaño*, illustrating different applications of the concept. If Quixote stands, in part, for Castilian Spain tilting at windmills, his disillusionment is a sobering, even shattering recognition that the country's long pursuit of empire has been, at last, an empty exercise.[11] The prescription, if any, is to try to avoid illusions in the future, to act on one's sense of the real, whether as a person or a nation.

Segismundo's series of *engaños* and *desengaños* at the hands of his manipulative father, King Basilio, leads to a different conclusion. Segismundo oscillates so violently between realities that he comes to understand the impossibility of distinguishing between dreams (or illusions) and wakefulness (or *desengaño*), as his most famous speech—his central speech of recognition—makes clear:

> . . .
> The king dreams that he is king, and lives
> With this illusion, commanding,
> Governing, disposing.
> And all the loud applause that he receives
> Is merely lent to him, written on the wind,
> And death transforms it soon enough
> To ashes—a powerful misfortune!
> Who would want to reign,
> Seeing that one has to wake up
> To the dream of death!

The rich man dreams his riches,
That only offer him more cares;
The poor man dreams he suffers
His misery and poverty;
He dreams—the one who is beginning to thrive,
He dreams—the one who toils and tries,
He dreams—the one who injures and offends;
And finally, in this world,
Everyone dreams the thing they are,
Though no one understands this.

I dream that I am here
Weighed down and shackled by these chains,
And I dreamed that in another state,
I saw myself much happier.
What is life? A frenzy.
What is life? An illusion,
A shadow, a fiction.
The greatest good is smaller than it seems,
Since all life is a dream,
And even dreams themselves are only dreams.

The conclusion that Segismundo draws, of course, is not one of paralysis or despair. Instead he finally wins through to an acceptance of his tutor Clotaldo's admonition that "even in dreams, you shouldn't forget to do what's right." Here *desengaño* has an uplifting effect. In losing his illusions, Segismundo gains the vision necessary to become King; his disillusionment is prelude to a higher order of civil life in the world of the play. It is not too great a leap to connect Calderón's construction of Segismundo's *anagnorisis*, his recognition of the necessity for positive ethical action, to Elliott's diagnosis of the national *desengaño* above.

Indeed the whole of *Dream* operates by means of layers upon layers of *desengaño*. Rosaura's disillusionment in love precedes, in fact incites, the opening action of the play. Her masculine disguise, donned in pursuit of honor lost, is another illusion, which will in turn force her father, Clotaldo, into a series of illusions, recognitions, and disillusionments. King Basilio—that somewhat more long-winded heir to Prospero—is consumed with an illusion that his wisdom can triumph over what is written in the book of fate; his defeat and disillusionment, so complete at the end of the play, can be read as a cautionary tale of the limits of human agency.

In a cape-and-sword comedy, a lighter burden attaches to the principle of *desengaño*. And yet the action of comedy can serve to suggest the same ethical dilemmas as the more serious philosophical drama, even though the stakes may be more personal. "Great reckonings in little rooms" have resonance beyond the household walls, and a marriage enabled, a family reconciled, or a fatal duel prevented stands figuratively for much larger values: the restoration of civic polity and the survival of the species.

Typically in comedy the field of vision is somewhat narrow, often focusing on the "little rooms" of the domestic scene, and that is the case in *The Phantom Lady*, composed in 1629, during Calderón's extraordinary first decade on the scene.

The deception and undeception take place for the most part in two nearby rooms of a single house, linked (probably: the critical literature is divided on this point, and the text is ambiguous) by a passageway that ends in a secret doorway, now disguised as a wall of glass panels. The imaginative space occupied by the "deceived" characters is more expansive, however, since at times they do not know, literally or metaphorically, where they are.

Yet tragedy seems to lurk in the shadows in a world where a severe code of honor, enforced to the letter, might easily be fatal—as indeed it is in other Calderonian works such as *Secret Vengeance for Secret Insult*. In fact the romantic hero of the play, Don Manuel, working through his options in a lengthy aside typical of the seventeenth century's "speech of justification," explicitly invokes the paradigmatic situation of the tragic hero—"every choice I make's a bad one"—as he resolves to stand his ground in defense of the no-longer-phantom lady at his side:

> . . .
> If I try to set her free
> And defend her with my blood,
> Letting my sword proclaim her innocence,
> Then I'll be doubly in the wrong,
> Since that's as much to say that I'm a traitor,
> That I've offended the whole house,
> And broken the code of hospitality.
> And if I prove my innocence
> By swearing out her guilt,
> That would be to say that she's at fault,
> And my honor won't allow that outcome.

Well, then, what should I do?
I make myself a traitor by defending her,
And I am a villain if I don't.
If I look out for her, I'm a faithless guest,
And I'd be less than human if I turned
Her over to her brother. In doing that,
I'd be ungrateful for a very noble love.
Well, every choice I make's a bad one—
So I might as well die fighting.

Apparently, catastrophe is at hand. Since this is finally a comedy, however, in a delightful subversion of the honor code's lethality, enforcing it actually serves to bring about the desired marriage, as Don Manuel's adversary returns to command the very union that the "phantom" lovers desire:

This lady is my sister; you must not take her
From my sight unless she becomes your wife.
If you agree, her hand is yours;
Take her away, and if you like, come back
To finish up this other business.

So: the phantom lady is revealed, family honor is satisfied, anger and fear are converted to joy and confidence. Finally all illusions yield to the power of *desengaño*. In *The Phantom Lady*, the principal illusion is created to bypass or subvert a key provision of the honor code; and since it is a comedy, both tonally and structurally, *desengaño* here results in the restoration of threatened honor and a round of weddings. But it is a close call. Like many of the greatest comedies, *The Phantom Lady* combines the Shakespearean imperative that "journeys end in lovers meeting" with a strong sense that death, the ultimate "journey's end," awaits one human misstep to stake its claim.

The Constant Prince: Mirror for a Troubled Time

El príncipe constante (The Constant Prince), also written in 1629, ranks as one of the greatest of the Golden Age's religious plays, and yet that label feels too restrictive to contain a play of historical heft, philosophical distinction, and above all poetic passion. Goethe is said to have remarked that "If poetry were to be lost from the world, this play alone could resurrect it once again." [12] Modern theater history has canonized Ryszard Cieslak's performance in

Grotowski's adaptation and production of the play, which originated in Poland in the mid 1960s and served as America's introduction to the Polish Laboratory Theatre in 1969, but the play has had very few productions on any level in the American theater.

The Battleground

Audiences of the twenty-first century may find resonance in the play's portrayal of the conflict between absolute religious faith and absolute political power set amid a fifteenth-century battleground between Islam and Christianity in which both sides are accorded dignity, respect, and courtly honor. The play is loosely based on the history of Portugal's disastrous attempt to take Tangier in Northern Africa in 1437, during the reign of Portugal's King Duarte I.[13]

Islamic and Christian forces had been engaged in a centuries-long struggle for the Iberian peninsula and parts of North Africa, and though enmities were profound, so was knowledge of each other's culture, politics, and religion. Muslims, Christians, and Jews did business, shared governance to a limited extent, and, for hundreds of years, avoided systematic forced conversions or expulsions (though those severe measures would come).

If the term *multiculturalism* had not yet been coined, the concept underwent perhaps its longest sustained test in medieval Spain. And it found its own contemporary expression: *convivencia*, literally "living together," came to describe the network of relationships—legal, economic, social, and religious— by which the rival cultures found it possible to interact with at least a measure of tolerance, especially during the twelfth and thirteenth centuries.[14] As the *reconquista* (reconquest) accelerated in the fourteenth century, Moorish controlled lands were reduced to a relatively narrow strip in the south containing the important cities of Málaga and Granada, which would not fall to Christian forces until 1487 and 1492, respectively.

This is the situation in which the combatants found themselves in 1437: the Christian area of the peninsula under divided control (Portugal and Spain have not yet been united under Ferdinand and Isabella); Moorish Spain reduced in scope but still influential; and both sides seeking religious glory and political advantage on a battleground that had shifted, in part, to Africa.

The surface action of *The Constant Prince* is deceptively simple: a Portuguese army comes to Africa to try to capture the Moorish city of Tangiers and extend Christian control in North Africa. In the course of battle Fernando is at first triumphant, capturing the Moorish general Muley and then releasing him when he discovers that his adversary is bound up in an all-consuming love affair. This generous action bonds the two forever, and Muley will struggle to repay the debt throughout the play.

When Fernando's fortune changes and he is captured by the King of Fez, the ransom for his release is a rich prize: the city of Ceuta, a Portuguese stronghold in Africa won at great expense some twenty years before the action of the play. This ransom is accepted by the dying King Duarte of Portugal, but rejected by Fernando himself, who remains "constant" in his Catholic faith and therefore will sacrifice himself rather than see a Christian city return to Muslim rule. No one—on either side—can quite believe that Fernando's faith will see him through the terrible degradation visited upon him by his captor. All parties to the offered ransom—except the Constant Prince—calibrate their strategies based on "rational" reactions such as aversion to suffering and fear of death.

But Fernando's constancy is beyond reason. His refusal to serve as ransom for Ceuta, and his consequent embrace of martyrdom, form the dramatic climax of the play. In his captivity he wastes away and finally dies, whereupon his ghost serves as inspiration to the Portuguese army that has returned, too late, to free him. The Christian forces win a decisive victory at Fez and reclaim Fernando's corporeal remains, secure in their belief that his spirit has found at last its proper home.

Throughout the action, and even beyond life, Fernando's constancy (of faith, behavior, and action) serves as the governing trope. He resolves his—and the world's—dilemma of conscience by simply (heroically) continuing to do what he said he would do, against all blandishments and counsel from his friends and enemies alike. The play, then, is easy to read as a chauvinistic encomium to the Catholic faith and the inherent rightness of Christian hegemony.

Intersecting with the straight line of the main action, however, are several strands of plot that, when taken together, reveal a more complex design that locates the primary value of the play in the *idea* of constancy itself. Constancy becomes almost a mirror image of honor, which, as we have seen above, is a pervasive theme in the *comedia*. I believe that Calderón locates constancy and honor not solely in Fernando, as commentators have traditionally claimed, but also in Muley, the Moorish general who begins as his mortal enemy and becomes his great and loyal friend, and in a different, more romantic vein in Fénix, the Princess of Fez, beloved of Muley. Examples of *inconstancy* are likewise to be found among both the Christian and Muslim characters.[15]

At first glance it goes against the grain to suggest that the cardinal virtue of the play is not the Catholic faith itself, but a character trait shared by Christians and "infidels" alike. Certainly earlier interpretations have not brought this view forward with confidence. But perhaps our own age has a less monocular perspective on the interplay of the three Abrahamic religions—Judaism, Christianity, and Islam—and certainly their conflicts and collaborations are foregrounded now in a way that seventeenth-century Spain would recognize.

The experiment in tolerance known as *convivencia* and the battles of the *reconquista* still echoed in the art, architecture, and social fabric of Castilian life in Calderón's day. Eight hundred years of Arabic/Islamic and Judaic thought could not be completely erased, although by Calderón's time their presence was certainly diminished by the program of forced conversions and eventual expulsion of Jews and Muslims by a church and state fearful of decline, clinging to notions of honor bound up in purity of blood (*limpieza de sangre*), and contending with internal and external threats to the empire.[16]

Is it possible that Calderón, master of dualities, understood both the declared necessity of these actions along with their inherent injustice and the cultural loss to his nation that they caused? Could the confluence of these unique historical circumstances with Calderón's particular habits of mind create the conditions under which he was able to craft a play of balanced judgments?

The Prince's Islamic adversaries generally appear in a sympathetic light. Initially, the King of Fez treats his royal Portuguese prisoner almost like a courtier, affording him freedom of movement in his luxurious captivity. If, later on, he is willing to imprison, humiliate, and starve Fernando, even forbidding anyone to succor him, he is pursuing a political and military objective through means not without precedent in the annals of conflict, and disturbingly recognizable in contemporary practice. Relentless (constant, even) in his pursuit of gain, nevertheless he does not wish to harm Fernando for harm's sake. And he is willing, even eager, to release him if the ransom terms are met.

Muley, the lovesick general, emerges as both a hero on the battlefield and a lover of high poetic imagination. His sense of honor, debt, and friendship to Fernando leads him—at great personal risk—to devise a means for the Infante to escape at night by ship. (This generous and daring offer is, of course, refused, even though it includes the release of all the Portuguese captives). Muley's paramour, Fénix, speaks the most lyrical, haunting poetry in the play, and in her fatalistic sense of destiny she comes closest to a tragic sensibility. These Moorish characters are every bit the equal of their Christian counterparts in eloquence, capacity to love, and intellectual distinction; and, I would argue (especially in the case of Muley, as we will see below), embody in varying degrees the play's titular value, constancy.

It cannot be accidental that the first use of the term (*ánimo constante*, constant soul) belongs to a Moor, the King of Fez:

> Well, whatever you have to tell me,
> Let me hear. A constant soul
> Can always find an equal place
> For good news and for bad . . .

The King, of course, proves to be truly constant only in the pursuit of his desired conquest, the city of Ceuta. Muley's constancy has two strands: the first is his unwavering love for Fénix, the confession of which binds him to Fernando in friendship, and the second, a direct result of the first, is his pledge to save the Prince even at mortal risk to himself. The imagery that describes Muley's pursuit of his love offers a vivid application of the process of constancy as he wears her resistance away like water falling on stone:

> . . .
> Just as water makes a mark on stone
> By its persistence—not by force,
> But simply falling, always falling, even so
> My tears at last began to work upon
> That stone-hard heart, harder than diamonds.
> I didn't gain the victory by excellence
> Or merit—just my love, my constant love,
> Which softened her resistance in the end.

Muley will persevere in this romance with unflagging constancy, and the play's sense of poetic justice will reward him in the end as the Portuguese Alfonso, in his victorious final disposition of loose ends, commands that Muley and Fénix should be married.

A more rigorous—or at least more physically dangerous—demonstration of Muley's constancy, however, comes as a result of his pledge of loyalty to Fernando in gratitude for being released from capture on the field of battle to pursue his love affair. This promise leads Muley to construct an elaborate plan for Fernando's escape from prison, which he details to him near the end of Act Two:

> . . .
> I'll break your chains;
> You will put to sea with all your fellow captives,
> And sail for home, sure of my safety here,
> Since it will be easy to believe
> You all escaped from prison.

So two great things will have been set free;
My honor and your life.

Muley's plan is ultimately foiled, not by stratagem, but by Fernando's refusal to jeopardize his friend's life to win his freedom. But the plan's conception and near execution reflect Muley's sense of constancy in friendship: note his use of "honor" in the last line above: another point at which constancy and honor face each other in the mirror.

Though Calderón's Catholicism (he would eventually take holy orders) might lead a reader to expect a more strongly biased worldview, one of the surprising and refreshing things about *The Constant Prince*—which is, in the end, a devoutly Catholic play—is its refusal to indulge in shallow stereotyping. Indeed it strikes the ear today as an affirmatively tolerant view of two cultures in mortal conflict, though just as surely written from the point of view of one of the combatant cultures. If the perspective of almost four centuries gains us any vantage point, it may be to look back in wonder at the cultural imagination of a great playwright who ought to be more a prisoner of his time and place than he turns out, happily, to be.

Metatheater Meets Metaphysics: *The Great Theater of the World*

Representing the *auto sacramental* in this volume is *El gran teatro del mundo (The Great Theater of the World),* probably composed about 1648. This is one of Calderón's most famous *autos*, considered along with *La cena del rey Baltasar* (King Belshazzar's Feast) of 1632 to be the finest expression of the form.[17]

The Great Theater of the World offers a metatheatrical allegory of humanity's role in a world where divine agency is visible and articulate. The Author (God) summons the World (in the guise of a sort of stage manager) to create a festival or pageant to celebrate the wonders of creation. The World responds with a plot summary of the three-act play he's planning, amounting to an elaborate if highly condensed retelling of the biblical history of creation and the generations of mankind. The first act, the "Law of Nature," ends with the Flood and the world's recovery, "Which once again reveals its true face, / Its fresh and newborn face, no longer wan and withered." The second act, the "act of the Commandments," features the parting of the Red Sea, Moses receiving the Laws, and ends in a cataclysm:

And then this second act will end
In a terrible eclipse. The Sun will seem
To flicker and almost die. Darkness and smoke.

A final paroxysm. The blue earth staggers.
Latitude and longitude tumble and are lost.
The mountains shake. The walls collapse,
Leaving all the transitory troubles
Of this world in ruins.

The third act will be called the "Law of Grace," but the World doesn't spend much time describing it, perhaps sensing the Author's desire to move the proceedings along. And yet the World is compelled to offer one last vision, of his own inevitable end, and it terrifies him:

To end our revels
The whole great scene and all its apparatus
Will dissolve in one pure flame, one ray of light:
Because light's the kind of theme our Author
Really likes. Wait! What am I saying?
Imagining it, I tremble, I am shaken;
We must delay this scene, this horrible end
So future centuries will never see it!

Finally, mindful of the Author's request for "a simple comedy of human life," the World begins to assemble the cast, costumes, and props necessary for the enactment of the Author's play.

A Casting Call

To create an acting ensemble to represent the panoply of humanity, the Author summons seven individuals. As they do not yet know what parts they are to play, they express a kind of undifferentiated desire for identity: one says:

Author! Here we are, obedient to your will.
We have no soul, no feeling,
No power, life, or reason;
We don't know who we are.

We're all unformed before you.
We are the dust at your feet.
Breathe on this dust and let us act our parts.

Another echoes:

> . . . if we're going to represent
> The world, please tell us who we're playing.
> We won't turn down our roles—because we can't.

The Author, after acknowledging that if it were left up to them, the actors would all choose roles " . . . where power and command / Come into play . . . " casts the players as a King, Beauty, a Rich Man, a Worker, Discretion, a Child, and a Beggar (*el Pobre*, literally the Poor One). The title of the play they will enact is *Do Good, for God Is God,* and the Author informs the cast that those who play their parts well (thus living up to the axiom of the title) will join him at " . . . a great banquet / And there, everyone will be equal" despite the seeming wide disparity in the social standing of their parts. Only the Child will not participate, since his role, the Author tells him, is "to die before you're born" to which the disappointed actor replies, "That won't be hard to memorize."

After some banter (reinforcing the piece's insistently metatheatrical strategy) about the necessity for rehearsal of a play with such high stakes—for example, Beauty asks " . . . how are we supposed to know / Our entrances and exits . . . ?" and the Beggar wonders "What if I go blank, forget my lines?" the Author acknowledges that although a sort of prompter has been provided, " . . . to correct / Whoever strays too far from the script," the human actors have free will to interpret their roles as they see fit. They must, in effect, improvise their lives within the overall mandate to "Do Good, for God is God."

The players don the costumes handed to them by the World and speculate as to how they are to make the best of the roles allotted them; this in turn allows the playwright to examine humanity through different lenses and from vantage points as divergent as the Beggar and the King. They extol their good fortune or lament their state according to their social type and class: the King wonders at the vastness of his empire, Beauty sings beauty's praises, the Rich Man arrogantly assumes that everything in the world is there for his profit and delight, while the Worker complains of the backbreaking labor he must do. In a display of class envy (and demonstrating economic principles with a contemporary ring) the Worker hopes for drought to create scarcity so that he can sell his crops at exorbitant prices and become the richest man in his district:

> . . .
> I'll tell you what: because
> I work and sweat, the people who depend
> On what I grow will have to pay the price

I want to charge. And if it doesn't rain
(When I beg God for drought and famine), then
My granary will make me rich! I'll be
The greediest man for miles hereabouts,
And everyone will need me, I'll grow fat,
And then—what should I do?

The Beggar, who depends on alms to live, offers each character the chance to exercise charity. But one by one, each refuses him. The Worker, again sounding like a certain stripe of contemporary politician, advises him in effect to get a job: " . . . And if you need a meal, here—take this hoe / And earn one for yourself—or dig one up." Finally Discretion, who represents religious devotion and a life of sacrifice, offers the Beggar a bit of bread before fainting (with hunger? with *weltschmerz?*) into the arms of the King.

As *Do Good, For God Is God* comes to an end, the characters return their costumes to the World in a manner consonant with their experience of the just-concluded play. The Beggar is not sorry to leave the world and its pain behind, whatever judgment may await; the King, Beauty, and Rich Man lament the loss of their privileged accoutrements. The Worker goes out in much the same manner as he came in: cantankerously. Discretion reminds the World that she takes her "sacrifices, love, and prayers" with her to the grave and so she cannot leave them behind like so many theatrical props. When the King asks why their departure feels much harsher than their entry into the play, the World offers an image that unites the cradle and the tomb:

Let me tell you why.
When somebody has something welcome
To receive, he holds his hands like this;
When it's something that he'd just as soon avoid,
He throws his hands up just like this;
And it's the same way with the world—
When it's your luck to be born, the cradle
Opens to receive you; and this same cradle,
Turning once again, becomes your tomb.
So the cradle bids you welcome, the tomb says farewell.

Interestingly, this language closely imitates a great speech of Fernando's in Act Three of *The Constant Prince,* as he makes his last attempt to explain his actions to his captor, the King of Fez. If we hear echoes of Shakespeare and prefigurations of Beckett in these metaphors ("we are born astride the grave"), it only serves to enlarge our sense of Calderón's belonging in their company.

In the final movement, the World summons the actors to a new theater, a "theater of truths," where the Author will mete out rewards and punishments as promised. When invitations to a heavenly banquet are extended to the worthy, The Beggar, Discretion, and the King—thanks to the kindness he showed Discretion in her moment of need—are granted immediate ascension, while the Worker and Beauty must pause briefly in Purgatory. The Child, who was never born and so never exercised free will, is consigned to a kind of limbo. The Author tells him:

> Because you did no action in the world,
> So now you receive neither reward nor punishment.
> You'll go into that darkened place, feeling nothing,
> Until finally, in time, you are born into sin.

Only the Rich Man, with his vainglory, ambition, and lack of care for others meets a painful end:

> Oh my God! In fire I fall, dragging my shadow
> So huge and fearsome that it blocks me from myself,
> And hard rocks hem me in on every side,
> Down, down into this dark cave.

The *auto* ends with a celebration, the "Heavenly Banquet" promised by the Author to the actors who play their parts well, and the singing of a hymn ("Tantum ergo") by Thomas Aquinas, whose ideas about natural law and free will exert a strong influence on the entire text.

Notes

1. See Henryk Ziomek, *A History of Spanish Golden Age Drama*, pp. 134–167.
2. For a full treatment of Ibsen's dialectical method and its Hegelian roots, see Brian Johnston, *The Ibsen Cycle*.
3. I am indebted here to ideas about genre formulated by Northrop Frye (in several works), William McCollom *(The Divine Average)* and, especially, Albert Cook *(The Dark Voyage and the Golden Mean)*.
4. J. H. Elliott, *Imperial Spain 1469–1716*, p. 310
5. See Ziomek, *op. cit.*
6. Eric Bentley, "The Universality of the Comedia," in *Hispanic Review* 38 (1970): pp. 153–154.
7. Michael McGaha, "Bridging Cultures," in Louise and Peter Fothergill-Payne, *Prologue to Performance: Spanish Classical Theater Today*, p. 89.
8. Elliott, *op. cit.*, pp. 222–224.
9. For a splendid treatment of the subject, see Edwin Honig, *Calderón and the Seizures of Honor.*
10. Elliott, *op. cit.*, pp. 299–300.
11. The temptation to call it "an impossible dream" is hereby resisted.
12. Quoted in Heinz Gerstinger, *Pedro Calderón de la Barca*, p. 106.
13. See Peter N. Stearns, ed., *The Encyclopedia of World History*, p. 250
14. See Richard Fletcher, *Moorish Spain*. This balanced and invaluable study offers essential background on the cultural matrix out of which the Golden Age emerged, and its relevance to *The Constant Prince* is even more direct.
15. See Leo Spitzer, "The Figure of Fénix in Calderón's *El príncipe constante.*" Reprinted in Bruce Wardropper, ed.: *Critical Essays on the Theatre of Calderón* (New York: NYU Press, 1965) pp. 137–160.
16. The *moriscos*, Muslims who had converted to Christianity, were subject to expulsion from Spain between 1608 and 1615, during Calderón's youth and adolescence. See Elliott, *Imperial Spain*, pp. 305–308.
17. See Ziomek, *op. cit.*, pp. 163–164.

THE PHANTOM LADY

(La dama duende)

 1629

CHARACTERS

DON MANUEL
COSME, A COMIC SERVANT
DOÑA ÁNGELA
ISABEL, A MAID
RODRIGO, A SERVANT
DON LUIS
DON JUAN
DOÑA BEATRIZ
CLARA, A MAIDSERVANT
SERVANTS

PLACE

The scene is Madrid.

Translation, 1992, revised 1997, 2003, and 2007. This translation was commissioned and produced by The Bowman Ensemble, Baltimore, Maryland, in 1992.

ACT ONE

A street. Enter DON MANUEL and COSME, who have been traveling.

MANUEL: We missed it by an hour—Madrid's great festival
    In honor of the Prince's baptism.
COSME: The way things are, an hour late
    Is all you have to be.
    If Pyramus had shown up an hour earlier,
    He wouldn't have found his Thisbe dead.
    And Romeo and Juliet—an hour
    Might have made the difference for them!
    But then of course we wouldn't have
    Those famous plays to enjoy,
    And that would be a shame.
    Now—since we missed the party,
    Let's not be late for our lodging—
    Or we'll have to sleep outside.
    And anyway, I'm dying to see this friend of yours,
    Awaiting you with bed and board
    Like you were some great man—
    Though I'm sure I don't know where
    That notion came from. But who am I to argue,
    When what we need is what he's got?
MANUEL: Listen, Cosme: Don Juan de Toledo
    Is my closest friend. We were at school together,
    And then we laid our books aside and took up arms—
    When the Duke of Feria made me a captain,
    I gave Don Juan my flag to bear.
    When he was wounded in the field,
    I nursed him back to health in my own bed.
    So, next to God, you see, he owes his life to me.
    When Don Juan heard that I was coming to Madrid
    To serve His Majesty, of course he offered me
    His hospitality. And since I didn't want
    To ask everyone I met along the street
    Where to find Don Juan,
    I left our horses and our luggage at the inn,
    Came out to look for him,
    Saw all the people dressed in costume,

Discovered what it's all about,
Wanted to get a look at it,
And that is why, more or less, we're late—
(Enter DOÑA ANGELA and ISABEL, veiled, in long overskirts.)
ANGELA: If you're a gentleman of honor
As your clothes suggest, protect a woman
Who comes to you in need.
Honor and life are at stake—
That gentleman there must not know who I am
And mustn't be allowed to follow me.
In the name of God, I beg you, save a woman
From a terrible misfortune—and maybe some day . . .
Good-bye! Good-bye, or it's all over for me!
(Exeunt the ladies, very quickly.)
COSME: Was that a lady or a tornado?
MANUEL: That was strange!
COSME: What are you going to do?
MANUEL: Can you even ask?
Can a man of my nobility
Do anything but defend the lady?
It seems to me, without a doubt, the man
Must be her husband.
COSME: What will you do?
MANUEL: I'll delay him with some business—
But if that doesn't work, I'll use force.
COSME: If you're looking for business, hold on—I've got an idea.
This letter from a friend—it'll be good for something.
(Enter DON LUIS and RODRIGO, his servant.)
LUIS: I've got to find out who she is,
Primarily because she's going to such trouble
To avoid me.
(COSME approaches and DON MANUEL moves back.)
COSME: Sir, even though it shames me to have to ask,
Could you do me the favor
Of reading the address of this letter for me?
LUIS: I'm not going to waste any spit on you.
COSME: *(Detaining DON LUIS.)* Well, if spit is all you need, I've got
plenty—
I can share some with you.
LUIS: Get out of here!

MANUEL: *(Aside.)* This street's so long and straight, she's still in sight!

COSME: As you live, sir—

LUIS: My patience is at an end. Go away!

　　(HE shoves COSME.)

MANUEL: *(Aside.)* The time has come. Now caution turns to courage.

　　Sir, that man's my servant. What could he have done

　　To deserve this treatment of you?

LUIS: I never respond to questions of that kind;

　　The answer never satisfies. Good day.

MANUEL: If I needed satisfaction from you, sir,

　　You'd better believe I'd get it, despite your arrogance.

　　My question—as to how you were offended—

　　Deserves a much more courteous reply.

　　And since I know the Spanish Court

　　Teaches courtesy to all its subjects,

　　You give it a bad name if a visitor to Madrid

　　Has to remind you of your lessons.

LUIS: Perhaps you'd like a lesson from me instead?

MANUEL: Hold your tongue—let your sword do the talking.

LUIS: Now you're making sense.

　　(THEY draw swords and fight.)

COSME: Who's winning? Can you tell?

RODRIGO: Bring out your sword.

COSME:　　　　　　　　　　　Sorry—she's still a virgin.

　　No one's proposed to her yet,

　　So I can't let her be seen outside.

　　(Enter DOÑA BEATRIZ, holding on to DON JUAN; and

　　CLARA, her servant, along with others.)

JUAN: Let me go, Beatriz!

BEATRIZ:　　　　　　　Don't do it!

JUAN: Look, he's fighting with my brother!

BEATRIZ: For heaven's sake!

JUAN: *(To DON LUIS.)* I'm at your side.

LUIS: Don Juan, desist. Your courage forces me

　　To play the coward. Noble stranger:

　　Though I'd pursue this quarrel by myself,

　　Now that I have help it would be craven to continue.

　　Go your way, sir—my honor keeps me from an unfair fight—

　　Especially with one who's shown

　　Such bravery and spirit. God be with you.

MANUEL: I appreciate your courage and your generosity.
　　　But if, by any chance, some scruple still remains
　　　Between us, you can find me at your pleasure.
LUIS: My best to you, sir.
MANUEL:　　　　　　　And mine to you.
JUAN: What's this I see and hear? Don Manuel!
MANUEL: Don Juan!
JUAN:　　　　　　　I'm frozen stiff—
　　　I don't know what to think!
　　　A brother, and a friend who's like a brother,
　　　In such a quarrel? Until I know the cause,
　　　I won't believe it. And I'll embrace him—
　　　The noble guest our house has been
　　　So anxiously expecting: Don Manuel.
　　　Brother, come here. You've fought as equals,
　　　And from this moment on you'll be fast friends
　　　Because you know each other's valor. Give me your arms!
MANUEL: Before I do, let me praise your bravery
　　　And say that I am at your service, Don Luis.
LUIS: Your friend forever—and I am ashamed
　　　I didn't recognize you: your courage
　　　Should have left no doubt.
MANUEL: Yours has left me with this little souvenir—
　　　A wound across my hand.
LUIS: I wish a thousand times that it were mine instead!
COSME: This battle's turned polite all of a sudden!
JUAN: You're wounded? Come and get it looked at.
　　　Don Luis, stay here with Doña Beatriz
　　　Until her carriage comes, and apologize to her
　　　For my discourtesy. Come, friend, to my house—
　　　We might better call it yours—where we'll take care of you.
MANUEL: But it's nothing.
JUAN:　　　　　　　Come quickly.
MANUEL: *(Aside.)* Too bad my first taste of Madrid's a bloody one!
LUIS: *(Aside.)* Too bad I couldn't find out who that lady was!
COSME: *(Aside.)* Too bad my master always thinks
　　　He has to play Don Quixote—
　　　He got what he deserved this time!
　　　*(Exeunt DON JUAN, DON MANUEL, and COSME. DON LUIS
　　　approaches DOÑA BEATRIZ, who is off to the side.)*

LUIS: The storm is past. And now, madam,
    Let the flowers in your countenance bloom again;
    They lie wilted, like your beauty,
    Under the icy hand of anxiety.
BEATRIZ: Where is Don Juan?
LUIS: He begs your pardon. His obligation
    To a wounded friend called him away.
BEATRIZ: Oh my God! I'm dead! Is it him?
LUIS: No, madam—not Don Juan.
    If my brother had been wounded,
    I would not be standing here myself.
    Don't be upset—why should the two of us
    Feel all the pain and sorrow while he feels none?
    It is unjust. My pain is seeing you
    So stricken by an imaginary hurt,
    All the more painful because it's not real.
BEATRIZ: Don Luis—please know that I am grateful
    For these fine words, assuming that
    They come from the heart, and are really yours.
    But I can't reply to them—
    I don't put much stock in words these days,
    If only because the Court puts too much stock in them.
    There—be thankful for my candor,
    Which you'll find in short supply at Court.
    God be with you.
    (SHE exits with her maid.)
LUIS: And with you, madam.
    I can't do anything right, Rodrigo.
    If I see a graceful woman and try to find
    A chance to meet her, first I am delayed
    By an idiot and then embroiled in a sword fight—
    And I don't know which is worse!
    So then I'm fighting, and my brother comes to help me,
    And sure enough my enemy turns out
    To be his best friend. He leaves me behind
    To mollify his lady, and she gives me
    Nothing but a thousand troubles.
    Just my luck: the veiled lady flees from me,
    An idiot torments me,
    A stranger tries to kill me,

My brother takes him to our house
Where he will be an honored guest,
And this other lady treats me like dirt.
RODRIGO: Of all these troubles, I think I know
What bothers you the most.
LUIS: You have no idea.
RODRIGO: What bothers you the most is—
You're jealous of your brother and beautiful Beatriz.
LUIS: You're out of your mind.
RODRIGO: Well, what is it, then?
LUIS: If I must speak of this—for your ears only—
What bothers me is how careless my brother is being,
Bringing a handsome young man to our house,
Rodrigo, where our lovely sister—
Recently widowed, beautiful, and young—
Lives so secretly that her only visitor
Is Beatriz, her cousin.
RODRIGO: I know she came to Court to try to settle,
In secrecy, some uncollected debts
Her husband left behind. And I know your brother
Has promised to keep her hidden safely here.
But since the rules of the game permit
No mention of her presence, what's the harm
In Don Manuel staying at your brother's house?
For one thing, his apartment opens to the street.
And then his other door, which normally connects
To the rest of the house, has been concealed by
A cabinet of glass—and the workmanship's so good
You'd never guess there'd ever been a door there.
LUIS: Do you see how reassured I am?
You're killing me with all this comfort!
You're telling me that all that stands between
This man and my sister's honor
Are some panes of glass that the first blow will shatter!
(Exeunt.)
DOÑA ANGELA's rooms in DON JUAN's house.
(Enter DOÑA ANGELA and ISABEL.)
ANGELA: Isabel, you'd better give me back
My widow's veil—that awful thing—
Bury me alive again in black,

Since that's what my bad luck seems to demand.

ISABEL: Put it on right now;
    If your brother were to come,
    And be the slightest bit suspicious,
    You wouldn't want to give yourself away
    By being dressed just like the woman
    He met today at Court.

ANGELA: Heaven help me! Here I am,
    Dying inside these walls, where even the Sun
    Can't find me—here, where I might as well be
    A prisoner, since in losing a husband
    I've simply been chained to a pair of brothers—
    And if I veil myself to venture out
    To enjoy the plays that everyone applauds,
    Steely-voiced authority calls it a crime!
    Who ever had such rotten luck, such unfair fate?

ISABEL: Don't be surprised, my Lady.
    Look at yourself—a widow, young, so beautiful,
    So charming, so alive—no wonder your brothers
    Have taken such precautions.
    This situation's ripe for crimes of passion,
    Especially at Court—oh, the young widows I've seen there,
    Trying to look so honest, so holy—
    I cross myself a thousand times for them,
    They're on the prowl for some young gentleman, I swear.
    Let's save this talk for some other time, señora.
    What about that handsome stranger
    Who became your champion today,
    The one who's now the caretaker of your honor?

ANGELA: You read my mind. I'm worried about that,
    But not for my sake—for his.
    After our conversation, when I heard
    The sound of sword fighting, I began to wonder—
    And maybe this was my imagination—
    Whether he had taken my request so seriously
    That he drew his sword on my account.
    I was crazy to implore him in that way,
    But when a woman's as upset as I was then,
    She doesn't stop to look before she leaps.

ISABEL: I don't know if you're the one

Who stirred him up—but after that
Your brother didn't chase after us any more.
ANGELA: Wait a minute—listen.
  (Enter DON LUIS.)
LUIS: Angela!
ANGELA: Brother of mine,
  Here you are all troubled and confused.
  Why? What happened? What's the matter?
LUIS: Everything's the matter! My honor's the matter!
ANGELA: *(Aside.)* Oh my God! He must have recognized me!
LUIS: And in that vein, I feel very strongly
  That certain people here don't hold
  Your honor in a high enough regard.
ANGELA: But—has something happened to disturb you?
LUIS: The worst thing, Angela, is when I come to you
  To ease my mind, I find I'm just as troubled
  As I was before.
ISABEL: *(Aside.)* Another scare?
ANGELA: But, brother, what could I have done to trouble you?
  Think . . .
LUIS: You're the cause—when I look at you . . .
ANGELA: Oh dear!
LUIS: Angela, our brother doesn't seem
  To take much care of you . . .
ANGELA: *(Aside.)* That's true.
LUIS: He only adds more cares
  To those you brought here with you.
  So it was no accident, I guess,
  That I took out my anger with Don Juan
  By fighting with his guest—you see, I wounded him
  (Prophetically enough) in a duel today.
ANGELA: Oh yes? What happened?
LUIS: I walked to the palace today, sister,
  And there I found a little crowd of carriages and men—
  Some friends of mine among them—
  Circled round a lady in a veil,
  All of them quite taken with her wisdom
  And her wit. But from the moment I arrived,
  She didn't say another word,
  Even after someone begged her to explain

Why my arrival should have cast this pall
Of silence over her.
This bothered me, of course.
So I tried to get a better look at her,
To see if I could recognize her.
She wrapped herself more tightly in her veil
And fled the scene. She disappeared.
I decided to give chase.
She ran, looking back to see if I still followed,
And her desire not to be discovered
Redoubled my desire to find her out.
We ran and ran until some man came up—
The servant of our guest, as it turns out—
And asked me if I could read a letter for him.
I told him I was in a hurry, and besides
I suspected he was stopping me on purpose,
Because the lady spoke to him as she ran by.
He wouldn't give up; kept chattering just to keep me there;
I said to him—I don't remember what I said.
Just then, our guest showed up, all soldier-like,
Defending his man. Of course we drew our swords and fought.
That's all there is—it could have been much worse.
ANGELA: Shame on the wicked woman who put you through that!
One of those scheming, plotting creatures—
I'll bet she didn't even know who you were,
In fact I'll bet she ran away
Just so you would chase her. This is why
I've always told you—as I hope you remember—
Not to fall for these nasty little women
Who are only out to get their thrills with men.
LUIS: What have you been doing this afternoon?
ANGELA: I've been here at home,
Entertaining myself by crying.
LUIS: Did our brother come to see you?
ANGELA: He hasn't been here since this morning.
LUIS: I won't tolerate his carelessness!
ANGELA: Well, you'd better let those feelings go—
Remember he's our elder brother,
And we eat from his table.
LUIS: If you can live with it, I guess I'll have to,

Since I'm only worried for your sake.
I'll go see my brother, and I'll even try
To be gracious to our guest.
(Exit DON LUIS.)
ISABEL: Well, my lady, what do you say now?
After that horrible fright you had,
The man who jumped to your defense—
and even took a wound for it—
Is right here as a guest!
ANGELA: Isabel, I suspected it as soon
As I heard about the quarrel,
But I still don't quite believe it.
How often does a man come to Madrid,
And as soon as he arrives
He finds himself confronted by a lady
Begging him to save her life,
Then getting wounded by her brother,
Only to become her other brother's honored guest?
These would be remarkable events,
Wouldn't you say? And even though it's all
Quite possible, I won't believe it until I see it.
ISABEL: Well, if that's truly what you want,
I know how you can get a look at him—
And even more than that, if you've a mind to.
ANGELA: You're crazy. How can I see him
If his room's so far away from mine?
ISABEL: There's a way to go between the rooms—
Now don't be afraid.
ANGELA: No, tell me—
Not so much because I want to see him,
But just because I want to know—
How can this be? I heard you but I don't believe you.
ISABEL: You know your brother had designed
A cabinet of glass to hide
The door between the rooms.
ANGELA: I see where you're going. We can make
A hole and get a look at our guest that way,
Just like folks who are too cheap to buy
A ticket to an outdoor theater.
ISABEL: I have more in mind than just a look.

ANGELA: Speak.

ISABEL: If you insist. Your brother had this cupboard
    Built of glass to conceal the doorway.
    But he made it portable so that he could
    Replace it later on. Anyone can move it easily.
    I should know: as I was fixing up the guest room,
    I leaned a ladder up against the cupboard,
    And wouldn't you know it broke loose?
    Lucky thing it was hung that way—
    Now anyone who wants can come and go
    Just by unlatching it.

ANGELA: Now look Isabel—suppose I want
    To get into that other room,
    So I've opened the latch.
    Couldn't it be opened then
    Just as easily from the other side?

ISABEL: Of course. So what we have to do
    Is fix it with two nails in such a way
    That we're the only ones who can open it.

ANGELA: Tell the servant to let you know
    When and if our gentleman goes out.
    I don't think his wound is grave enough
    To keep him in.

ISABEL: You mean you're going in there?

ANGELA: I have this urge—a foolish one, I know—
    To find out if he's the one who saved my life.
    Because if I have cost him both trouble and blood—
    His wound will satisfy me on that score—
    And if I can find a way to keep it secret,
    I mean to offer him my gratitude.
    Let's go: I'll take a look at this wall of glass,
    And if I can get into his room—
    Without his finding out—I'll pay him back.

ISABEL: This has the makings of a great story.
    But what if he goes and tells it?

ANGELA: He won't do that. He's a gentleman,
    Whose courage, discretion, and charm
    Are all of equal standing.
    Everything he's done, from the first moment we met,
    Has filled my heart with noble feelings.

His bravery in the fight—his gracious style—
His obvious intellect—I wouldn't worry for a minute
That a man with such enormous gifts
Would ever spill my secret.
(*Exeunt.*)

DON MANUEL's room, which includes the cupboard made with shelving into which glass panels have been set; a brazier, etc.

(*Enter DON JUAN, DON MANUEL, and a SERVANT with candles.*)
JUAN: For my sake, won't you please lie down?
MANUEL: The wound's so small, Don Juan, I'd say it looks
    Just like a tiny little lady's ribbon on my hand—
    More an ornament than anything to be concerned about.
JUAN: My luck has really been put to the test.
    I'd never be able to stand the thought
    That you came here as my guest only to be injured,
    And then by my brother's hand, too—
    No matter how blameless he may be.
MANUEL: He's absolutely blameless—and what's more,
    He's quite a gentleman, and to be frank
    I envy his style of swordplay. I look forward
    To being his humble servant and his great friend.
    (*Enter DON LUIS and a SERVANT carrying a tray on which is placed a sword and scabbard.*)
LUIS: I am yours, sir, and to show how much
    Your injury grieves me, I offer you my life.
    And furthermore, here's the guilty instrument—
    I can't keep it. Here it is, sir, the sword that wounded you.
    I lay it at your feet. Take it up,
    And use it to exact whatever vengeance you require.
MANUEL: You're courteous and courageous too: in fact
    You conquer me in both arenas.
    I accept your sword, because as long
    As it is at my side, I'll need
    No further lessons in bravery.
    I'm sure my life is safe from this day forth;
    This sword's the only thing I feared, and now it's mine.
JUAN: Well—Don Luis has taught me a few things
    About how to treat a guest. Now it's my turn

To offer you another gift.

MANUEL: I can never hope to repay all these favors—
As long as you keep trying to top each other
In showing me your courtesy!
(Enter COSME, loaded down with valises and cushions.)

COSME: Two hundred thousand devils,
Set loose from their infernal fires,
Or two hundred thousand dragons,
Or I don't care who does it,
Can run me all around the sky
And leave me torn to pieces—
Just as God, who's got his own good reasons
For saying so, would insist they do—
If I wouldn't rather live like a hermit
In Galicia or a hundred miles from nowhere
In rural Asturias than one more minute
Here in this court.

MANUEL: Control yourself.

COSME: How can I? I'm just one of the characters.

MANUEL: What are you saying?

COSME: I'm saying what I'm saying.
The man who makes friends with his enemy
Is a traitor.

LUIS: Wait wait wait. What enemy?

COSME: A fountain, and especially the water in it.

MANUEL: That's what's bothering you?

COSME: Coming down the street, loaded down
With all your cases and your cushions,
I stumbled up against the drainage ditch
Around this fountain, see, and so I dragged
Everything down with me, as the saying goes,
Into the mud. Who'd want it now? No one I know.

MANUEL: Get out of here—you're drunk.

COSME: If I were drunk, look here, I wouldn't be
So angry at the water. I might have liked it.
I read this book once where a thousand fountains flowed,
And the water could become anything it wanted,
Any shape or substance. So it wouldn't surprise me,
After all, if when I fell into the water
It changed suddenly to wine.

MANUEL: Once he gets started, he generally won't finish
    For a year or so
JUAN: He's in rare form.
LUIS: I'd just like to know how you could read
    That book, when you couldn't read the letter—
    The one you stopped me on the street to ask about?
    Why so shy all of a sudden?
COSME: Because I can read books, you see,
    But, and I'm kind of ashamed to admit it,
    Not letters.
LUIS: That's a good answer.
MANUEL: In God's name, gentlemen, please don't encourage him.
    You'll find out soon enough he's just a fool.
COSME: I've got a lot of jokes,
    And you can have as many as you want.
MANUEL: Since it's not too late yet,
    There's an important visit I'd like to make.
JUAN: I'll expect you soon for supper.
MANUEL: Cosme—open up these bags
    And set my clothing out—
    But first be sure it's nice and clean.
JUAN: If you want to lock your door,
    Here's the key to your room.
    I've got a master key, in case I come home late.
    Those are the only keys—
    And this is the only entrance to your room.
    If you leave your key in the lock,
    They'll come make up your room every day.
    (Exeunt, and COSME remains behind.)
COSME: Come here, my little bag of tricks—
    First I want to spend some time with you,
    So we can see how much we managed to filch
    Along the road. Because you know those wayside inns—
    They're not quite as careful about things there
    As people are at home, where every little item
    Is guarded, counted, inventoried.
    On the road, there's opportunity.
    A fellow can always find work for his hands—
    In someone else's pockets.
    (HE opens a valise and pulls out a purse.)

You've found your true calling, my dear!
You began this day a maiden,
And now look at you—fat and ready to deliver.
I'd count the money, but why waste the time?
I don't have to answer to anyone for it.
I didn't sell a flock of sheep
On orders from my master,
So he won't be wanting an accounting.
Whatever's there, that's what I've got.
There's my master's valise. I ought to open it
Right up and get his clothes set out.
That's what he ordered me to do.
But just because he ordered me,
Does that mean I have to do it right away?
Not at all. I'm a servant;
I don't have to do something
Just because my master wants it done.
I feel a need to make a little
Liquid pilgrimage instead.
Do you want to do that, Cosme?—
Do I!—Well, Cosme, let's go!
Pleasure before business,
And my master will never know!
*(HE exits. DOÑA ANGELA and ISABEL enter by removing
the fasteners from the glass panel.)*
ISABEL: As Rodrigo said, the room is empty.
The guest went out with your brothers.
ANGELA: Would I be doing this otherwise?
ISABEL: You see how easy it is to get in here?
ANGELA: It seemed impossible, Isabel,
But you were right—we had no trouble
Opening the panel, and now we can
Come and go with no one the wiser.
ISABEL: And tell me again—why are we here?
ANGELA: We're in here simply because you told me
That we could get in. Of course,
If it turns out that the gentleman really is
The one who risked his life for me,
Then I'd like to leave some token
Of my gratitude for him.

ISABEL: Your brother really fixed this room up nicely.
　　　Look—there's a sword lying on that desk.
ANGELA: Come here. Did they put my writing-case in here?
ISABEL: That was one of your brother's crazy ideas.
　　　He had me bring in everything the gentleman might need
　　　For writing, not to mention
　　　Something like a thousand books.
ANGELA: There are two valises on the floor.
ISABEL: And they're open. Madam—
　　　Do you want to see what's in them?
ANGELA: Yes, yes. I'm curious, for some reason,
　　　To see what kind of clothing he brought with him.
　　　You know, his jewels, his dressy things.
ISABEL: A soldier won't have brought that kind of stuff along.
　　　(THEY discuss everything they pull out, and toss the items around the room.)
ANGELA: What's this?
ISABEL: A bunch of papers.
ANGELA: Love letters?
ISABEL: No, legal briefs—
　　　They're bundled together—very heavy.
ANGELA: That's right—if they were from a woman,
　　　They would be much lighter.
　　　Let's not waste time on these.
ISABEL: Here's some underwear.
ANGELA:　　　　　　　　　　Does it smell nice?
ISABEL: It smells clean.
ANGELA:　　　　　　　That's the best perfume of all.
ISABEL: These things have three good qualities:
　　　They're white, and soft, and very very fine.
　　　But Madam, look at all these different instruments
　　　Inside this leather bag—what are they for?
ANGELA: Show me. Ah, yes. Here's a tooth-puller.
　　　Here's a pair of tweezers. Oh—and these are curling irons—
　　　One for his hair and another for his moustache.
ISABEL: Item: brush and comb.
　　　Listen, would a farsighted guest
　　　Forget to bring his shoe trees?
ANGELA: Why do you ask?
ISABEL:　　　　　　　'Cause here they are.
ANGELA: Is there more?

ISABEL: Yes, madam.
    Item: a second bundle of papers—
ANGELA: Give them here. These are from a woman,
    And there's more than just letters—A portrait!
    Yes, here it is.
ISABEL: What's so astonishing?
ANGELA: Just look at it—beauty is fascinating,
    Even when it's only painted.
ISABEL: It looks to me as if
    You'd rather not have found it.
ANGELA: What a fool you are!
    All right, no more staring now.
ISABEL: What are you going to do?
ANGELA: I'm going to write him a letter. Take the portrait.
    (SHE begins to write.)
ISABEL: Meanwhile, I'll get a feeling for the servant.
    Here's some money. Just small change,
    Common coins, no royalty here.
    I ought to play a trick on him, like this:
    I'll take this lackey's money
    And replace it with some coals.
    They'll say: "that woman is some kind of devil!"—
    Never thinking that it's November,
    And there's a brazier in the room.
ANGELA: I'm finished writing. Where do you suggest
    That I should leave it so my brother
    Won't see it if he comes in?
ISABEL: There, under the pillowcase.
    That way he can't miss it when he goes to bed,
    And no one else will see it.
ANGELA: That's very good advice.
    Put it there, and let's get all
    These other things cleaned up.
ISABEL: Look out—someone's key is in the lock!
ANGELA: Well, leave everything as it is,
    And let's get out of here. Quickly, Isabel!
ISABEL: Abracadabra!
    (THEY exit through the wall of glass, which remains as it was.
    Enter COSME.)
COSME: Now that I've served myself,

I don't mind serving my master again
At my customary bargain rate.
But—who's been in here going through our things?
In Christ's name, this place looks like the town bazaar,
With all our stuff on sale! Who's here?
My God, there's nobody here,
Or if he is, he isn't talking.
I guess he's not responding
Because he knows I don't much care
For long-winded answers.
Well, whatever the case may be, for good or ill,
If I had to tell the truth I'd have to say
I'm quivering with fear right about now.
But then again—as long as my money's safe,
Let him come back and throw the rest around
As much as he wants!
(HE looks over the money-bag.)
But—what's this? Oh my God!
He changed my money into charcoal!
Little ghost, little phantom, whatever you are,
Whatever you might be,
Come back and get this money you've left behind—
Take it, I don't need it—but why, oh why
Did you have to take the stuff I stole?
(Enter DON JUAN, DON LUIS, and DON MIGUEL.)
JUAN: Why are you shouting?
LUIS: What's the matter?
MANUEL: What's happened? Speak.
COSME: This is a cute little show you're putting on!
       As if you didn't know!
       Sir—if you've already got a goblin for a tenant,
       Why did you invite us in to share his room?
       I was gone for one brief instant,
       And coming back I found the place like this—
       Clothing scattered everywhere,
       Just like at an auction.
JUAN: Anything missing?
COSME: No, nothing's gone.
       Just some money of mine—it was turned into charcoal,
       Right here in this purse.

LUIS: I follow you now.

MANUEL: What kind of stupid joke is this?
It's not funny, and it's not clever!

JUAN: It's not even good; it's just impertinent!

COSME: That's because it's not a joke, in God's name!

MANUEL: Oh, shut up! It's always this way with you.

COSME: That's true. But another of my ways is
To have my wits about me most of the time.

JUAN: Well, good night, Don Manuel, and sleep well—
Unless our goblin-guest decides
To disturb your slumber. And tell your servant
To work a little harder on his jokes.
(Exit.)

LUIS: It's a good thing you're as valiant as you are, sir,
Since you seem to have to draw your sword a lot,
To extricate yourself from all the trouble
This fool gets you into.
(Exit.)

MANUEL: You see how they talk to me because of you?
Since I put up with you, the whole world
Calls me crazy! Everywhere we go,
I take a thousand snubs on your behalf.

COSME: Now that you're here alone with me,
Why would I still want to play a joke on you?
It's only fun to knock your master down
When someone's watching. If what I said
Was wrong, may two thousand devils take me away.
Someone else—I don't know who, I swear—
Must have wrecked this room.

MANUEL: You just want to excuse yourself
For your own stupidity—come on,
Put away all this stuff you threw around,
And get ready for bed.

COSME: Sir, make me a galley slave if—

MANUEL: Silence! Shut up, or by God I'll break your head!
(HE goes into the alcove.)

COSME: And I would just hate that. Now then:
Time to get my house in order again.
Oh, in heaven's name, I wish the trumpet
Would sound the Last Judgment of the wardrobe,

Then we could watch them all
Get up and hop right in at the first note!
(DON MANUEL returns with a piece of paper.)

MANUEL: Cosme, get me some light.

COSME: What's going on, sir?
Did you run into somebody in there?

MANUEL: I was turning back the covers, Cosme,
To get into bed, when I found this sealed letter
Under my pillowcase.
What's even more surprising is the address.

COSME: Who's it to?

MANUEL: To me, but in the strangest fashion.

COSME: What does it say?

MANUEL: It goes like this: *(Reads.)* "No one must open me;
I'm for Don Manuel alone."

COSME: God help you, sir, if you don't believe me now!
Don't open it! Stop right there!
First you've got to have it exorcised!

MANUEL: Cosme, what's stopping me is surprise, not fear—
When someone's amazed it doesn't mean they're afraid.
(Reads.)
"I feel some concern for your welfare, having been the source of your
danger. And so, with gratitude and regret, I beg you to advise me whether
you are well, and also how I may be of service to you. If you should have
occasion to respond to either question, leave your reply where you found
this letter, remembering that secrecy is vital: for the moment your two
friends know of this, I lose both life and honor."

COSME: Very strange!

MANUEL: What's strange?

COSME: Doesn't this surprise you?

MANUEL: No, because I began
To see it clearly before this.

COSME: What?

MANUEL: It's clear enough that the veiled lady,
Who fled from Don Luis so blindly
And so fearfully, was his mistress—
He's a bachelor, Cosme, so I assume
She's not his wife. And knowing that,
How difficult could it be for her
To have a way into her lover's house?

COSME: All right, that makes good sense.
　　But my fears are way ahead of you.
　　Let's say she is his mistress—
　　In which case, good for you, sir—
　　Still, how could she have known what would happen
　　In the street, and had a letter
　　Waiting for you here?
MANUEL: She could have written it after it happened,
　　And given it to a servant.
COSME: Even if she did, how did it get here?
　　Nobody's been in here since I got back.
MANUEL: It would have been before that.
COSME: All right. But look at the whole picture—
　　The letter, the clothing thrown around—
MANUEL: Look and see if these windows are closed.
COSME: Oh yes—barred and bolted.
MANUEL: That makes me wonder even more—
　　Now I have a thousand new suspicions.
COSME: Like what?
MANUEL:　　　　　　I don't know quite how to put it.
COSME: Well, what are you going to do?
MANUEL: I'll write her an answer—and make it seem
　　That neither fear nor wonder even crossed my mind.
　　I have no doubt that we'll discover who the courier is.
COSME: And we can't say a word about this to our hosts?
MANUEL: No—I couldn't harm a woman
　　Who has shown such confidence in me.
COSME: So then—you'll offend her lover instead?
MANUEL: Not at all. All I know is that as long as
　　I don't wrong her, I'll be doing right.
COSME: No, sir; there's more here than meets your eye.
　　With every word you say my doubts
　　And my suspicions just increase.
MANUEL: How so?
COSME: You see letters coming and going from here,
　　And the more you try to figure it all out,
　　The less certain it all becomes.
　　What do you want to believe?
MANUEL: That somebody's had the art and craft to make
　　Or find an entrance and an exit to this room,

To open and close some hidden door in here.
I might lose my mind trying to figure this out, Cosme,
But I won't believe it's supernatural.
COSME: So there are no phantoms?
MANUEL: No one's ever seen them.
COSME: Familiar spirits?
MANUEL: Just imagination.
COSME: Witches?
MANUEL: None.
COSME: Sorceresses?
MANUEL: Stupid!
COSME: Succubi?
MANUEL: No.
COSME: Enchantresses?
MANUEL: Not a one.
COSME: Magicians?
MANUEL: Ridiculous!
COSME: Necromancers?
MANUEL: Triviality!
COSME: Possessed people?
MANUEL: You're crazy!
COSME: By God, I've got you now—what about devils?
MANUEL: Well, they don't seem to do much in the world.
COSME: Are there souls in Purgatory?
MANUEL: Souls who are in love with me
    And write me letters?
    This is the most incredible stupidity!
    Get away from me, you're wearing me out.
COSME: So then: what have you decided to do?
MANUEL: I'll keep a watch by night and day—
    And I'll get to the bottom of this mystery
    Without the need for phantoms or familiars.
COSME: For my part, I just assume some devil
    Brought that letter, and that he'll be back as soon
    As he's had a chance to go out and have a smoke.

END OF ACT ONE

ACT TWO

An outer room in DOÑA ANGELA's apartment.

(Enter DOÑA ANGELA, DOÑA BEATRIZ, and ISABEL.)

BEATRIZ: These are amazing things you're telling me.

ANGELA: Twice as amazing when you hear
    The whole story. Where did we leave off?

BEATRIZ: You were telling how you got
    Into his room through the wall of glass,
    And that it was much easier
    Than you thought it would be;
    Then you wrote him a letter,
    And the next day you went back and found
    Your answer right where you expected it.

ANGELA: I'll tell you something else—
    I've never seen a letter written
    In such a courteous and gallant style.
    He manages to strike a tone
    That's exalted and yet graceful—
    Almost like Don Quixote
    Writing to his Dulcinea.
    Here's the letter, Beatriz—
    Tell me if it doesn't charm you too.
    (SHE reads.)
    "Most beautiful lady, whosoever thou may'st be, that smilest on this
    heartsick knight and would console him, I beg thee to make known to me
    where I may find that arrant knave, that pagan evil-doer, who holds you
    in his spell, so that I may make a second sortie in your name, my former
    wounds being now healed, and in the last great battle bring a just death to
    your tormentor, else die in the attempt, for what is life unless I can be
    your protector? The giver of light preserve thee, and not forsake me.
                      —*The Knight of the Phantom Lady.*"

BEATRIZ: You're right—his language fits
    The whole adventure perfectly!

ANGELA: I was sure his answer would be cautious—
    Full of doubts and questions—
    But now I see how easily he takes to it,
    I'll answer him in the same style,
    And here's how I'll begin—

BEATRIZ: Stop—no more.
 Here comes your brother, Don Juan.
ANGELA: He'll come all right, playing the gallant lover
 To the hilt, talking of nothing
 But what a pleasure it is to see you, Beatriz,
 And what an unexpected honor
 To speak with you under his roof,
 And so on and so forth . . .
BEATRIZ: Well, that won't exactly bother me,
 If the truth must be told.
 (Enter DON JUAN.)
JUAN: There's nothing bad but what some good will come of it,
 As the old proverb says, and I see it once again
 When I remember how my blessings
 Spring from your troubles. I know,
 My beautiful Beatriz,
 Your father's anger brought you here,
 Unwillingly and discontentedly, to our house.
 It saddens me that I should find such joy
 Because of your great sorrow.
 Still, I cannot feel anything but gladness,
 Since love has power to turn evil into good,
 Much like the asp who, when he bites,
 Injects both venom and its antidote.
 You are most cordially welcome to our house.
BEATRIZ: You've mixed up your condolences and flatteries
 So well, I hardly know which one to answer.
 I came because my father's quite upset,
 But of course you'll have to take the blame for that.
 All my father knows is that I spoke
 With a gentleman from my balcony last night—
 He doesn't know the man was you.
 So until his anger passes,
 He sent me to stay here with my cousin,
 Whose virtue he trusts completely.
 I'll say only this, and this will be enough:
 I value my misfortunes too;
 Because I also feel love's various powers,
 Much like the Sun whose rays may wither
 One poor flower only to make another bloom.

ANGELA: Well—it's clear that this is going to be
   One of those days when lovers spare
   No expense of words. Maybe they'll let me
   Have a few of their compliments on the cheap.
JUAN: Do you know what I think, sister?
   To get back at me for all the trouble my guest
   Has put you to, you've found a guest
   Of your own to put me to the same.
ANGELA: You're right. I did it just to put you to
   The trouble of entertaining her.
JUAN: This is the kind of vengeance I enjoy.
   (HE starts to go.)
BEATRIZ: What are you doing, Don Juan? Where are you going?
JUAN: On an errand for you, Beatriz;
   I could only bear to leave you on your own behalf.
ANGELA: Let him go.
JUAN: God be with you.
   (Exits.)
ANGELA: Yes, that guest of his has caused me trouble,
   But it's far too soon for us to understand
   How much trouble, or what kind.
   The situation's much the same with you
   And brother Juan—so it seems that, guest for guest,
   We're even.
BEATRIZ: Now then—I can bear his absence
   For a while only because I've got to know
   The rest of your story.
ANGELA: I won't keep you waiting.
   We've been exchanging letters, he and I,
   And I tell you—his are such a brilliant mixture
   Of seriousness and wit,
   I've never seen the like of it.
BEATRIZ: What do you think he makes of you?
ANGELA: That I must be Don Luis's mistress,
   That I'm in hiding from him,
   And that I've got another key to his room.
BEATRIZ: There's just one thing that bothers me.
ANGELA: What's that?
BEATRIZ: This man knows someone must be carrying
   These letters back and forth—why hasn't he caught you?

ANGELA: Because I'm one step ahead of him.
    A man is posted by his door,
    Who tells me when he comes and goes.
    So that way Isabel can go in
    When she's sure the room is empty.
    Today, for instance, the servant's been there waiting,
    But we haven't gotten any signal yet.
    Before I forget, Isabel, take this basket
    In there with you when you get the chance.
BEATRIZ: Another quibble. Why do you give him
    Such credit for his brilliance, when he can't
    Figure out the simple secret of the wall
    After so many chances?
ANGELA: Every secret's simple when you know
    The answer to it.
BEATRIZ: All right, just one more question.
ANGELA: Ask away.
BEATRIZ: What do you think you'll get
    From all these crazy goings on?
ANGELA: I don't know. I could tell you that it's just
    To show my gratitude, and fill the time a little,
    As long as I'm locked up here in my solitude;
    But it's more than that—
    Because, knowing full well how stupid
    And how foolish this all is, I've let myself
    Grow jealous of a woman's portrait
    That he keeps with him in there.
    I've even planned to go in there and take it,
    First chance I get. And there's more yet:
    I don't know how to tell you, but I'm resolved
    To see him and speak to him as well.
BEATRIZ: And let him find out who you are?
ANGELA: Jesus and all the angels, no!
    Not that he would ever reveal it;
    He'd never be such a traitor to his hosts.
    Besides, the thought that I am
    Don Luis's mistress is what makes him write me
    In such a timid, courteous, flowery way.
    No, I don't have to put myself in that position.
BEATRIZ: Then how is he ever going to see you?

ANGELA: Here's the most amazing part of the plan:
    I'll walk right into his room without his seeing me,
    And he'll come into mine without
    The slightest idea where he is.
ISABEL: Time to write the other brother's name
    Into the stage directions: here comes Don Luis.
ANGELA: I'll finish later.
BEATRIZ: The stars must really have great power—
    Look at how, in men of equal strengths and merits,
    Heaven has arranged it
    So that one attracts and the other repels!
    Let's go—I don't want anything to do with Don Luis.
    (THEY start to go, and DON LUIS enters.)
LUIS: Why are you leaving like this?
BEATRIZ: Because you've arrived.
LUIS: So then the purest light, that taught the Sun to shine,
    Flees at my appearance? Does that make me the night?
    Well, blame it on your beauty, then,
    If I seem to lack the courtesy to leave.
    I won't beg pardon of you, since I know
    You're too severe to grant it.
    If only for revenge against your scorn,
    My love grows greater. The more profoundly
    You abhor me, the deeper is my love for you.
    There's just one remedy for this affliction;
    You'll have to learn to love, or teach me how to hate.
    You teach me scorn, I'll teach you tenderness;
    You teach me insults, I will teach you kindness;
    You, contempt, and I, affection;
    You, forgetfulness, I, a faithful heart.
    And even if you wipe all thoughts of us away,
    Still I, granted grace by the God of love,
    Will love enough for both of us.
BEATRIZ: You complain so beautifully—still,
    Even if I wanted to respond in kind,
    I couldn't do it—just because it's you.
LUIS: You've treated me so badly, I'm afraid
    I'm learning something of the language of disdain.
BEATRIZ: Well, good; it's time you used it.
    Perhaps you'll drive away

Anyone who speaks nicely to you.
(*SHE starts to leave, but DON LUIS stops HER.*)
LUIS: Listen—if this is how you mean
    To take revenge, we'll suffer together.
BEATRIZ: I'm tired of listening to this.
    For God's sake, cousin, why don't you stop him!
    (*SHE exits.*)
ANGELA: How little spirit you must have,
    To want to put yourself through that!
LUIS: Oh, sister—what should I do?
ANGELA: Give up—forget her.
    Loving someone who hates you in return
    Isn't love—it's death.
    (*Exeunt ANGELA and ISABEL.*)
LUIS: Oh yes—how am I supposed to forget her?
    And why should I? How am I at fault?
    Just let her do one nice thing for me,
    Speak a gentle word,
    Then I'll immediately forget her, thank you.
    But not when she's insulted me like this.
    The wiser heads among us have a saying:
    Forget kindnesses, since they don't last;
    But remember insults—because they never go away
    Unless we force them to—by taking vengeance.
    (*Enter RODRIGO.*)
RODRIGO: Where've you been?
LUIS: I don't know.
RODRIGO: You look sad. Won't you tell me why?
LUIS: I had a talk with Doña Beatriz.
RODRIGO: Say no more; I can read her answer in your face.
    But where did that happen? I haven't seen her anywhere.
LUIS: The little tyrant's here—my sister's guest
    For a little while. Every day my brother
    Cooks up another plot against me.
    And every day someone else shows up
    To be my personal tormentor.
    First Don Manuel, and now, as you see, Doña Beatriz.
    The heavens have arranged it very nicely:
    I'm simply to be jealous of everyone and everything—
    How else can you explain it?

RODRIGO: Take care that Don Manuel doesn't hear you—
    He's coming.
    (Enter DON MANUEL.)
MANUEL: *(Aside.)* Who else has ever experienced
    All these extraordinary things?
    Who in the world? Now, heaven, show me
    How to discover whether this woman
    Really has been Don Luis's mistress,
    And what kind of cunning craft she's got
    To keep this intrigue going.
LUIS: Don Manuel, my lord.
MANUEL: My lord Don Luis.
LUIS: And where have you just come from?
MANUEL: The Palace.
LUIS: Of course—I'm sorry—
    How could I have even asked a man
    Of your high station where he goes
    Or comes from; it's clear as day
    That every road leads you directly
    To the Palace; as it were, the center
    Of your universe.
MANUEL: If the Palace were my only destination,
    I wouldn't be in such a hurry—
    But my duty now takes me on a longer route.
    His Majesty left this afternoon for the Escorial,
    And that means I have to go to him tonight
    With my dispatches, which cannot risk delay.
LUIS: If I can be of any service,
    You know I'm ready to do anything—
MANUEL: I'm deeply grateful to you—
LUIS: You know this isn't just flattery—
MANUEL: I know you truly want to help me—
LUIS: *(Aside.)* I do—to get you out of here
    As fast as ever I can.
MANUEL: But I shouldn't keep a man like you
    From the pursuit of his own pleasures;
    I'm sure you've more enjoyable things to do,
    And my affairs would just be in your way.
LUIS: You wouldn't talk like that if you had heard me
    Just now, speaking to Rodrigo.

MANUEL: Well, don't I have it right?

LUIS: Yes, but not how you imagine.

> Although it's true my heart cries out
> For a beautiful lady, her only answer is disdain,
> And all my strength is powerless against that.

MANUEL: You paint such a helpless picture of yourself!

LUIS: But I'm in love with a great lady—

> And my fate's against me.

MANUEL:　　　Are you joking?

LUIS: If only I were, in heaven's name!

> But I was born under such unhappy stars
> That this beauty flees from me
> Like lovely twilight flees advancing darkness,
> And even so her rays set me afire.
> Do you want to see just how extreme
> My bad luck is? All right—
> I was following this lady, spurred by love
> And jealousy, and she asked someone to stop me
> In the street—just think of it.
> Most people use third parties as go-betweens,
> But she—she uses one to get away from me!

(Exeunt DON LUIS and RODRIGO.)

MANUEL: What more needs be said?

> A woman fled from him and asked
> Another person to detain him!
> At least this clears up one doubt—
> If she's that lady, she is not his mistress.
> He wouldn't let her live here if she hated him.
> But now here's a thornier question:
> If she's not his mistress, and she doesn't live here,
> How does she carry on this correspondence?
> Now one mystery dies and another one is born.
> What should I do? Even my confusion
> Is confused! And yet, by heaven,
> That's no surprise—a woman is involved!

(Enter COSME.)

COSME: So where's the phantom, sir?

> Maybe you've seen him around here?
> I'd sure be glad to know he's neither here
> Nor there.

MANUEL: Speak softer.

COSME: Because I've got a lot of things to do
    In our room, and I can't go in there.

MANUEL: Well, what's the matter?

COSME: I'm afraid.

MANUEL: Should a man be afraid?

COSME: No, sir,
    But you see before you one's who's got good reason.

MANUEL: Just stop this nonsense, now, and get me a light—
    I've got some things to take care of,
    Some letters to write, and then tonight
    We're leaving Madrid.

COSME: I see how it is—
    You talk like this because you're just as scared as I am.

MANUEL: I've told you before I don't care about that,
    And in fact when you start talking to me about it
    I immediately begin thinking of other things.
    And so you see it's just a waste of time.
    Get the light ready while I
    Say good-bye to Don Juan.
    (HE exits.)

COSME: You can bet I'll do that.
    I'll get some light ready for the phantom.
    It's time we started looking after him;
    I doubt he likes to be left in the dark.
    There ought to be a candle around here
    And I'll light it in that lamp that's flickering over there.
    Now careful, Cosme, careful!
    Between one thing and another, I'm shivering with fear.
    (HE exits.)

DON MANUEL's room.

(Enter ISABEL through the cupboard, with a covered basket.)

ISABEL: They're out, just like the servant told me.
    Now I'll put this basket full of linens where she wanted it.
    Oh dear! It's black as night in here
    And even so I'm afraid of my own shadow.
    I'm trembling all over, God help me!
    I'll bet I am the first phantom

Who ever called on God for help.
Oh oh. I can't find the desk.
What's this? Now I'm so confused
I've lost my feeling for the room.
I don't know where I am, or where the table is.
What should I do now? Heavens!
If I can't figure out how to get out of here,
And they find me here, it's all over.
Now I'm really frightened!
I feel like someone's opening the door,
And now I see he's carrying a candle.
Well, that's it then—it's all over!
I can't hide, and there's no way out.
(Enter COSME with a candle.)

COSME: Phantom? Oh Phantom, just in case
You enjoy being begged,
Like all the phantoms from the best families do,
I humbly beg you not to mix me up
In any more of your many wonderful tricks.
And I have four reasons why.
The first one, I know for myself;
*(COSME walks around and ISABEL follows behind, making sure
he doesn't see her.)*
The second, you know for yourself;
The third, a word to the wise, as the saying goes,
And the fourth, because of this song:
O great Phantom Lady
Please take pity on me
I'm just a boy, upon my chin
There is no trace of stubble
And what is more, I'm all alone
And I'm not worth your trouble.

ISABEL: *(Aside.)* Now at least I've got my bearings again.
And he hasn't seen me.
If I could just snuff that candle out,
I'm sure I could get out of here
Before he got it lit again.
He'll hear me, all right, but he won't see me,
And that's the lesser of two evils.

COSME: Fear's a great music-teacher:

I could never sing before!

ISABEL: *(Aside.)* Here goes nothing!

(SHE hits him and snuffs out the candle.)

COSME: Oh God! Last rites! I'm dead!

ISABEL: Now for my escape.

(As ISABEL starts to leave, enter DON MANUEL.)

MANUEL: What is this? Cosme!

Why are you here in the dark?

COSME: The phantom's killed us both:

The candle with a breath and me with a blow.

MANUEL: Fear makes you believe these crazy things.

COSME: Well, I pay for my beliefs!

ISABEL: *(Aside.)* Now where's that door?

MANUEL: Who's there?

(ISABEL runs into DON MANUEL, who hangs on to the basket.)

ISABEL: *(Aside.)* Bad to worse: I've managed

To run into the master now as well.

MANUEL: Bring some light, Cosme.

Whoever it is, I've got him.

COSME: Well don't let him go.

MANUEL: I won't.

Hurry up with that light.

COSME: Hang on tight.

(HE Exits.)

ISABEL: *(Aside.)* He's only got hold of the basket.

I'll leave it with him.

Because now I found the panel. Good-bye.

(SHE exits, leaving him holding the basket.)

MANUEL: Whoever you are, you stay right there

Until we get some light in here.

Because if you don't, by God,

I'll make a pin-cushion of you with my sword here.

But wait—all I'm holding onto now is air,

And all I can put my hands on is some clothing,

Nothing with any weight to it at all!

What's going on? God help me,

Now I'm completely confused!

(Enter COSME with some light.)

COSME: Bring the phantom over here to the light.

But—where'd he go? Wasn't he caught?

What did he do? Where is he? What's going on, sir?
MANUEL: I don't know what to say.

    He left me this bundle of clothing and fled.
COSME: And what do you say to this?

    You just finished telling me that you had him,

    And now he's gone with the wind.
MANUEL: Here's what I say: the same person

    Who has discovered how to come and go

    From here at will was hidden here tonight,

    And to escape, snuffed out your candle,

    Left me with this basket, and got away.
COSME: Where'd he go?
MANUEL: Through the door, I guess.
COSME: You'll make me go completely mad.

    By God, I caught a glimpse of him myself

    While he was killing me and blowing out my candle.
MANUEL: What did he look like?
COSME: Like a great big friar,

    With a huge cowl, which tells me

    He was a Capuchin phantom.
MANUEL: That's your fear playing tricks on you again.

    Bring that light over here, and we'll see

    What our little friar's brought us. Get me that basket.
COSME: You want me to touch that basket from hell?
MANUEL: Pick it up, I tell you.
COSME: My hands are dirty, sir, with candle-wax,

    And I'd just ruin that taffeta covering.

    Much better to leave it on the floor.
MANUEL: Fresh linen, and a letter.

    Let's see if this friar is discreet.

    (Reads.)

    "In the short time you've been living in this house, it has not been
possible to make up more linens; however, as they are made up, they'll be
brought to you. As for what you have said, that you believe I am the
mistress of Don Luis, let me assure you that not only am I not such a one,
but can never be so. I'll leave the rest until I see you, which will be soon.
God save you."

    Well. This phantom's been baptized, at least.
COSME: So you see—it is a friar-phantom after all.
MANUEL: It's getting very late. Get our things together,

And put these papers in a pouch, ready for our journey.
In the meantime I will leave a proper answer
For my phantom.
*(HE gives his papers to COSME, who puts them on a chair, and
DON MANUEL writes.)*
COSME: I'd like to leave these right here, sir,
So they'll be close at hand.
Meanwhile, sir, may I just stop
For one second and say:
Now do you believe in phantoms?
MANUEL: Idiot! You're talking nonsense!
COSME: Nonsense? You've seen the phantom at work—
The wind brings gifts to your hands
And you still doubt it? You may be right, though,
Since everything works out just fine for you,
While I, who believe in the phantom,
Get left out.
MANUEL: How do you mean?
COSME: I'll prove it, like so: if our clothes
Get thrown around, you see it and can laugh,
But I'm the one who has to pick them up,
And that's no little job.
Someone leaves you letters,
And comes for your replies,
But he comes to get my money
And leaves me coals instead.
You get sweets brought to you, which you eat
As hungrily as any priest, while I
Stand by like a poor pimp, and cannot touch them.
Someone brings you shirts, collars, and handkerchiefs,
Which comfort you, but frighten me
When I try to figure out how they get in here.
And when we both are in the room,
Look at what happens: you get a basket
Full of soft clothing, while I get clobbered.
That phantom puts kid gloves on for you, sir,
But saves his iron fist for me.
So let me have my beliefs;
At least my suffering will purify me,
Which is more than I can say for you,

Who tries to deny what happens right before his eyes.

MANUEL: Pack the bags, and let's go.

I'll be waiting for you in Don Juan's room.

COSME: Yes sir.

MANUEL: Lock the door, and take the key.

If someone needs to enter, Don Juan has another one.

This isn't a good time to be leaving here.

I can't decide which affair is more important.

One involves my family's honor and my livelihood,

The other's just a matter of pleasure;

And so, between these two extremes,

Honor takes priority;

Everything else is insignificant.

(Exeunt.)

DOÑA ANGELA's room.

(Enter DOÑA ANGELA, DOÑA BEATRIZ, and ISABEL.)

ANGELA: So that's what happened to you?

ISABEL: I thought the game was over—

If they had seen me there,

They would have found out everything—

But, as it is, we're safe, since I escaped.

ANGELA: That's amazing.

BEATRIZ: It should even help the scheme,

Since he wound up with the basket in his hands

And no one in the room.

ANGELA: And now,

If I can arrange to meet him

In the way I told you, I don't doubt

He'll lose his head completely.

BEATRIZ: Angela, these tricks would fool

The sharpest man alive.

Your plan is excellent:

He wants to speak to you, of course,

But he has no idea where you are.

He finds himself somehow in the presence

Of a lady who just happens to be beautiful,

Rich, and famous, except he hasn't got

The slightest idea who she is or where she lives.

Finally he's blindfolded and led
In and out of the room so that he loses track
Of where he is—who wouldn't be amazed?
ANGELA: Everything's ready. If you weren't here,
Tonight would be the night.
BEATRIZ: Don't you think I could keep your secret?
ANGELA: No, cousin, that's not the reason.
It's just that as long as you are in the house,
My brothers won't go out, because they're both
So madly in love with you, they simply
Have to worship every silver ray
That twinkles from the star that they adore,
As they might put it.
And as long as they stay here,
I don't dare put my plan in action.
(Enter DON LUIS just to the wings.)
LUIS: *(Aside.)* Oh God—who among us knows the secret
Of how how to hide his heart!
Who can hold his thoughts in check,
Stifle his voice and legislate his feelings!
Not I, at least not yet. But from this day on,
I've got to try to teach myself
To conquer passion and keep my wits about me.
BEATRIZ: I'll tell you how to manage things
So I can stay without throwing off your plan.
Because, you see, I really wouldn't
Want to miss this scene.
ANGELA: Tell me.
LUIS: *(Aside.)* What are they talking about? It sounds
Like one voice telling secrets to itself.
BEATRIZ: We'll say my father's sent for me,
We'll make a show of leaving, and when
Everybody thinks I've gone,
I will return . . .
LUIS: *(Aside.)*   Now, in heaven's name,
What new torment is she planning?
BEATRIZ: And hide myself where I can see
Everything without disturbing you . . .
LUIS: *(Aside.)* What's this now, cruel fate?
BEATRIZ: Which will be a lot of fun for me.

ANGELA: And later on, what will we say
 When they see you here again?
BEATRIZ: Come on now—don't you think
 We'll have enough ingenuity left over
 To think up one more little lie?
LUIS: *(Aside.)* I'll bet you do. Why must I listen to this?
 Now I've got a fresh new pain to conquer.
BEATRIZ: And so—in total secrecy,
 I'll see how this amazing love turns out.
 Because when I'm well hidden,
 And the household's all tucked in,
 He'll pass from room to room without a chance of scandal.
LUIS: *(Aside.)* Now I understand your plan exactly.
 And though I may live a coward,
 My death will be a brave one.
 She wants to see my brother secretly—
 While I burn up with passion.
 And these enemies of mine in here
 Conspire to conceal this from me.
 Well, by heaven, I'll find a way
 To wreck their little love-plot. When she's hidden,
 I'll think of some excuse to search the house—
 I'll turn it upside down and inside out
 Until I find her, and just let them try to stop me.
 Nothing else can drown the fire that consumes me.
 It's jealousy's last resort, I guess—
 To spoil other lovers' joy.
 Now all the saints in heaven give me strength!
 For though I burn with love, I die of jealousy.
 (HE exits.)
ANGELA: That's well thought out. A perfect plan.
 Tomorrow, we'll announce that you've gone home.
 (Enter DON JUAN.)
JUAN: Sister! And beautiful Beatriz.
BEATRIZ: We've missed you.
JUAN: Those words resound so sweetly in my soul
 That I begin to feel jealous
 Of my own happiness. It is impossible
 That my humble love for you is worthy

Of such a show of care—and so
I envy myself, and by myself am envied,
As my happiness and I are left to wonder
On whom this radiance is truly meant to shine.
BEATRIZ: Don Juan, I do not want to contradict you,
Since you've framed such an elegant reply
To such a simple statement—
Except that you've been gone so long,
I think you had forgotten all about me.
No doubt you had some better entertainment—
So maybe it's my turn to feel envy;
Though not, as in your case, of myself.
JUAN: If I wouldn't risk offending both of us,
Beatriz, I might satisfy you
By telling you that I have been
With Don Manuel, my guest, who just tonight
Has left Madrid.
ANGELA: Oh my God!
JUAN: What's so startling in that, sister?
ANGELA: Good news and bad can be equally surprising.
JUAN: I'm sorry you feel that way—
Because he returns tomorrow.
ANGELA: *(Aside.)* That gives my hopes a second life.
(Aloud.)
I was taken by surprise
Simply by the thought that our
Troublesome guest would be gone
As quickly as he came.
JUAN: I don't see where he gave you any cause
To complain—in fact I think what bothers you
And Don Luis is that
I take such pleasure in our guest.
ANGELA: I won't answer that, although
There's plenty I could say. But no—
I wouldn't want to spoil the game,
And when lovers' cards are being dealt.
Three at the table is one too many.
(Aside to ISABEL.)
Come with me, Isabel. I have to get

That portrait out tonight; we can do it easily
With no one there. Have a candle ready for me,
And we'll slip in unobserved. I just can't stand
The thought that a gentleman who writes me letters
Should have the portrait of another woman.
(Exeunt DOÑA ANGELA, and ISABEL.)
BEATRIZ: I don't believe I owe you such kindness.
JUAN: I'll prove my love is worthy of your faith
If I may speak.
BEATRIZ: Go ahead.
JUAN: Attend and listen.
Beautiful Beatriz, my faith is so true,
My love so strong, my affection so rare,
That even if I didn't want to love you,
Against my wishes I would love you anyway.
Regard my life this way:
If I could forget you, I would do it,
So that afterwards I could choose
To fall in love with you again;
My love would be a pleasure, not a duty.
And yet, whoever loves a woman,
Because he can't forget her,
He has no other choice, he's lost his will.
I cannot forget you, beautiful Beatriz,
And I'm sorry when I see how proud my star,
My fate, is of this great victory:
Your love has conquered me completely.
BEATRIZ: If the choice were really yours to will,
And the force of fate the impulse of a star,
It would take a stronger will to live
In freedom from that delirium, that madness.
And so I find I cannot trust your kindnesses,
For if my faith, which is impossible to brush aside,
Sees my will acting on its own,
It would deny that it was truly mine in heaven's name.
In that brief and lovely instant of forgetting
Only to fall in love again,
I'm afraid I'd feel my affection falter.
And so I'm pleased to see I am not partial
To forgetting you, since I find

I could not love you
While I was trying to forget you.
(Exeunt.)

The street.

(Enter DON MANUEL, following the fleeing COSME.)
MANUEL: In God's name, if I didn't think—
COSME: So think!
MANUEL: That it would be disgraceful of me to hit you—
COSME: Remember how well I've served you, sir,
    And how every Catholic's allowed one mistake.
MANUEL: Who else would put up with you, I ask you, who?
    One mistake? You left behind the thing
    We really need, the one thing I insisted
    That you not forget!
COSME: But that's why I forgot it,
    Because it was so important.
    Would I ever forget something unimportant?
    Heavens no! I was being so careful
    With those papers, I put them aside
    In a special place, and all my special pains
    Are what got me into trouble.
    If I hadn't set them out for special packing,
    I would have simply packed them with the rest.
MANUEL: Good thing you remembered
    Before we got all the way there.
COSME: I had this awful feeling,
    But I wasn't sure what for.
    I figured it was something stupid,
    Until it hit me. I knew right then
    It was those papers I had taken such good care of.
MANUEL: Tell the boy to wait here with the mules;
    We don't want to wake everybody up.
    I've got my key, so I can get in the room
    And find the papers without being noticed.
    (COSME goes out and comes right back in.)
COSME: Let's think about this for a second, sir.
    It would be a terrible mistake
    To try to find those papers in the dark;

You'll surely make a lot of noise that way.

And where can we get a light, except Don Juan?

MANUEL: You are so unbelievably annoying!

Now you want me to yell and scream

And wake Don Juan? Haven't you got it through your skull

That we'll just have to find our way by feel?

You remember where you left the papers, don't you?

COSME: Oh, no problem there.

I left them on the table—

I could find them blindfolded.

MANUEL: So open the door!

COSME: See, what I'm worried about is this:

I don't know where the phantom will have put them.

I mean, when have I ever put anything down

And later found it where I left it?

MANUEL: If we can't find the papers,

Then we'll ask for a candle.

I'm not going to put our host

To any more trouble unless we have to.

(Exeunt.)

DON MANUEL's room.

(Enter DOÑA ANGELA and ISABEL through the wall of glass.)

ANGELA: Isabel, the house is all in bed—

Sleep, after all, steals half our lives

If we let it—and our guest is gone,

So now's the time to get that portrait

I saw the first time I was in here.

ISABEL: Careful—don't make any noise.

ANGELA: You go lock up my room,

And until you come back I'll just stay put—

Don't worry, I'm not taking any chances.

ISABEL: Wait for me here.

(Exit ISABEL, closing the wall of glass. Enter, in the darkness, DON MANUEL and COSME.)

COSME: *(Speaking softly to his master in the doorway.)*

It's open.

MANUEL: Step softly.

COSME: Would you believe I'm frightened?

You'd think this phantom could at least
Light a candle for us.
ANGELA: Now's the time to light the lamp
I brought along—no one's looking, after all.
(DOÑA ANGELA, across the room from DON MANUEL and
COSME, brings out her lantern and lights it.)
COSME: *(Aside to his master.)* The phantom's never been so obedient before.
He lights right up, just for the asking!
See how much the phantom likes you, sir?
When you come in, he lights his lamp;
He blew mine out.
MANUEL: Heaven help me!
This is truly supernatural.
That light appearing right on cue—
No human could do that.
COSME: Now do you see what I mean?
MANUEL: I'm petrified! Let's get out of here.
COSME: So now you're mortal too—you're in a fright.
ANGELA: Over there I see the table, and some papers.
COSME: It's moving toward the table.
MANUEL: In God's name, I don't know what to think!
COSME: See how it leads us right to what we're looking for,
And yet we can't tell who is carrying the light?
(DOÑA ANGELA takes the candle out of the lamp, puts it in a
candlestick on the table, takes a chair, and sits with her back to them.)
ANGELA: I'll just put the light right here
And have a look at these papers.
MANUEL: Wait now—in the reflected light I see it all.
I've never seen such supreme beauty in my life!
God help me, what is all this? What should I do?
COSME: She's taking her time, that's for sure.
Ah—she moved the chair.
MANUEL: She's an image of the most rare beauty—
As if the master painter of them all
Had done her portrait.
COSME: That's true—
He's the only one who could have done it.
MANUEL: Her eyes shine with more than just the candlelight.
COSME: That's also true—they have
An unearthly glow, like Lucifer's.

MANUEL: Each strand of her hair is a ray of sunlight.

COSME: Stolen from up there.

MANUEL: Each curl, a star.

COSME: No doubt they are:
    She grabbed some of them too, on her way here,
    from Paradise, Purgatory, or Hell.

MANUEL: I've never seen such absolute perfection!

COSME: I'll bet you wouldn't say that if you could see her feet.
    These types, you'll find, have cloven ones.

MANUEL: Astonishing beauty! She's a lovely angel,
    Nothing less!

COSME: An angel, sure,
    But with that foot defect I pointed out.

MANUEL: What does she want with my papers, do you suppose?

COSME: I imagine she's looking through them for you
    To find the ones you want, save you the trouble.
    She's a very handy phantom.

MANUEL: God in heaven, show me what to do.
    I've never been a coward until tonight.

COSME: I, on the other hand, have often been one.

MANUEL: I feel like I'm bound in chains of ice—
    I can't move or think—I've got to break this spell!
    (HE goes to HER and grabs HER.)

ANGELA: *(Aside.)* Oh, my! He didn't really leave!
    He's got the better of me now!

COSME: In God's name—(Devils hate that)—tell us . . .

ANGELA: *(Aside.)* But I'll play along . . .

COSME: Who are you, and what do you want from us?

ANGELA: Noble Don Manuel Enríquez,
    For whom a great blessing is reserved,
    Let go of me, lest you lose the great bounty
    Heaven has in store for you.
    I wrote to you this evening, and in that letter,
    Told you that we should soon meet,
    Anticipating this very occasion.
    Since I have kept my word,
    Choosing the most human of forms in which
    To appear to you, go in peace and leave me here.
    The time is not yet come for you to understand me.
    Tomorrow you shall know all.

And hear this: not a word to anyone,
If you do not wish to forfeit your great good fortune.
Go in peace.
COSME: "Go in peace," she said, sir—
What are we waiting for?
MANUEL: *(Aside.)* These silly fears made me lose
My reason for a minute. But now I've got
My courage back, and I'm going to crack
This case right now.
(Aloud.)
Woman: whoever you are (and I won't believe
you're anything but a woman), by God, I mean
To find out who you are, how you've gotten in here,
To what end, and why.
And I don't mean to wait until tomorrow
For this "great bounty." If you're a devil, speak as a devil;
Or if you're a woman, speak that way.
COSME: It's all the same.
ANGELA: Don't touch me, or you'll lose your fortune.
COSME: The devil has a point. Don't touch her—
After all, she's not a harp or a lute.
MANUEL: If you are a spirit, my sword will soon tell us:
(Draws his sword.)
Even if I run you through, I cannot hurt you.
ANGELA: Oh! Drop your sword, hold your bloody hand!
You don't want to kill a poor unhappy woman.
I confess that's what I am.
And if it is a crime to be in love,
I don't think it's a capital offense.
Please don't stain your sword
With my innocent blood.
MANUEL: Tell me who you are.
ANGELA: Now I'll have to tell you;
And now I won't be able to bring my love,
My desire, my true devotion, and my faith
To its just conclusion. But we're in mortal danger
If they hear or see us; because, believe me,
I am more than I seem.
And so we have to lock the doors
And the alcove too; that way, no one passing by will see our light.

MANUEL: Cosme, get some light so we can lock the doors.
You see now? She's a woman, not a phantom.

COSME: Didn't I say it's all the same?

(*Exeunt DON MANUEL and COSME; ANGELA goes to the wall of glass.*)

ANGELA: Isabel locked the other side—I can't get out!
And now I'll be forced to tell the truth,
Since our guest has caught me here.

(*Enter ISABEL through the wall of glass.*)

ISABEL: Psst! Madam! Psst!

ANGELA: About time!

ISABEL: Your brother's asking for you.

ANGELA: Let's go. Lock the panel behind us.
Oh, my love—you'll just have to live
With your doubts a while longer.

(*DOÑA ANGELA and ISABEL exit through the wall of glass, as
DON MANUEL and COSME return to the room.*)

MANUEL: Now the doors are all locked, madam,
You may continue—tell us who—
But, what's this? Where is she?

COSME: Like I'm supposed to know?

MANUEL: Did she go into the alcove? Take a look.

COSME: Oh, sir, it would be rude of me
To go ahead of you.

MANUEL: I'll search the room. Let go of that light, I tell you.

COSME: I tell you, here it is.

(*DON MANUEL takes the candle from COSME, goes into the alcove,
and comes back out.*)

MANUEL: Cruel luck!

COSME: At least we know
She didn't use the door.

MANUEL: But how did she escape?

COSME: We'll never know. Now do you see
What I've been telling you—
That she's a devil, not a woman?

MANUEL: By God, if I have to go over every inch
Of this room I'll find whatever trick she's using—
Some trapdoor, some picture frame
Covering a secret passage,
Even a hidden hole in the ceiling!

COSME: The only thing I see is that glass wall there.

MANUEL: No—we needn't worry about that—
    As you can see it's just a cabinet—
    No doubt about it. We'd better keep on looking.
COSME: I don't like to be so nosy.
MANUEL: I'm still not prepared to believe
    She is a phantom—she feared my sword.
COSME: Yes, and she foretold our coming back
    To see her here tonight.
MANUEL: She certainly seemed ghostly at first,
    When she showed herself in that fantastic light;
    But her fear was human, her caution was womanly;
    And yet she disappeared like an illusion,
    Vanished like a spirit.
    If I allow free rein to these thoughts, by God—
    I won't know any more what to doubt, and what to believe!
COSME: I do.
MANUEL: What?
COSME: She's a devil-woman;
    And that's nothing new.
    Women are devils all year, after all—
    Why shouldn't the devil be a woman
    Once to get even with them?

END OF ACT TWO

ACT THREE

DOÑA ANGELA's room.

(Enter DON MANUEL, in the dark, with ISABEL leading him.)

ISABEL: Wait for me here; my mistress
    Will be in to see you later on.
    (SHE exits, closing the door as she goes.)
MANUEL: This is a pretty good plot!
    Did she lock the door?
    Yes. Has anyone ever known such exquisite agony?
    I came back from the Escorial,
    Only to find a letter from
    This same enchanting pilgrim,
    This celestial wonder who, last night
    When she lit her lamp, plunged me
    Into the darkest doubt! Here's what she said:
        "If you dare to come and see me, go out this evening, along with
        that servant of yours. Two men will be waiting for you in the
        cemetery (that's the strange part!) of Saint Sebastian's church, with
        a sedan chair."
    And she wasn't kidding. I got in the chair,
    We ran around until I lost all sense
    Of where I was, and finally they let me off
    Before a grim and horrid doorway,
    Through which I stepped, alone and in the darkness.
    Then a woman appeared—
    At least she seemed to be a woman—
    Who led me without speaking, in the darkness,
    By touch alone, from room to room.
    And here I am.
    (A glimmer of light.)
    Now I see some light—
    It's coming through a keyhole.
    Ah—but there's the lady. If I could read ahead,
    I'd say there's an adventure coming up.
    (HE peers through the keyhole.)
    What an ornate room! What lovely women!
    What an exquisite table! How fine the ladies are!

What extraordinary beauty!

(Enter all the WOMEN [DOÑA ANGELA, DOÑA BEATRIZ, and maids] carrying napkins, hors d'oeuvres, and water. Each one curtseys before DOÑA ANGELA, who is richly dressed, as they pass her.)

ANGELA: *(Aside to Doña Beatriz.)* Since my brothers think that you've gone home,

As long as you stay hidden here with me,

You're safe—they have no reason to come in here.

BEATRIZ: *(Aside to Doña Angela.)* And what's my part?

ANGELA: *(Aside to Doña Beatriz.)*　　　　　For right now, play my servant;

Later on, you get to be the audience,

And witness everything that happens.

(Aloud to Don Manuel.)

Are you very tired of waiting for me?

MANUEL: No, my lady. When one awaits the dawn,

One knows that the cold and dismal night

Must be endured; and in that knowledge,

Pain becomes a pleasure, even as

The longer one must wait,

The more one cherishes the day.

And yet, your beauty shines so brilliantly

That night is banished; the Sun will rise,

But you will outshine it as well,

Just as the night is overtaken

By the smiling rays of dawn,

The dawn by morning light,

And morning light is conquered

By the burning heat of noon.

All these are nothing now:

The one true god of light is here,

So night and day have ended their career.

ANGELA: Although I want to thank you for that lovely speech,

I feel I must chastise you a bit

For taking liberties with fact.

This place is not like Heaven,

Where every ardent thought's accompanied

By a matching blast of rhetorical wind,

But rather a modest little house,

In which we take all such pronouncements

With a grain of salt. I'm not the dawn;

She always smiles and I, I must confess, do not.
I'm not like morning light, I'm sad to say,
Nor do I shine a noontime sun
Upon the truth that I adore so much.
I really don't know what I am,
Except I'm not the dawn, the morning light,
Or noontime sun. Today I neither shine
So brightly, nor weep a river of tears.
And so, Don Manuel, I beg you,
Say of me just this: that I was and am a woman,
Who has granted only you among all men
This extraordinary favor.

MANUEL: But that's not much. Although I've come to see you,
I could argue that I feel more pain than pleasure
In the visit. In fact, I am offended.

ANGELA: Offended by me?

MANUEL: Yes. Because you won't entrust me with your name.

ANGELA: All I ask is that you don't demand that from me;
It's the one thing I cannot tell you.
If you want to come and speak with me,
The one condition is that you don't attempt
To find out who I am.
Today I present myself as an enigma—
I'm not what I appear, nor do I look
Like what I really am.
As long as I am hidden, we can see each other;
But once your curiosity about my name
Is satisfied, you'll cease to love me,
Though I will still love you.
When death picks up his paintbrush,
He sometimes makes a picture
That looks one way in a certain light,
And quite different when the light is changed.
Just so, my portrait, made by Love the painter,
Contains my image in two lights;
You see me now in one, and love me;
I fear that when you see the other one,
Your love will turn to something worse.
Anyway, the most important thing
For you to know about me is that

I am not Don Luis's mistress, as you thought;
I want to put that doubt to rest forever.

MANUEL: Then, madam, what moved you to flee from him
So urgently?

ANGELA: It might have been
Some feminine principle I hold,
That would have been compromised
If Don Luis had recognized me.

MANUEL: All right, at least tell me how
You got into my room.

ANGELA: Now's not the time for you to know that;
It's another inconvenient matter.

BEATRIZ: *(Aside.)* Here's where I make a graceful entrance.
(Aloud.)
As Your Excellency can see,
The sweets and sparkling water are served . . .
(The LADIES bring napkins, glasses of water, and sweets.)

ANGELA: What a gross *faux pas*! What impertinence! Fool!
Who's "Your Excellency" here?
Are you trying to trick Don Manuel into believing
That I am some great lady?

BEATRIZ: No, I . . .

MANUEL: *(Aside.)* That little slip relieves me
Of a great many doubts; I already thought
She was a noblewoman, which was why
She hid herself so thoroughly—
And she had the money to ensure
Her secret stayed intact.
(DON JUAN's voice is heard calling from offstage; everyone is thrown into confusion.)

JUAN: *(Offstage.)* Open this door, Isabel.

ANGELA: *(Aside.)* Oh heavens! Who's making that noise?

ISABEL: I'm dead!

BEATRIZ: *(Aside.)* I'm frozen solid!

MANUEL: *(Aside.)* God help me!
Will my bad luck never end?

ANGELA: Sir, that's my father at the door.

MANUEL: What should I do?

ANGELA: You've got to find a hiding place.
Isabel, take him to that other room,

You know the one I mean, and hide him.
You understand?

ISABEL: We'll go there at once.

JUAN: *(Offstage.)* Will you never get around to opening this door?

MANUEL: Heaven stand by me now,
Or I lose my life and honor both
With one roll of the dice.
(Exeunt DON MANUEL and ISABEL.)

JUAN: *(Offstage.)* I'll knock the door down, then.

ANGELA: You can hide in the hallway, Beatriz—
They won't find you there.
(Exit BEATRIZ and enter DON JUAN.)

ANGELA: Now what are you doing in my room
At this late hour, and what are you
Making such a scene about?

JUAN: First you tell me, Angela,
What kind of dress is that
For the hour and the place?

ANGELA: Since my situation calls for mourning,
I thought I'd try to cheer myself a bit
By putting on something nicer, that's all.

JUAN: No doubt. Women always cure their griefs
By dressing up; they let their jewels
Nurse them back to health.
But this seems inappropriate for you.

ANGELA: What does it matter if I dress this way
In my own room, where no one comes to see me?

JUAN: Tell me, did Beatriz go home?

ANGELA: Yes, her father finally got over his temper.

JUAN: That's all I need to know.
I'm going to see if I can speak with her tonight.
God be with you—and remember,
This dress just isn't right for you.
(HE exits.)

ANGELA: God be with you—and get out of here!
(Enter BEATRIZ.)

BEATRIZ: Well, we dodged that one.
So your brother's going to look for me.

ANGELA: Before we stir the house up any further,
And Don Manuel comes back to find me,

Let's go to a private room where we can have
Some peace and quiet for a moment.
BEATRIZ: If this works out in the end,
  We'll all be calling you the Phantom Lady.
  (Exeunt.)

DON MANUEL's room.

(Enter DON MANUEL and ISABEL though the wall of glass.)
ISABEL: You've got to stay put, and not make any noise;
  People can hear you.
MANUEL: I'll be a statue.
ISABEL: Heaven help me shut this panel—
  I'm so afraid, I'm shaking.
  (SHE exits.)
MANUEL: Oh my God. Imagine going to a place
  Where you're completely ignorant of everything—
  So you can't sense when you're in danger,
  You can't anticipate the traps
  That may be set for you—a risky situation.
  So where am I? Far from my familiar room
  At Don Juan's place, in a house I've never seen,
  Whose owner is—at least—one of nobility,
  And the place is full of terrifying shadows.
  What's this? It looks like someone's
  Opening a door over there.
  Yes, and now he's coming in.
  (Enter COSME.)
COSME: Praise be to God, tonight I can
  Get to my room a little easier,
  And I don't have to be afraid of anything,
  Even though I'm going around without a light.
  After all, since my lord the phantom's
  Got hold of my master, what could
  He possibly want with me?
  (HE runs into DON MANUEL.)
  Well, he wants something from me after all.
  Who's there? Who is it?
MANUEL: Be quiet, I tell you,
  Whoever you are, if you don't want me

To slice you into ribbons.

COSME: I'll be as quiet as a poor relation
    At a rich man's dinner.

MANUEL: *(Aside.)* No doubt this is a servant who wandered in here.
    Now I'll find out where I am.
    (Aloud to COSME.)
    Tell me, whose house is this? Who owns it?

COSME: Sir, the owner and the house belong to Satan;
    Because there's a certain person living here
    They call the Phantom Lady, who—by the way—
    Is a demon in woman's flesh.

MANUEL: And who are you?

COSME: You might call me a valet, or a serving-man;
    In reality I'm a subject, a slave, who for some reason
    Has been made to suffer through these evil spells.

MANUEL: And who's your master?

COSME: He's a crazy man,
    A scatterbrain, a fool, a simpleton,
    A real lost soul: and if you want proof,
    He's fallen head over heels for that lady.

MANUEL: And what's your master's name?

COSME: Don Manuel Enríquez.

MANUEL: Jesus and all the Saints!

COSME: And I'm Cosme Catiboratos.

MANUEL; Cosme—it's you? But—how did you get in here?
    This is your master! Tell me—
    Did you follow behind my sedan-chair?
    Did you come in here, like I did,
    To hide in this apartment?

COSME: This is a pretty game now!
    Tell me—how did *you* get here?
    Didn't you go charging off by yourself
    To your mysterious graveyard rendezvous?
    Well then, how did you get back here so quickly?
    And how about this—how'd you get in here
    When I've had our only key the whole time?

MANUEL: Wait—tell me—what room is this?

COSME: Yours, or else the devil's.

MANUEL: By God, you're lying!
    Just this minute I was far away from here,

In a completely different house.

COSME: Well, there's our phantom at work again,
   Without a doubt, because I've told you
   Nothing but the truth.

MANUEL: You want to make me lose my mind!

COSME: You need your eyes opened a little wider?
   Go through that door into the alcove, then come back,
   And you'll be sure of where you are.

MANUEL: Good idea. I'll go take a look.
   (HE exits.)

COSME: Oh, Ladies and Gentlemen!
   When are we going to be through
   With all these obvious complications and contrivances?
   (Enter ISABEL through the wall of glass.)

ISABEL: *(Aside.)* So Don Juan's come back.
   He and Don Manuel had better not
   Run into each other tonight;
   I'll get Don Manuel away.
   (Aloud.)
   Psst! Sir! Psst!

COSME: *(Aside.)* Even worse! Those "Pssts" give me sciatica!

ISABEL: My master's gone to bed now.

COSME: *(Aside.)*   Which master's that?
   (Enter DON MANUEL.)

MANUEL: It's my room, all right.

ISABEL: Is that you?

MANUEL: Yes, it's me.

ISABEL: Come with me.

MANUEL: All right, whatever you say.

ISABEL: Nothing to worry about, nothing to be afraid of.

COSME: Help, sir, help! The phantom's taking me away!
   *(ISABEL takes COSME by the hand and takes him out through
   the wall of mirrors.)*

MANUEL: Won't we ever figure out this mystery?
   You're not answering? What an idiot!
   Cosme, Cosme!—Oh my God,
   I can touch the room's four walls, but no Cosme.
   Didn't I just speak with him here?
   How could he have vanished in such a flash?
   Wasn't he here? All right:

I am now, truly, losing my mind.
Even so, it's obvious
Someone got in here somehow.
I'll hide in the alcove and wait until
I find out who this beautiful Phantom Lady is.
(HE exits.)

DOÑA ANGELA's room.

*(All the WOMEN enter, one with candles, another with some boxes,
and another with a pitcher of water.)*

ANGELA: *(To Doña Beatriz.)* Now that my brother's gone off to look for you,
And Isabel is bringing Don Manuel here,
Everything should be ready. He'll find this tableau
Waiting for him when he comes.
Now, ladies, places please.

BEATRIZ: I've never seen anything like this.

ANGELA: Are they coming?

MAIDSERVANT: Yes, I hear their footsteps now.
(Enter ISABEL, leading COSME by the hand.)

COSME: *(Aside.)* Poor me! Where am I going? These jokes
Aren't funny anymore. But wait a minute—
All of a sudden I'm staring at a gallery
Of the most extraordinary beauties!
Am I Cosme, or Amadis of Gaul?
Am I really little Cosme?
No—suddenly I'm Paris of Troy,
And these are all my Helens!

ISABEL: Now here he comes. But—what do I see? Sir! . . .

COSME: *(Aside.)* All right, now I really believe it, I'm under a spell,
And I'm hanging on to my soul by a whisker.

ANGELA: What's this, Isabel?

ISABEL: *(Aside to her mistress.)* Madam, it seems that when I went to get
Don Manuel right where I left him, and I told him not to move,
I picked up his servant instead.

ANGELA: Don't try to sugar-coat your error, Isabel.

ISABEL: It was dark.

ANGELA: Now everything will be revealed,
There's no stopping it.

BEATRIZ: *(Aside to ANGELA.)*   Wait—we can fool him

Even better now.

(Aloud.)

Cosme.

COSME: Great lady.

BEATRIZ: Come over here.

COSME: I like it over here.

ANGELA: Come on now—don't be afraid.

COSME: A valiant man like me, afraid? Hmpf.

ANGELA: So then why don't you come over here?

    (COSME goes over toward them.)

COSME: *(Aside.)* Now there's no getting out of it—

    It's become a point of honor.

    (Aloud.)

    Respect always grows faster with

    Some fear and trembling going before,

    To pave the way, you know.

    Even Lucifer himself wouldn't scare me

    All that much if he dressed up as a woman.

ANGELA: Now get a hold of yourself;

    Have a sweet, take a drink of water.

    Fear can make you thirsty.

COSME: I'm not thirsty.

BEATRIZ: Come here. You've got two hundred leagues to go,

    You know, to make the journey home.

    (Noise of someone calling.)

COSME: Heavens! What do I hear?

ANGELA: Is someone calling?

BEATRIZ: Yes.

ISABEL: *(Aside.)* The worst is yet to come!

ANGELA: *(Aside.)*   Oh my poor soul!

LUIS: *(Within.)*   Isabel!

BEATRIZ: *(Aside.)*   Heaven help me!

LUIS: *(Within.)*

                  Open up!

ANGELA: *(Aside.)* For every catastrophe,

    I've got a brother.

ISABEL: It's now or never!

BEATRIZ: I'll go hide.

    (SHE exits.)

COSME: *(Aside.)* That one's got to be the real Phantom.

ISABEL: *(To COSME.)* Come with me.

COSME: You bet I will.

    (Exeunt.)

    (The door opens and DON LUIS enters.)

ANGELA: And what do you mean by coming in here?

LUIS: My troubles bring me here,

    To intrude on others' pleasures.

    I just saw Beatriz's sedan-chair

    In the house, and so I know she's back;

    I also know my brother's around here somewhere.

ANGELA: Well, get to the point: what do you want?

LUIS: I heard footsteps in the rooms above me,

    So I thought there must be people here.

    I only came up to be sure

    I was mistaken about that.

    (HE raises a portiere and discovers BEATRIZ.)

LUIS: Beatriz, you're here?

BEATRIZ: Yes, I'm here. I had to come back,

    Because my father got upset with me again—

    It seems he's always angry nowadays.

LUIS: You're up to something, I can see that much—

    What's with all these plates, and sweets, and glasses?

ANGELA: Why are you so curious about

    How women entertain themselves

    When they're alone?

    (ISABEL and COSME make a noise at the wall of mirrors.)

LUIS: And that noise there—what's that?

ANGELA: *(Aside.)* I'm dying!

LUIS: By God, there are people around here

    Somewhere after all! My brother

    Better not be hiding from me like this.

    (HE moves away from the wall of mirrors to get a candle.)

    Oh my soul! I only came in here

    To spoil a love affair, spurred on by foolish jealousies.

    But now it's becoming a matter of honor!

    I'll take this candle—no doubt another bad idea—

    And its light will uncover everything,

    Including my lost honor.

    (HE exits.)

ANGELA: Oh, Beatriz, we're lost if he runs into them!

BEATRIZ: If Isabel's got them safely
　　Into Don Manuel's room by now,
　　You've got no need to worry—
　　The secret of the wall is safe.
ANGELA: Yes, but wouldn't it be rotten luck if Isabel,
　　In all the turmoil, doesn't lock the panel,
　　And somehow he gets through it?
BEATRIZ: You need to find a safer place to hide.
ANGELA: I'll make use of your father,
　　Just as he did of me;
　　If one problem brought you here,
　　Another one carries me away.
　　(Exeunt.)

DON MANUEL's room.

(Enter ISABEL and COSME through the wall of mirrors, and DON MANUEL through another door.)
ISABEL: Come in quick.
MANUEL: 　　　　　　　I hear someone
　　In the entry hall again.
　　(Enter DON LUIS with a candle.)
LUIS: By God, I see a man there!
COSME: 　　　　　　　　　This is bad.
LUIS: How did this wall of glass become ajar?
COSME: Oops. There's a light. I'll make use
　　Of this convenient table that I've found.
　　(Hides.)
MANUEL: It's come to this. *(Puts his hand on his sword.)*
LUIS: Don Manuel!
MANUEL: 　　　Don Luis! What now?
　　This is impossibly confusing!
COSME: *(Aside.)*
　　It's good to hear him say so finally—
　　I could have told him that a thousand times!
LUIS: You're an unworthy gentleman—worse, a villain!
　　A traitor, a faithless guest,
　　Who tramples on the hospitality
　　And honor of a man who holds you
　　In such high esteem—

(Draws his sword.)
>   If you dare to be so vulgar,
>   Let's see you use that infamous sword of yours.

MANUEL: I'll use it only to defend myself—
>   I'm so confused by what you say—
>   I hear you, see you, try to understand,
>   And I cannot. You may try to kill me,
>   But you won't be able to,
>   Because the cruel misfortunes of my life
>   Have already made me immortal;
>   No, you cannot kill me, because the pain
>   You have inflicted with your words
>   Has gone before your sword and done the deed.

LUIS: Deeds, not clever words,
>   Are your only answer now.

MANUEL: But stop—just think a moment—
>   Is there any other way that I can
>   Satisfy you, Don Luis?

LUIS: What satisfaction could there be
>   After what you've done to me?
>   If you've used the secret door to enter
>   That wanton woman's room, how will I ever
>   Get satisfaction for so great an insult?

MANUEL: Don Luis—may your sword run through my breast
>   A thousand times if I ever knew
>   Anything about a door,
>   Or that there was an entrance
>   To any other room from here.

LUIS: Well then—what were you doing
>   Shut up in here in the dark?

MANUEL: *(Aside.)* How should I answer that?
>   *(Aloud.)*
>   I was waiting for a servant.

LUIS: When I saw you hiding here—
>   Are you saying my eyes deceived me?

MANUEL: Yes—they'll trick you more than any other sense.

LUIS: And so my eyes were lying to me—
>   Were my ears mistaken too?

MANUEL: Yes they were.

LUIS: So everything lies, you only tell the truth,

You're the one who—

MANUEL: Stop right there—
    Because before you have a chance to speak,
    Or think, or even imagine what to say,
    I'll take your life. I'm just the one to do it, too.
    Friendship now gives way to the laws of honor.
    If we've got to fight, let's do it properly.
    We'll share the light so that it shines
    The same on both of us; now lock the door
    That you so rashly entered by,
    While I secure this other one.
    We'll put the key between us on the floor
    So that the survivor can make his escape.

LUIS: I'll block the wall of mirrors with this table;
    Then no matter how hard they try,
    No one can get in here.
    (HE picks up the table and finds COSME.)

COSME: *(Aside.)* The plot thickens.

LUIS: Who's this here?

MANUEL: Of all the rotten luck!

COSME: Nobody here.

LUIS: Tell me, Don Manuel, isn't this the servant
    You were waiting for?

MANUEL: Now's not the time
    To sort this out. I know I'm right;
    Believe what you want about me.
    Once our swords clash, only the victor
    Will be left alive.

LUIS: Come on then, let's fight.
    What are you waiting for?

MANUEL: Now you offend me even more.
    I was just considering what to do
    About my servant; if I turn him loose,
    The world will know exactly what we're doing
    In an instant, but if I keep him here,
    I'd have unfair advantage,
    Since he would surely fight
    At my side.

COSME: I won't, if that'll help.

LUIS: This alcove has a door—

Shut him up in there and we'll be equal.

MANUEL: Good thinking. Get in there and don't come out.

COSME: To make me fight would be the real challenge—
They're going to too much trouble
To get me not to fight.
(HE exits.)

MANUEL: Now we're alone.

LUIS: Let the duel begin.
(THEY fight.)

MANUEL: I've never seen such a steady hand!

LUIS: I've never seen such a strong thrust!
(DON LUIS loses his sword.)
I'm defenseless now. You've disarmed me.

MANUEL: That's no blemish on your courage,
It's just an unlucky accident.
Go look for another sword.

LUIS: You are courteous as well as valiant.
(Aside.)
Fortune! What should I do
In an awful mess like this,
When he's taken my honor, conquered me,
But let me live?
I've got to think—to find some proper way
To pay him what I owe him.

MANUEL: Aren't you going for your sword?

LUIS: Yes, and if you'll wait for me,
I'll be back soon.

MANUEL: Late or soon, I'll be here.

LUIS: God save you, Don Manuel.

MANUEL: And you as well.
(Exit DON LUIS.)

MANUEL: Now I'll lock the door and put the key away
To make sure no one gets in here.
My thoughts are in a whirl—I was right
About that passageway; and now it's clear
She's Don Luis's mistress, as I thought.
In fact, everything's turned out exactly
As I thought it would—but then,
When do one's misgivings ever lie?
(COSME sticks his head out above the door.)

COSME: Oh, sir! Now that you're alone,
  I beg you, sir, let me out of here.
  I'm afraid the phantom will come
  Looking for me here, and this alcove
  Is so small I can't even hide from myself.
MANUEL: I'll let you out, but only because
  My brain is so exhausted
  That nothing can upset me—even you.
  (DON MANUEL goes into the room with COSME.)
  (Enter DOÑA ANGELA, veiled and not wearing slippers;
  DON JUAN remains in the doorway.)
JUAN: You'll stay right here until I'm satisfied
  I know just why you left the house at this late hour.
  You will not be allowed in your own room,
  Ungrateful creature, until I've formed my own conclusions
  About what's happening, without your interference.
  (Aside.)
  I'd better post a servant outside the door
  To warn Don Manuel away if he returns.
  (HE exits.)
ANGELA: Oh, my unhappy life! One misfortune
  Follows hard upon another.
  I might as well be dead!
  (Enter DON MANUEL and COSME.)
COSME: Let's get out of here right away.
MANUEL: What are you afraid of?
COSME: I'm afraid that woman is a devil
  And that she's not through with me.
MANUEL: Look—we know who she is now,
  And besides, one entrance is blocked by a table
  And the other's locked—how do you think
  She'd get in here?
COSME: However she wants.
MANUEL: You're an idiot.
  (COSME sees DOÑA ANGELA.)
COSME: Jesus, Mary, and Joseph!
MANUEL: What is it?
COSME: You-know-who has joined us,
  Just like that.
MANUEL: Woman, what are you—an illusion

Or a ghost who's come to kill me?
Tell me how you got in here.
ANGELA: Don Manuel . . .
MANUEL: Tell me!
ANGELA: Listen carefully.
Don Luis, upset, knocked on my door.
He came in, thought things through,
And calmed himself a bit,
But then ran out again,
In a bigger frenzy than before.
He tore apart the house until he found you,
And then I heard the clatter of your swords
In combat. I knew the end had to be fatal
For one of you, and not knowing what to do,
I left the house. The stillness of the frigid night
Became a pale image of my sorrow.
I began to walk around, falling down,
Picking myself up, wandering
Without a purpose or a plan,
Until I found myself back in my old
Familiar prison cell, my room.
Where else should a poor unhappy soul end up?
And who should be there, on the threshold—
You see how heaven weaves the web of our misfortunes—
But Don Juan, my brother! I tried in vain
To keep my silence, not to tell him who I was;
And yet he stood there, like a snow-capped volcano,
All ice and fire, ready to explode.
Then he caught a glint of light
From some jewels in my necklace—
He heard the rustle of my clothes—
Not the first time we women have been betrayed
By things like that—and he imagined
I was his mistress. He flew to me
Just as a moth does to the flame,
To be consumed willingly in the fire—
But he found, instead, a cold shadow
Of his star in me. He tried to speak,
But couldn't, for such deep feeling
Is always mute. Finally, in a voice

So choked with sadness that his lips
Could hardly form the words, he asked
Why this insult had been thrust upon him.
I wanted to reply, but my emotion
Silenced me as well.
Fear is no great friend to reason;
And as I tried to find excuses
To put a better color on my guilt,
I found I couldn't say a word.
When innocence attempts to speak,
The words come late, or not at all—
And so, by keeping silent, you affirm
(Or seem to, anyway) the very crime
You would deny. "Go on," he said,
"My wanton sister, the first blot
On the ancient honor of our house.
I'll lock you up, safely hidden,
While I think about the meaning of this insult."
And so I was once again imprisoned
With my sorrows, until heaven sent you
To relieve them. For love of you,
I played the phantom in my house.
For your honor's sake, I buried my heart's secret
In a living tomb; because
I didn't want to lose you,
I didn't dare speak to you face-to-face.
My intention was to love you,
My only fear, to lose you.
My concern was for your safety.
The purpose of my life is to obey you,
My soul to find you, my desire to serve you,
And my plea is, finally, to persuade you
To stand by me in my present danger.
MANUEL: *(Aside.)* Like some Phoenix, my troubles rise again
Out of the cold ashes.
How can I find my way in this abyss,
The labyrinth of my own soul?
She's Don Luis's *sister*, and all along
I thought she was his mistress. Oh, heavens—
If I was so afraid to offend him

Where only pleasure was concerned,
What will happen now when it's a matter
Of his honor? This is unjust!
All right: she's his sister.
If I try to set her free
And defend her with my blood,
Letting my sword proclaim her innocence,
Then I'll be doubly in the wrong,
Since that's as much to say that I'm a traitor,
That I've offended the whole house,
And broken the code of hospitality.
And if I prove my innocence
By swearing out her guilt,
That would be to say that she's at fault,
And my honor won't allow that outcome.
Well, then, what should I do?
I make myself a traitor by defending her,
And I am a villain if I don't.
If I look out for her, I'm a faithless guest,
And I'd be less than human if I turned
Her over to her brother. In doing that,
I'd be ungrateful for a very noble love.
Well, every choice I make's a bad one—
So I might as well die fighting.
    (To DOÑA ANGELA.)
Don't be afraid, my lady. I'm a noble gentleman,
And you're with me now.
    (A knock at the door.)
COSME: Sir, someone's knocking
MANUEL: That'll be Don Luis, who went
    To get a sword. Well, open it.
ANGELA: Poor me! My brother!
MANUEL: Have no fear; my valor will defend you.
    Stand behind me now.
    *(DOÑA ANGELA places herself behind DON MANUEL, and COSME
    opens the door. Enter DON LUIS.)*
LUIS: I have returned. But—what's this I see?
    Traitress!
    (As HE sees DOÑA ANGELA, HE draws his sword.)
MANUEL: Put up your sword, Don Luis.

As you know I've been waiting here since you left;
And then—somehow—this lady entered.
She tells me she's your sister.
I give you my word as a gentleman:
Until this moment, I had no idea of that.
Suffice to say, although perhaps it was
An error on my part, I spoke to her
Without knowing who she was.
And now I must lead her to safety
At the risk of my life and soul:
Our duel, you'll agree, must take place alone,
Behind locked doors, to avoid a scandal.
Once having freed her, I will return
As our quarrel demands. To one who cares
About his reputation, his honor and his sword
Are his most important armaments.
I let you go to get your sword;
Now let me go in service of my honor.

LUIS: I went for my sword only so that
I could lay it at your feet,
Complying with the debt of gratitude
I owed you. But now you give me a new cause,
And I find I'm ready to fight again.
This lady is my sister; you must not take her
From my sight unless she becomes your wife.
If you agree, her hand is yours;
Take her away, and if you like, come back
To finish up this other business.

MANUEL: I will return, but given the example
Of your prudence and your constancy,
My only business now is
To throw myself at your feet.
(HE kneels.)

LUIS: Rise, Don Manuel. Get off the floor.

MANUEL: And in further compliance with your judgment,
I give your sister my hand.
(Enter DON JUAN.)

JUAN: If all that's missing is someone
To give the bride away, here I am.
I was on my way to where I'd left my sister

When I heard some angry voices;
Now I find they've changed to happy ones.

(Enter, through a different door, BEATRIZ and ISABEL.)

BEATRIZ: And why stop there? We're not quite finished yet!

JUAN: But—Beatriz—you're here in my house again?

BEATRIZ: I never left; I'll tell you all about it later.

JUAN: We should seize this moment, which calls to us so clearly.

COSME: Thanks be to God, the phantom's revealed herself.

(To DON MANUEL.)

Tell me something—was I drunk the whole time?

MANUEL: If you're sober now, you may marry Isabel today.

COSME: To do that, I'd have to be really drunk.

Anyway I can't.

ISABEL: Why not?

COSME: Because I wouldn't want to waste our time
On things like that. What we should really do
Is beg pardon now for all our faults,
And tell these good people there
That our humble author thanks them,
And asks them for their hands.

END OF *THE PHANTOM LADY*

THE CONSTANT PRINCE

(El príncipe constante)

 1629

CHARACTERS

The Portuguese

    DON FERNANDO, PRINCE, INFANTE OF PORTUGAL
    DON ENRIQUE, PRINCE
    DON JUAN COUTIÑO
    DON ALFONSO, LATER KING OF PORTUGAL
    BRITO, A GRACIOSO
    PORTUGUESE SOLDIERS
    CAPTIVES

The Moors

    THE KING OF FEZ, AN OLD MAN
    MULEY, A GENERAL
    CELÍN, SERVANT TO THE KING
    TARUDANTE, LATER THE KING OF MOROCCO
    FÉNIX, THE INFANTA OF FEZ
    ZARA, SERVANT TO FÉNIX
    SOLDIERS
    COURTIERS

PLACE

The scene is North Africa: Fez, Tangier, and their environs. The principal action takes place in the year 1437.

ACT ONE

The Garden of the King of Fez

Offstage, we hear the voices of male CAPTIVES in a song of lamentation.

CAPTIVES: *Our songs are played*
 On instruments of iron,
 These chains that hold us prisoner.
 Under the weight of years
 Even the great ones yield;
 For to Time, great Time
 The hardest conquests
 Seem as nothing.
 (Enter FÉNIX, attended by ZARA, who is dressing her.)
ZARA: Now that you've come,
 The pure light of dawn
 Can no longer claim
 That it illuminates this garden;
 That task is yours now.
 The flowers cannot boast
 Of their sweet smell,
 Nor the rose that its purple is as deep
 Or the jasmine so white.
FÉNIX: The mirror.
 (ZARA gives her a mirror.)
FÉNIX: What good is beauty
 (And mine deserts me anyway.)
 If I lack happiness?
ZARA: What are you feeling?
FÉNIX: If I knew what I feel, from that same feeling
 I would fashion some relief. But I don't know
 The nature of my pain. Sometimes it's sadness,
 Today it's melancholy. All I know
 Is that I feel; I know I feel something,
 But I don't know what it is;
 It must be some illusion of the soul.
ZARA: You cannot shake your sadness here;
 These gardens, which spring adorns with roses
 Big as statues, and temples made of jasmine,

Are still not beautiful enough for you.
Go down to the sea. There you'll find
A beauty big enough to match your own.
FÉNIX: But this won't make me happy,
This contest of the sea and land,
A battle of reflections in a mirror
To see who is more splendid—
The flowers or the breaking waves,
The waves or the flowers;
Because the garden, jealous of the sea's
Thundering waves, will try to imitate
Their motion; a sweet confusion
Comes of all this jealousy:
The garden then becomes a sea of flowers
And the sea, a garden of rolling waves.
Without a doubt, my pain is great;
So great that nothing can assuage it,
Not field, sky, earth, or sea.
(Enter the KING with a portrait.)
KING: If by chance your sickness,
Born of the fever of your beauty,
Permits you to call a truce to your sadness,
Then look upon this beautiful original
(Because you can't call something
A mere portrait that has such soul and life).
This is the Prince of Morocco, Tarudante,
Who's coming to lay his crown at your feet.
The picture is merely his ambassador,
And I don't doubt that even though
This diplomat is mute, he brings
A real embassy of love.
I have high hopes of his protection:
He's promised me ten thousand horsemen
For the conquest of Ceuta, which I'm now preparing.
Allow yourself to love the one who will
Be crowned the King of all your beauty
Here in Fez.
FÉNIX: *(Aside.)* Allah protect me!
KING: Why does this news seem to chill you so?
FÉNIX: *(Aside.)* Because it's my death sentence.

KING: What did you say?

FÉNIX: My lord,
  You know you've always been
  My mentor, my father, and my King,
  So what should I say?
  (Aside.)
  Oh, Muley!
  You've lost your one best chance!
  (Aloud.)
  My silence best portrays
  My great humility.
  (Aside.)
  My soul would be a liar if I thought it,
  My voice would be one if I spoke.

KING: Take the portrait.

FÉNIX: *(Aside.)*   Forced to do it,
  My hand will take the portrait,
  But not my heart.
  (A cannon shot is fired.)

ZARA: That salute is for the entrance of Muley,
  Returned today to the Sea of Fez.

KING: That's good.
  (Enter MULEY carrying a general's staff.)

MULEY: My Great Lord, I am at your feet.

KING: Muley, it's good you're home.

MULEY: Whoever finds his way to port
  And finds a radiant dawn waiting there,
  A daughter of the sun, that man can say
  With all his heart he's glad to be home.
  Give me your hand, my Lady,
  So that this royal favor
  Can shine on one who plans new triumphs
  In your name, who left to do great deeds
  And who returns more bound to you than ever . . .
  (Aside.)
  Heaven help me! What do I see?

FÉNIX: You, Muley, are truly welcome.

MULEY: *(Aside.)* Not if I believe my eyes, my welcome
  Seems more ill than well.

KING: Muley, what's the news from the sea?

MULEY: A test of your capacity to suffer.

KING: Well, whatever you have to tell me,
  Let me hear. A constant soul
  Can always find an equal place
  For good news and for bad . . .
  Sit here, Fénix.

FÉNIX: I obey.

KING: Be seated, everyone. Now go ahead,
  And I command you: don't hide anything.
  (All sit.)

MULEY: *(Aside.)* There's nothing I can hide—
  And nothing that I say will matter anyway.
  (Aloud.)
  I sailed, as you commanded,
  With two small ships, Great Lord,
  To survey the Barbary Coast.
  My mission was to land
  At that famous city called Ceuta,
  Which heaven took from you,
  Perhaps because Muhammad was rightly angered
  By the weakness of our arms.
  For now we see that Portuguese banners
  Fly from her towers, a constant insult
  To the eye, an obstacle to reverence,
  A painful bit in the mouth of our pride.
  Heaven may yet concede the victory to you,
  Although a greater need is now upon us:
  The arms that you prepared
  To conquer great Ceuta now must go
  To Tangier, which cries out for rescue.
  I know this, because at sea one morning
  I discovered, far across the water,
  A heavy swarm of ships—a Portuguese armada.
  Facing such a fearsome enemy,
  I turned my ships around
  As quickly as I could (knowing full well
  That retreat is often the root of victory);
  And made it to the shelter of a cove
  Where I could avoid the awesome enemy.
  They passed by without seeing us.

Now from this fleet, one ship was straggling,
For, as I later learned, a storm had ripped
Through every ship, and left just this one
Wounded, torn, and broken; and so she staggered,
Plunging this way, blundering that way,
At each turn on the point of sinking or
Staying afloat. I approached the ship.
Though my Moorish colors identified me
As an enemy, the will to live
So stirred some of the men that they began
To improvise a ladder out of ropes and cables,
Crossing over from their danger to the safety
Of my prison; some remained behind,
Insulting those who made their escape, shouting
That to live with honor is to live eternally,
And—Portuguese vainglory at its finest—
Still resisting to the end.
One sailor gave me a picture of their plan.
He said that this armada had sailed from Lisbon
Bound for Tangier, determined to lay siege.
The King of Portugal sends his two brothers,
Enrique and Fernando, with fourteen thousand
Soldiers, and a thousand strong war-horses.
We must defend the city:
Take arms yourself, bear Muhammad's scourge,
So that upon the sandy shores of Africa,
The Portuguese crown will find an unhappy grave.
Our scimitars will make green fields
And blue seas run blood red.
KING: Be silent now. Tell me no more;
    I am already filled with deadly fury.
    Muley: take our best horsemen
    And move along the coast, while I
    Prepare a larger force behind you;
    You can occupy our foe in skirmishes,
    Delaying them from gaining ground,
    And in so doing, show the quality
    Of blood that is your heritage. Meanwhile
    I will quickly come with the rest of this great
    Army that you see among these fields;

One great and bloody day will put an end
To so much pain: Tangier will never fall to them,
And Ceuta will once again be mine.
(Exits.)

MULEY: Fénix, now that I must go to die,
I wish to say a word about the sickness
That is killing me; and even though
I fear the loss of your respect, I must admit
My pains are caused by jealousy,
And jealousy is never courteous.
What portrait—oh, my lovely enemy!—
Do I see in your hand?
Tell me, who's the fortunate one?
Who? . . . But wait a minute,
Don't let your tongue speak such an insult:
Even though I don't know who it is,
It's bad enough to see it in your hand
Without hearing it from your lips.

FÉNIX: Muley, although I wish to give you leave
To love me, you have none to injure and offend.

MULEY: That's true, Fénix. But the Heavens
Know that jealousy can triumph over
Every other power in the world.
With great prudence, caution, even fear,
I served you, desired you, and loved you.
And so I could be silent when it came to love;
Now that jealousy takes hold,
I can't, Fénix, I simply can't.

FÉNIX: Your fault does not deserve an answer from me;
But even so, I want to satisfy you,
For an injury between the two of us requires
Explanation. Now I'll give you one.

MULEY: You really will?

FÉNIX: Yes.

MULEY: God will grant you
Happiness!

FÉNIX: This portrait has been sent to me . . .

MULEY: By whom?

FÉNIX: Tarudante, Prince of Morocco.

MULEY: Why?

FÉNIX: Because my father, ignorant of my care . . .
MULEY: All right.
FÉNIX: Would like for these two kingdoms . . .
MULEY: Don't say another word.
    This is the explanation, the satisfaction
    That you promised me?
    God grant you evil news, not good!
FÉNIX: But how am I at fault?
MULEY: You took the portrait.
FÉNIX: Could I have avoided it?
MULEY: Of course!
FÉNIX: And how?
MULEY: You could have invented something.
FÉNIX: Oh, like what?
MULEY: You could have died. That's just what I
    Would do for you.
FÉNIX: It was done by force.
MULEY: More like weakness.
FÉNIX: By violence.
MULEY: Not by violence.
FÉNIX: What then?
MULEY: It was my absence.
    The grave where my hope is buried.
    And so as not to see your fickleness
    Confirmed without a doubt, I'll go away
    As soon as possible; and you,
    Fénix, will no doubt kill me once again.
FÉNIX: Your absence is commanded now—you must depart . . .
MULEY: My soul's already gone.
FÉNIX: . . . for Tangier, while
    I wait for you in Fez where finally
    All your complaints will find an end.
MULEY: They will, if my ill fate allows it.
FÉNIX: Good-bye—for we must part now.
MULEY: Listen: will you, can you, let me leave
    Without giving me that picture?
FÉNIX: The King forbids it.
MULEY: Let it go—it's only right
    That from your hand I seize
    The one who seized me from your heart.
    Exeunt.

The Beach at Tangiers.

Within, the sound of a trumpet, noise of disembarkation, and enter DON FERNANDO (the Constant Prince), DON ENRIQUE, DON JUAN COUTIÑO, and Portuguese SOLDIERS.

FERNANDO: Beautiful Africa, I have to be the first
    To step onto your sandy shore,
    Because in the pressure of my footprint
    Your neck will feel the powerful force
    That will at last subdue you.

ENRIQUE: In the soil of Africa I'll make the next
    Bold stand—
    (HE falls.)
    Heaven help me! My evil omens
    Follow me all the way here.

FERNANDO: Enrique, put aside the misgivings
    You feel; no, this fall is a good omen,
    Because the land rewards you like a Lord,
    Opening its arms to you.

ENRIQUE: The field's deserted—the minute they saw us,
    All the troops departed.

DON JUAN: Tangier has closed its gates.

FERNANDO: Everyone's retreated to find safety.
    Don Juan Coutiño, explore the area with care:
    Before the sun offends us with its fury,
    We'll make our first salvo against the city.
    We'll tell them that they'd best not undertake
    A vain defense, because all that they will gain
    From that are blood and fire.

JUAN: You'll soon see me at the city's gates.
    (Exits. Enter BRITO, the gracioso.)

BRITO: Thank God I've got a spring
    Back in my step, and here on land
    I can go wherever I want,
    Without quivering from hand to foot!
    Not like at sea, where you are stuck
    Inside a wooden monster who's a rotten judge
    Of which way to go or what to do.

At sea, there's no escape from death,
Even at a full gallop—nowhere to run!
Ah, my lovely earth! I don't want to die in water.
Come to think of it, I don't want to die on land:
Not until the Judgment Day.

FERNANDO: What are you saying, Brito?

BRITO: I'm rewriting a funeral oration.
I'm preaching a panegyric
To the water, this stuff I used to hate;
But ever since I learned
That wine is partly water,
All my anger's gone, and now
Is drowned, you might say, in the distant past.

ENRIQUE: Why do you listen to this fool?

FERNANDO: Why not, if he's amusing? Why should you
Deprive yourself of all these things?

ENRIQUE: My soul is full of fears;
My luck's dead set against me.
Ever since leaving Lisbon, all I've seen
Are images of death.
Barely two days out, the sun
Was blotted out by storms,
And the fierce and furious sea
Threatened to destroy our fleet.
If I look at the sea, I seem to find
A thousand shadows; in the sky,
Instead of a blue veil I see blood;
In the pleasing air all I can make out
Are terrible night-birds; and on the land
All I see are graves, into which I,
In my misery, trip and fall.

FERNANDO: Now let me decipher the cause of your
Quite accidental melancholy.
The storm took one ship from us,
Which tells us that we set sail
With more than enough
To do what we set out to do;
If we imagine monsters in the water
Or terrifying birds floating on the wind,
We didn't bring them here; and if they're real,

Doesn't that foretell a bloody end
To the monsters who live here?
These vile omens are for the Moors
Who believe in such things, not for Christians
Who maintain a proper doubt.
We two are such; we come to glorify
Our faith in God; His will be the honor,
His the Glory, if we triumph.
And if we die, to fear the punishment
Of God is proper; we come to serve Him,
Not offend: we are Christians, and should
Act as such. But—what's this?
(Enter DON JUAN.)

DON JUAN: My Lord,
When I approached the city walls as you commanded,
I saw a troop of horsemen
Charging along the road from Fez
So quickly that they seemed to me to be
Riding birds, not brutes.
The air gives way before them,
They hardly touch the ground;
And so you cannot say whether they run or fly.

FERNANDO: Let's go receive them, with our muskets
In the lead; afterwards, the horsemen
In their usual style, with lance and harness.
Come on, Enrique! This occasion offers us
A good beginning! Take heart!

ENRIQUE: I am your brother! These accidents
Don't frighten me, any more than I'll be frightened
When I look Death in the face.
(Exeunt all but BRITO.)

BRITO: I'll set a constant guard on Headquarters—
Where my health and safety are stationed.
What a brave skirmish!
Now they're charging, the attack is on!
I'd better get myself some cover.
(Exit. Sound of arms within.)

Another part of the beach.

(Enter DON JUAN and DON ENRIQUE, fighting with several MOORS.)

ENRIQUE: After them—the Moors have turned
 Their backs and run!

JUAN: These fields are filled with spoils,
 Of horses and of men.

ENRIQUE: Where's Don Fernando, do you think?
 Why hasn't he appeared?

JUAN: He was so embroiled in the action
 That we've lost sight of him.

ENRIQUE: Let's look for him, Coutiño.

JUAN: You'll always have me at your side.
 (Exeunt.)
 (Enter DON FERNANDO with MULEY's sword in hand, and MULEY
 with his shield.)

FERNANDO: On this deserted plain, which seems to be
 One mass grave, if not in fact a theater
 Of death, only you, brave Moor, still stand;
 You fought with strength and brilliance,
 And yet your eyes betray some deeper anguish:
 I think the cause of your sadness
 Must lie elsewhere; because in freedom's name
 It's neither just nor decent that someone
 Who is so fierce in battle should cry so tenderly.
 And so, if there is any comfort in
 Telling one's troubles to another, then
 While we make our way toward my people
 I want to offer you such comfort as I can,
 If I am worthy of the favor.
 So with all courtesy, I ask you,
 What's the matter? For I know
 Already that being taken captive
 Isn't all. When you speak about your pain
 It's lessened, if not conquered altogether,
 And I, the one who's had the greatest part
 In this, your accident of fortune, want
 To be the one to offer consolation
 If you will consent to be consoled.

MULEY: You are valiant, Spaniard, and equally as courteous.
 You win victories by speech
 As surely as you do by sword.

My life was yours when, with your blade,
You conquered me as I stood among my people;
But now, as you subdue me with your words,
My soul is yours as well; by arms and words
You've made me captive twice.
I'd rather not repeat my griefs aloud—
And yet I must obey your will.
Besides, I want to tell you what I feel
Because of who I am, and who you are.
I am the nephew of the King of Fez,
Sheik Muley is my name; when I was young
I came to Fez to serve the King, my uncle.
But there began my pains and my misfortunes;
And all my happiness came to an end.
All to an end.
I came to Fez, and found a beauty
Living in the house next door,
And fell in love.
This love constantly increased
As we grew up together.
When we were young,
Our love was not the blinding kind,
But it aimed subtler arrows
At our young hearts.
Just as water makes a mark on stone
By its persistence—not by force,
But simply falling, always falling, even so
My tears at last began to work upon
That heart of stone, that heart of diamond.
I didn't gain the victory by excellence
Or merit—just my love, my constant love
Which softened her resistance in the end.
And for a happy while I lived this way,
Although the time was brief—enjoying
A thousand amorous delights under a sky
Grown gentle with soft breezes and sweet air.
But then I went away, to my destruction:
For in my absence another lover came
And killed me. Or he might as well have.
Now he's delighted; I am miserable;

He's beside her; I'm away.
I'm a captive, he is free.
You'll easily see the contrast in our fates
Since you have taken me captive:
Perhaps you'll also see why I lament.
FERNANDO: Valiant and gallant Moor:
If you adore her as you tell it,
If you idolize her as you say,
If you love as strongly as you claim,
If you're wracked with doubting fears
And still you love, I tell you that you suffer
Happily. I don't require any other ransom
For your freedom but that you take it.
Go home, and tell your lady that a knight
Of Portugal offers you up to be her slave;
And if she wishes to be obliged to me
For some repayment, tell her this:
Pay the debt with love, and keep the interest.
Now your horse, which fell exhausted,
Seems rested and refreshed;
And because I understand what love is,
And know the perils of absence and delay,
I don't want to hold you any longer:
Mount your horse and go.
MULEY: My voice can say nothing in reply:
To such a liberal offer
The best response is simply to accept.
But tell me, Portuguese, who you are.
FERNANDO: A nobleman, nothing more.
MULEY: You show that well, whoever you may be.
For good or ill, I will always be your servant.
FERNANDO: Take the horse. It's getting late.
MULEY: I only hope that someday I can repay you
For all these favors.
FERNANDO: You can: Enjoy them!
MULEY: Because in the end, good deeds are never lost.
May Allah protect you, Spaniard.
FERNANDO: If Allah is God, may he go with you.
(A noise within of drums and trumpets.)
What trumpet stirs the air so boldly?

And from the other side, the sound of drums.
Together they make the music of Mars.
(Enter DON ENRIQUE.)

ENRIQUE: Oh, Fernando! I've been hurrying to find you!

FERNANDO: Enrique, what's the news?

ENRIQUE: Those echoes come
    From the armies of Fez and Morocco;
    Tarudante's coming to the aid of Fez,
    And the King himself follows with his people,
    Which puts us right between both armies.
    So we're surrounded, both besieging and besieged.
    If we turn our backs on one, we'll have no chance
    To defend against the other: What can we do?

FERNANDO: What can we do? Die well,
    With constant hearts and souls. Are we not
    Two Masters, two Princes, when it would be
    Enough to be two Portuguese? Enough that
    No trace of fear would ever cross our faces?
    Now let us die for our faith, as we
    Came here to do.
    (Enter DON JUAN.)

JUAN: Our expedition is in disarray.
    We're losing ground.

FERNANDO: There's no time now
    To talk of means and ends—
    We must take arms and seek our remedy
    In battle, since the armies that surround us mean to end
    Our struggle—for Christ and Portugal!

JUAN: To war, to war!
    (Exeunt, drawing their swords to give battle. Enter BRITO.)

BRITO: Now we're stuck in the middle between two armies,
    And there's no remedy for that.
    No remedy. What a wicked phrase!
    If only the eternal key that unlocks heaven
    Would open that door just a crack
    So that from out of this great danger, one could slip—
    Someone who came here not knowing
    The why or wherefore of it all—
    But feigning death seems like the thing to do,
    So from now on I'll be dead.

(HE falls down on the ground.)
(Enter a MOOR, attacking DON ENRIQUE.)

MOOR: Who is this that defends himself so well,
  Against my arm that falls upon him like
  A lightning bolt from heaven?

ENRIQUE: Even though I stumble, fall, and die
  Upon the Christian corpses, my hands
  Won't lose their strength and I won't fail:
  Let this advise you who I am.
  (THEY step over BRITO and exit.)

BRITO: God be with him—and I hope he always steps so carefully!
  (Enter DON FERNANDO, retreating from the KING and other MOORS.)

KING: Give up your sword, proud Portuguese.
  If I can keep you alive and in my power,
  I promise to be your friend. Who are you?

FERNANDO: A knight: that's all I'll tell you. Now let me die.

JUAN: *(Within.)* Onward, my Fernando—

KING: Hearing this name, what's left to hope for?
  Put up your arms; I need no more of
  Joy or glory on this day. This prize
  Is victory enough. If fate has sentenced you
  To prison, or to death, Fernando, give
  Your sword now to the King of Fez.
  (Enter MULEY.)

MULEY: What's this I see?

FERNANDO: I would give it only to a King; indeed
  It would be useless to deny it.
  (Enter DON ENRIQUE and DON JUAN.)

ENRIQUE: My brother taken captive!

FERNANDO: Enrique, stop.
  Don't add more sorrows with your words.
  Although our luck seems to turn against us,
  Sometimes fortune goes that way.

KING: Enrique, Don Fernando is in my power,
  And even though I could demonstrate my
  Advantage now by putting you to death,
  My only purpose here is to defend myself;
  Your blood would not bring half so many honors
  As will the sparing of your lives.
  To speed the ransom from the King,

Go now to Portugal—Fernando
Will stay here, in my power, until the day
That you return to free him. But tell Duarte
That any ransom is in vain unless
He returns Ceuta to my hands.
And now, your highness, to whom I am
Indebted for this great honor,
Come with me to Fez.

FERNANDO: I follow your illustrious highness.

MULEY: *(Aside.)* Oh, Heavens! Now my feelings overflow,
Torn between friendship and jealousy!

FERNANDO: Enrique, I remain a prisoner.
I do not fear my fate, nor any evil.
Tell our brother to behave
Like a Christian prince regarding my misfortune.

ENRIQUE: And who would doubt his greatness of heart?

FERNANDO: I charge you with this—I say that he
Must act like a Christian.

ENRIQUE: And I pledge to return as such.

FERNANDO: Give me these arms.

ENRIQUE: You are the prisoner, and yet you place
Me in your bonds.

JUAN: I should stay here with you;
Don't send me away.

FERNANDO: Loyal friend!

ENRIQUE: Unhappy day, when I must leave you.

FERNANDO: Say to the King . . . better yet, don't say a word.
In great silence, fearing nothing, carry
These tears to the King my brother.
(THEY exit; enter two MOORS, who see BRITO playing dead.)

FIRST MOOR: This Christian's dead.

SECOND MOOR: To prevent the plague, we'd better
Throw these bodies in the sea.

BRITO: You're leaving your skulls wide open
To slashes and blows—
(HE rises and begins attacking them.)
Because even though we're dead,
We're still Portuguese!

END OF ACT ONE

ACT TWO

A mountainside near the gardens of the King of Fez.

(Enter FÉNIX.)

FÉNIX: Zara! Rosa! Estrella! Will no one answer me?
    (Enter MULEY.)
MULEY: I will, because to me, you are the sun,
    So I must be your shadow,
    And shadow always follows sun.
    I heard the sweet echo of your voice and hurried
    Across the mountain to ask you:
    What's the matter?
FÉNIX: Listen now, while I
    Attempt to explain myself to you.
    I came here, exhausted, after hunting
    A wild beast; and in the freshness of this garden
    I found peace and rest. I had barely
    Given up my soul to the murmuring
    Soft solitude when I felt a stirring
    Among the leaves; I made myself alert,
    And soon I saw an old African woman,
    A spirit in a human shape,
    Her face a wrinkled, distant frown,
    A living skeleton whose cold, wild form
    Was like a sculpture carved from a tree
    Still covered in rough bark.
    She took my hand; I put down roots right then,
    Became a tree trunk just like her.
    One touch made the blood in my veins turn icy;
    So did the horror of the voices that ran
    Swiftly all around me, hard to understand.
    And yet I could make out this much:
    "Unhappy woman! Inescapable misfortune!
    You are beautiful, yes, but beauty has a price,
    And that is someone's death!" That's what she said;
    Now all I do is wait for the fulfillment
    Of that cold prophecy, that oracle —
    For that will be, as well, the end of my own life.

For now I know my beauty's price is death
For someone else!
(SHE exits.)

MULEY: It's easy to decipher
This dream, this illusion—the images
Might as well describe the pain I feel.
You have to give your hand to Tarudante.
But even though I die to think of it,
I'll keep my wrath contained; and yet
I'll see to it that he will not enjoy
Your love unless he kills me first.
It could be that I will lose you,
But I cannot lose you and still live;
And then your price will truly be
The value of one death,
Because you'll see me die
Of love, of envy, and of jealousy.
(Enter TWO CAPTIVES and DON FERNANDO.)

FIRST CAPTIVE: From the garden, hard at work, we saw you
Going to the hunt, Fernando, and all of us
Together come to throw ourselves at your feet.

SECOND CAPTIVE: Sharing your pity is the only consolation
That heaven offers us here.

FERNANDO: Friends, give me your arms;
God knows I wish my arms could give you liberty
Before my own is won.
But think of this as one of heaven's favors.
Our bad luck will certainly improve.
Let that idea help you endure the hardships
Of the moment—we know our fate will change.
Oh, God! It's vile that all I have to give
Is counsel, nothing more. My friends,
Please pardon me. I expect some help
From Portugal at any time; it will
Be here quickly, and all my fortune
Will be yours; if they release me from
Captivity, I tell you now, you all
Are coming with me. Now go with God,
Back to your labors, and refrain
From angering your masters.

FIRST CAPTIVE: The sight of you makes our slavery blessed.
SECOND CAPTIVE: May you outlive the Phoenix by a century!
   (Exeunt CAPTIVES.)
FERNANDO: My soul's so full of pity it can
   Hardly bear to see them leave without
   Some favor from my hands.
MULEY: And here am I, observing the simplicity
   And love you show these captives.
FERNANDO: Their misfortune pains me
   As if it were my own; from their misfortune
   I am learning how to be unhappy.
   Someday that may prove necessary.
MULEY: Does your Highness really say this?
FERNANDO: From being born a Prince, I've come to be
   A slave. And I suspect that I will come
   To a more miserable state.
   For if I'm living as a slave,
   I've already endured the longest fall—
   From Prince to prisoner—now there's only
   The slow decline of one who is held captive.
   One day summons forth another day,
   And that one summons yet another,
   All chained together, in pain and lamentation.
MULEY: I wish my pain were less than yours; you see,
   Although Your Highness is a captive today,
   Tomorrow you'll return to your country.
   But my hope is in vain, because my fortune,
   Although it's more changeable than the moon,
   Can never change for the better.
FERNANDO: I'm practically a courtier here at Fez
   And I have never heard another word
   About the love you told me of before.
MULEY: I've hidden all those favors deep within.
   I swore to their owner that I'd keep them
   Safely concealed; but, for friendship's sake,
   Without breaking my oath, I'll tell you this.
   My bad luck, and my pain as well,
   Have stayed pent up inside me all this time.
   My love is a Phoenix that can never die.
   And so no matter what I see or hear,

A Phoenix is in all my thoughts. My suffering
In love, in all my fears and feelings? Phoenix.
When I mistrust my misery, that's the Phoenix too.
When I believe I'm worthy of her, yet
All the while fearing that I'm not,
Even in this, a Phoenix is my hope.
Phoenix is all my love and all my care;
Now, since I have told you of this Phoenix
As a lover and a friend, I've spoken—
And kept silent.
(HE exits.)

FERNANDO: He managed to declare his love quite prudently;
If Fénix is the cause of all his pain
I can't compete with that; my pain is common.
I don't deserve any special sympathy,
Since many have suffered just as much
And their lives are filled with troubles.
(Enter the KING.)

KING: I've come here to the foothills
In pursuit of you, Your Highness,
So that before the sun has hidden itself away
In tones of pearl and coral, you might enjoy
The combat between a tiger and my hunters
Who have surrounded it.

FERNANDO: My lord,
You think up new delights to please me
As if someone were keeping score of them.
If this is how you entertain your slaves,
They'll never miss their homeland.

KING: When I hold captives of such qualities
That they bring honor to their master—
I have ample reason to treat them well.
(Enter DON JUAN.)

JUAN: Great lord, a Christian galley's in the harbor,
Wearing signs of mourning black.
(Enter DON ENRIQUE, in mourning, with a piece of paper.)

ENRIQUE: *(To the KING.)* Give me your arms, great lord.

KING: Your Highness brings good news?

FERNANDO: Oh, Don Juan, my death is certain now!

KING: Oh, Muley, my happiness is certain!

ENRIQUE: Give me license to embrace my brother.
>   Ah, Fernando!
>   *(THEY embrace.)*
FERNANDO: My Enrique,
>   What kind of suit is this? But stop:
>   Your eyes have told me quite enough,
>   Your tongue needs add nothing to the tale.
>   Don't cry; if you have come to tell me
>   That my slavery is to be eternal,
>   That's the thing I most desire:
>   You could have asked for a reward,
>   And instead of mourning and sadness,
>   Dressed in festive clothing.
>   How is the King, my lord? If he is well,
>   I have no other care. Why don't you answer?
ENRIQUE: If we feel our sorrows twice when they're repeated,
>   I wish for you to feel them only once.
>   *(To the KING.)*
>   Hear me now, great lord;
>   For even though this mountain makes a rustic
>   Sort of palace, here I beg of you
>   To give me audience.
>   Broken and shattered, the armada that so proudly
>   (But with such vain pride) came here across
>   The waves to Africa, has once again
>   Returned to Lisbon, leaving behind in sorrow
>   A captive—the Infante. From the moment
>   Duarte heard the tragic news, a sadness
>   Fell upon his heart, and thus it grew
>   From its first lethargic melancholy
>   To a more fatal state, making liars
>   Of those who say that sorrow cannot kill.
>   It killed the King. He is in Heaven.
FERNANDO: Oh my God! This is the cost of my
>   Imprisonment?
KING: Allah knows that this misfortune
>   Pains me. Please go on.
ENRIQUE: In his last will,
>   The King my lord commanded that Ceuta
>   Should be given to you in exchange

For the Infante. And so, with all the powers
Of Alfonso, the heir, the star that shines
Now in the absence of the sun, I come
To hand that city over, and so . . .
FERNANDO: Stop!
Don't go any further: stop, Enrique.
These are unworthy words, not only
For a Portuguese Infante, or a knight
Who bears the cross of Christ, but even
For the vilest man, a barbarian who never
Saw the eternal light of Christian faith.
My brother, who is now in heaven—
If his last will contained this clause, it's not
Meant to be taken at its word,
But only to show how deeply he desired
My liberty. And you should seek this liberty
By other means, peaceful or violent.
Because to say "Give him Ceuta" is to say,
"To free Fernando, you must do the impossible."
How could a King who's Catholic and just
Possibly hand over to a Moor
A city that has cost him his own blood,
As he was the first to place our colors
On the battlements, armed only with
His sword and shield? And that's the least of it.
A city that makes Catholic confession
To our Lord; a city filled with churches,
Consecrated to holy worship with love
And reverence; would it be a Catholic action,
Would it stand for Christian piety,
If these sovereign temples,
Instead of being filled with golden light
Would see instead nothing but the shadows
Of the Ottomans? Their crescent moons
Eclipsing our bright sun? A tragedy.
Would it be right to change the chapels
Into stalls, the altars into mangers?
Or, heaven forbid, into mosques?

Here my tongue grows mute, I lose my breath,
I'm overcome with pain; because the thought
Breaks my heart, and my whole body trembles.
It wouldn't be the first time that a stable
Had given shelter to our Lord. But mosques—
That would be to write an epitaph,
A memorial to our immortal shame,
Saying this: "Here God had a home,
And today was thrown out by the Christians,
So they could give it to the Devil."
And what will become of the Catholics
Who live there? Must they hide their faith,
Or practice new, ungodly rites and customs
So as not to lose all that they hold dear?
Should so many lives end in miserable captivity
In trade for one whose loss is not important?
Who am I? Am I more than a man?
If being born Infante sets me apart,
Look now—I am a captive. If I lack
The trappings of nobility, it is because
I am a slave. That's what I am. And anyone
Who calls me an Infante is mistaken.
I lost myself in battle, lost myself;
And so I died. I died, and so
It makes no sense that many lives must perish
To redeem this one dead man.
See how these vain powers, now torn in pieces,
Become like shards of sunlight, sparks of flame—
(HE tears the paper that DON ENRIQUE brought.)
King, I am your slave; use me as you will.
I do not want my freedom.
It is not available to me.
Enrique, return to your country;
Say that you left me buried in Africa;
For I will live my life as if that were
The truth. Christians! Fernando is dead;
Moors, a slave remains with you;
Captives, a new companion now is joining
Your ranks of suffering.

Heavens, a man restores your holy churches;
Mountains, on you there lives a sad someone,
Who soon will be the equal of your beasts;
Wind, a poor man's cries must sound as loud
As you do in their race around the world;
Earth, a corpse now makes his grave within
Your entrails. For King, brother, Moors, Christians,
Sun, Moon, stars, Heaven, Earth, wind,
Mountains, wild beasts, everyone must know
That today a constant Prince, amid
The worst misfortunes and the sharpest pain,
Exalts the Catholic faith, reveres the law of God.

KING: You thankless wretch, ungrateful
For the glories and the grandeurs of my kingdom,
You dare deny me now the thing I've most desired?
You know you are my slave, you call yourself
A slave and you confess it; and so I must
Begin to treat you like a slave. Your brother
And your friends will see how a vile slave
Will bend and kiss my feet.

ENRIQUE: What misfortune!

MULEY: How painful!

ENRIQUE: What misery!

JUAN: What a pity!

KING: You are my slave.

FERNANDO: That's true,
But your revenge in this is small; for if
A man goes free upon the earth for his
Life's journey, at the end of all his travels
He returns to her, there's no escaping that.
Besides, I'd rather offer thanks to you
Than blame, because you teach me shortcuts
To my rest, which draws ever closer.

KING: Being a slave, you cannot hold a title
Nor collect a tax. Today Ceuta
Is in your power: if you admit yourself
A captive, and confess that I'm your master,
Why don't you give it to me?

FERNANDO: Because it's God's, not mine.

KING: Don't you believe in obedience to your master?
    Well then, I command you by this precept
    To hand the city over to me now.
FERNANDO: Heaven commands that a slave obey his master
    When the order is a just one; if the master
    Demands some sinful action from his slave,
    The slave has no obligation to obey;
    Because even a commanded sin is still a sin.
KING: You must die.
FERNANDO: That would give me life.
KING: Well then, you'll live like you were dying.
    I'll prove that I can be severe.
FERNANDO: I'll prove I can be patient.
KING: But you'll never have your liberty.
FERNANDO: And Ceuta never will be yours.
KING: *(Calling to a servant.)*   Ho!
    (Enter CELÍN.)
CELÍN: My lord.
KING: From this point on,
    This captive will be treated like the others:
    Have him tend my horses, baths, and gardens;
    No longer dressed in silks,
    But rough and humble woven cloth;
    He'll eat black bread and drink brackish water;
    He'll sleep in a damp, dark dungeon,
    And so will everyone who serves him—I extend
    This sentence to his vassals and his train.
    Take all of them away!
ENRIQUE: I weep for this!
MULEY: What misfortune!
JUAN: What sadness!
KING: You will see, barbarian, you will see:
    You are patient; I am severe. Which will last
    The longest?
FERNANDO: You'll see indeed,
    For what's inside of me is all eternity.
    (THEY take him away.)
KING: Enrique, you have my word; I permit you
    To return to Lisbon and leave this sea

Of Africa behind you. When you reach Portugal,
Tell them the Infante tends my horses.
If they object, tell them to come and set him free.
ENRIQUE: And so they will. For if I leave him
In this unhappy misery, with my heart
In torment that I cannot share his pain,
I leave only so that I can come again
With force enough to win his liberty.
KING: Very well; do what you can.
MULEY: *(Aside.)* Now the moment has come to show my loyalty;
I owe my life to Fernando, and I will pay the debt.
(Exeunt omnes.)

The King's garden.

(Enter CELÍN, leading in FERNANDO, dressed as a captive.)
CELÍN: The King commands you to attend here
In this garden, and to obey his law.
FERNANDO: My patience is greater than his severity.
(Enter other CAPTIVES, and one sings while others dig in the garden.)
FIRST CAPTIVE: *To the conquest of Tangiers,*
Against the Moor Muley,
The King sent Don Fernando,
His brother, the Infante.
SECOND CAPTIVE: *(To FERNANDO.)*
Captive, why are you so upset? Don't cry,
Take comfort; for the Master said that we
Would soon return to our homeland and live
In freedom once again. No one will have
To stay behind on this sad ground.
FERNANDO: How quickly this illusion will be lost!
SECOND CAPTIVE: Take comfort now and help me water all
These flowers: take these pails and bring me water
From that pool.
FERNANDO: I want to obey. And so I'll try.
You've given me a proper task to do,
Asking me for water, since my cares
Will flood a field with the torrent of my tears.
(HE exits.)
(Enter DON JUAN.)

JUAN: Tell me, friend, and Heaven bless and keep you,
  If you've seen the master Don Fernando working in this garden.
FIRST CAPTIVE: We have not seen him.
JUAN: I can't hold back my tears.
  (Enter DON FERNANDO with the buckets of water.)
FERNANDO: Mortals, don't be horrified to see
  A Prince of Portugal insulted
  In such a miserable way.
  It just reflects these miserable times.
JUAN: But my lord, is your Highness really come
  To such a state of sadness? It breaks my heart.
FERNANDO: God bless you, Juan, but it pains me greatly
  That you found me here; I wanted to conceal
  My true identity and lose myself
  Among my people, fellow captives all,
  In our poor and miserable servitude.
FIRST CAPTIVE: My lord, I beg forgiveness for having been
  So blind and idiotic not to know you.
SECOND CAPTIVE: Give us, lord, your feet to kiss.
FERNANDO: Rise, my friend; look and see; I live
  A humble captive, just like you.
JUAN Your Highness . . .
FERNANDO: What "highness" does one have
  Who lives so lowly now? Never treat me
  As anything but an equal from now on.
JUAN: Why doesn't the lightning strike from Heaven
  And kill me now?
FERNANDO: Don Juan—remember you are noble,
  And should not behave this way. Have you begun
  To lose your trust in Heaven? Prudence, valor,
  And gallantry are required of you now.
  (Enter ZARA.)
ZARA: Fénix, my mistress, is coming to the garden,
  And commands that you create a lovely
  Garland for this basket with your flowers.
FERNANDO: I hope that I can bring it to her;
  I want to be the first in every service.
FIRST CAPTIVE: We'll all help you collect them.
ZARA: We'll wait for you to bring them here.
FERNANDO: Don't do me any courtesies: your sorrow

And mine are equal now. But it's our luck
If not today, tomorrow then, that death
Will truly equalize us all. So it's important
Not to leave undone today
What otherwise we'd have to do tomorrow.
(All the captives exit, making courtesies toward the Infante; enter FÉNIX.)
FÉNIX: Did you order them to bring me flowers?
ZARA: I did.
FÉNIX: I need their colors here to cheer me up.
ZARA: My lady, why are you so melancholy?
FÉNIX: What I saw was not a dream; I saw
    My own misfortunes. When a troubled person
    Dreams, perhaps, of joy, or treasure,
    There's no doubt that it's a dream.
    But if that person dreams of some great ill,
    And then it's put before you— dreaming ill
    And finding ill the moment you wake up—
    I have no hope of pity.
ZARA: If you feel like this now, what sorrows
    Will you have left over when you die?
FÉNIX: All my misfortunes come to that—the price
    Of one man's death. Who has ever seen
    Such pain! Must I live by someone's death?
    Who will this dead man be?
    (Enter DON FERNANDO with the flowers.)
FERNANDO: I.
FÉNIX: Oh heavens!
FERNANDO: What do you wonder at?
FÉNIX: I wonder at the sight and sound of such a fortune.
FERNANDO: You wouldn't swear it's true, but Fénix, I,
    Who humbly wish to serve you,
    Bring you flowers from the garden;
    Hieroglyphs of fortune, let me call them,
    That are born with dawn's first light
    And perish with the day.
FÉNIX: That's true. But tell me, who is responsible
    For this change in your condition?
FERNANDO: My fortune.
FÉNIX: Is it so severe?

FERNANDO: So powerful.

FÉNIX: You bring me pain.

FERNANDO: Don't let it frighten you.

FÉNIX: Why not?

FERNANDO: Because a man is born a subject
    To both fortune and death.

FÉNIX: You're not Fernando?

FERNANDO: Yes I am.

FÉNIX: Who put you in this state?

FERNANDO: The law of slavery.

FÉNIX: Whose law?

FERNANDO: The King's.

FÉNIX: But why?

FERNANDO: Because my life is his.

FÉNIX: I'm sure
    That he respects you.

FERNANDO: That was true,
    And just as true that now he hates me.

FÉNIX: Is it possible that it has taken
    Only one day to drive apart twin stars?

FERNANDO: To stand in for the stars you speak of,
    I bring these flowers. Let them be a warning
    To all of humankind:
    How much can change in a single day!
    The roses waken early so that they
    Can flower with the dawn; and then they bloom
    Only so that they can grow old and die;
    They find their cradle and their grave in one
    Single bud. Just so men see their doom,
    Being born and dying the same day;
    Centuries pass, but really they were hours.

FÉNIX: You've filled me with horror and fear, and now
    I neither wish to see nor hear you; you must be
    The first poor soul from whom another soul,
    Just as unfortunate, must flee.

FERNANDO: And the flowers?

FÉNIX: If you have found hieroglyphs in them,
    Tear them up, break them apart,
    They alone will know my anguish and my rage.

FERNANDO: What fault do the flowers bear?

FÉNIX: Impersonating stars.

FERNANDO: So you no longer want them? Why?

FÉNIX: These points of light, these sparks
 That make a show of feeding
 On the sun's splendors, they live
 To cause us pain. They are nocturnal flowers.
 Although they're very beautiful, their ardor
 Is ephemeral; for if one day is an entire age
 In the world of flowers, so one night
 Is an epoch for the stars.
 What endurance can mankind
 Hope for, what changes will we see,
 When our fortunes flow from stars that every night
 Are born anew, and every morning, die?
 (Exeunt FÉNIX and ZARA.)
 (Enter MULEY.)

MULEY: Until Fénix left I've waited over here;
 Even the most ardent eagle sometimes
 Flies from the light. Are we alone?

FERNANDO: Yes.

MULEY: Listen.

FERNANDO: Noble Muley, what do you wish?

MULEY: I want you to know that in my heart—
 In the heart of a Moor—there's loyalty and faith.
 I don't know how to begin my story.
 I'm not sure I can describe how I've felt
 The wild swings of fortune in the world,
 The unjust devastation, the inconstant disdain,
 The cruel example of the times.
 And there's grave risk to me
 If I'm seen talking to you here;
 Because the King's decree is that no one
 Is to treat you with respect. And so, I trust
 My pain to speak more clearly than my voice,
 And like a slave I come to throw myself
 At your feet. I am yours.
 I do not come, Infante, to offer you my favor,
 But to pay a debt that is now due.
 You gave me life; and now I come
 To give it back; for doing good

Is a kind of treasure, to be hoarded
Until the need is greatest.
Because terror has me now in shackles
I want to tell you quickly what I've done.
Tonight, I have arranged a boat for you;
In the windows of your dungeon
I will place instruments to unlock
The fetters that you wear.
Later, outside the walls, I'll break your chains;
You will put to sea with all your fellow captives,
And sail for home, sure of my safety here,
Since it will be easy to believe
You all escaped from prison.
So two great things will have been set free;
My honor and your life.
And because it might be necessary
To purchase some good will during your voyage,
Here are some jewels, whose value is uncountable.
So, Fernando, this act will rescue me from prison too:
And paying such a debt will be a blessing
To this noble, faithful servant.
FERNANDO: I'd wish to thank you for my freedom now,
    But the King is coming toward the garden.
MULEY: Has he seen you with me?
FERNANDO: No.
MULEY: Well then;
    He'll have no reason to suspect anything.
    (HE exits.)
    (Enter the KING.)
KING: *(Aside.)* What's so secret between Muley and Fernando?
    Why should one depart as soon as he
    Sees me, while the other stands pretending he's alone?
    There's something here to be afraid of.
    And my fears will seek security.
    (Aloud.)
    It pleases me—
MULEY: Great Lord, I'm at your feet.
KING: —To find you here.
MULEY: What is your command?
KING: It pains me that Ceuta is not mine.

MULEY: Conquer it, and crown yourself with laurel;
That city is ill-prepared to defend itself
Against your valor.

KING: I plan to bring it to my feet by means
Of a more domestic sort of warfare.

MULEY: Such as?

KING: Such as this: I will humiliate
Fernando, putting him in such a state
That he himself will turn Ceuta over.
You know as well as I, friend Muley,
That I have reason to suspect
That Fernando is not completely secure
In Fez. The captives, seeing him in such
A humbled state, will pity him so much
That they will rise up in a riot to free him;
Besides which, he has always had powerful
Friends who would assist him; and gold will break
The strongest guards so easily.

MULEY: *(Aside.)* I'll support this notion now, so when it happens
I'll be beyond suspicion.
(Aloud.)
Your fears are just;
I'm certain that they wish to free him.

KING: I've thought of only one remedy for this.

MULEY: And what is that, my Lord?

KING: Muley, you must guard him. I place him wholly
In your charge; you will let nothing sway you,
Neither fear nor interest. You are the Infante's
Governor; see that you guard him well;
Because no matter what should happen,
He's your responsibility. *(Exits.)*

MULEY: Beyond a doubt the King has heard our plans.
Allah defend me!
(Enter DON FERNANDO.)

FERNANDO: What afflicts you?

MULEY: Did you hear?

FERNANDO: I heard it all.

MULEY: Then why do you ask me what afflicts me
When you see me in such blind confusion,
In a pitched battle between friendship and honor,

My duty to my friend against my duty to my King?
If I am loyal now to you, I must be traitor against him;
And I would be ungratefully disloyal to you
If I am faithful to my lord.
What should I do when at the very moment
I arrive to free you, he puts his trust in me
To keep you captive? And what if the King
Has found the master key of our great secret?
Help me think this through; advise me;
Tell me what you think I ought to do.

FERNANDO: Muley, love and friendship are of inferior grade
To loyalty and honor. Nobody stands equal
To the King; so my advice is that you serve him;
Do not think of me. I am your friend,
And to secure your honor,
I'll guard myself as well; if anyone
Comes to offer me my freedom, I will
Not accept it, on my life; because
Your honor must be safe with me.

MULEY: Fernando, don't advise me with such courtesy.
I owe my life to you, and I want to pay that debt.
So, all that I've prepared tonight
I'll carry out. Be free, while I
Remain behind to suffer death for you;
Be free, and after that I will fear nothing.

FERNANDO: Would it be just for me to be so cruel,
So tyrannous to the man who pities me
So greatly? To slay his honor
When he offers me my life? No, no.
Now I wish for you to judge my cause,
And my life as well: advise me now in turn.
Shall I take my liberty from one
Who stays behind to suffer in my place?
Should I make him be cruel to his honor
In order to be liberal to me?
How do you advise me?

MULEY: I can't decide.
I don't dare say yes or no. Not no, because
I will bear the weight of speaking that one word
Forever; not yes, because I am convinced

That if I answer yes I will be giving bad advice.
FERNANDO: And yet, advise me; because I, in service
   To my God and to my law,
   Will be a constant Prince in slavery here in Fez.

END OF ACT TWO

ACT THREE

A room in a small palace of the Moorish King.

(Enter MULEY and the KING.)

MULEY: *(Aside.)* Now that there's no hope of rescue, since
    The King has placed Fernando under heavy guard,
    I want to turn his deprivations to some use:
    That is the law of a true friend.
    (Aloud.)
    My Lord, since I have served you, as you know,
    On land and sea, I hope that I have earned
    Some place in your good graces such that
    You might listen and attend
    To something of great weight.
KING: Speak.
MULEY: Fernando . . .
KING: Not another word.
MULEY: Is it possible that you won't hear me out?
KING: I will not. In saying "Fernando"
    You have offended me already.
MULEY: How?
KING: When you plead on his behalf, you deny me
    Any chance of giving what you ask.
MULEY: Since I am his guardian, my Lord, don't you wish
    To have my full report of his condition?
KING: Speak then; but do not look for pity.
MULEY: Fernando is reduced to such a miserable state —
    A trash heap, so debased and humble
    That it is not fit for you to hear about;
    Sick, poor, and crippled,
    He begs for alms from those who pass.
    But he receives next to nothing,
    Because you gave the order that nobody
    Should give him food.
    He's come to such extremes that now starvation
    Cripples him; his sickness rips away
    All traces of his former majesty.
    Passing the frigid night in a hard dungeon,

He remains constant in his faith; and when
He comes out into the pure light of day
The captives, grieving at their task, put him down
Upon a miserable piece of matting,
Which sits upon a—must I name it?—
A dung heap.
You see his smell is such
That none can stand to have him near their home;
And so everyone turns away from him, or flees,
No one speaks to him or offers sympathy,
No one hears his cries, except one servant
And one faithful gentleman who dare
To comfort him in his strange and painful journey.
These two divide their rations with him,
So that they barely have enough to feed themselves.
And yet your people even punish these two souls
For taking pity on their master.
But there is no crueler punishment for these two
Than to be parted from their lord; while one
Goes off in search of food, the other
Stays behind to offer simple comfort
In whatever way he can to ease his pain.
Bring an end to this severity;
Take up the Prince, my lord,
Whom you have placed in such fierce distress
That pity now no longer can describe it;
The only word is horror.
KING: Very well, Muley.
    (Enter FÉNIX.)
FÉNIX: My lord, if ever I have earned some grace
In your affection through my humble service,
Today I come to beg a favor from your majesty.
KING: What can I deny to you?
FÉNIX: Fernando . . .
KING: Very well; there's no more need to speak of it.
FÉNIX: Everyone who sees him in his state
Is horrified by it; all I ask of you
Is mercy . . .
KING: Stop, Fénix! Wait a moment. Think about it.
Who insists that Fernando should die?

And that his end should be so miserable?
If by being faithful to his cruel fate
He suffers drawn-out and cruel punishments,
He's the one who passed the cruel sentence,
Not I: it was none of my design.
Doesn't he hold the means of escaping all
His misery right in his own two hands?
Because in his hands he holds Ceuta; if he
Gives that up to me, he'll free himself
From all these pains and punishments.
(Enter CÉLIN.)

CÉLIN: My Lord, two Ambassadors have come,
Requesting audience with you;
One from Tarudante of Morocco,
The other from the Portuguese Alfonso.

FÉNIX: *(Aside.)* Can my pains grow any greater?
There's no doubt that Tarudante sends for me.

MULEY: *(Aside.)* Now, Heavens, all the hopes I had are lost.
Friendship and jealousy have killed me;
Everything lost in a single day.

KING: Let them come in. Fénix, sit with me
Here upon the dais.
(CÉLIN exits; the KING and FÉNIX sit. ENTER DON ALFONSO and
TARUDANTE, as Ambassadors, each by a separate door.)

TARUDANTE: Generous King of Fez . . .

ALFONSO: King of Fez most high and powerful . . .

TARUDANTE: Whose fame . . .

ALFONSO: Whose life . . .

TARUDANTE: Will never die . . .

ALFONSO: Will last forever . . .

TARUDANTE: *(To FÉNIX.)* And you, the bright dawning of this sun . . .

ALFONSO: This sunset's sunrise,
So to speak . . .

TARUDANTE: In spite of passing ages, may you endure . . .

ALFONSO: In spite of time itself, long may you reign . . .

TARUDANTE: So that you'll have . . .

ALFONSO: So you'll enjoy . . .

TARUDANTE: Much happiness . . .

ALFONSO: Laurels . . .

TARUDANTE: High praises . . .

ALFONSO: Great triumphs . . .
TARUDANTE: No harm . . .
ALFONSO: Many blessings . . .
TARUDANTE: Tell me, Christian, why
    Are you so bold to speak while I am speaking?
ALFONSO: Because no one speaks before me.
TARUDANTE: I should have first place; when allies meet,
    Strangers do not take precedence.
KING: Now that's enough. You may both approach
    The dais and sit here with me. We'll let
    The Portuguese speak first, since he is of
    Another faith, and deserves the honor.
ALFONSO: I will be brief; Alfonso of Portugal,
    The justly celebrated King,
    Sends you good health, and prays that since Fernando
    Will not allow Ceuta to be given
    For his ransom, your Highness will accept
    Gold and silver worth the value of
    Two great cities to reclaim his liberty.
    This he begs of you in a friendly way;
    But if you won't consider it, he must then
    Rescue him with arms, the effect of which
    Will be to fill the seacoast hereabouts
    With a thousand well-armed ships;
    And he swears that by blood and fire he
    Will free the Prince and conquer you, leaving
    This countryside so bloodied
    That if the sun rises on these
    Verdant emerald fields, when it sets,
    This same land will be colored ruby-red.
TARUDANTE: Although as an ambassador it's not
    My place to offer a reply, when it
    Touches my King, I step into the breach;
    And thus for your part you can say
    To Don Alfonso: "Come!" And when he does,
    He'll see these fields run with hot purple agony,
    The blood of Portugal.
ALFONSO: If you, Moor, were my equal, it could be
    That we would see this fight reduced to one

Between two valiant youths;
But tell your King to come, if he pretends
To seek fame in battle, and I'll tell mine
To do the same.

TARUDANTE: You've almost said that you
Were he, and being so, Tarudante
Will know precisely how to answer you.

ALFONSO: Well then: I'll await you in the field.

TARUDANTE: I'll see you don't have long to wait;
Because I'm lightning.

ALFONSO: And I am wind.

TARUDANTE: I am a volcano, pouring out flame.

ALFONSO: And I am Hydra, casting fire aside.

TARUDANTE: I am fury.

ALFONSO: I am death.

TARUDANTE: Don't you tremble when you hear me speak?

ALFONSO: When you look upon me, don't you fear to die?

KING: My lords, your Highnesses, now that anger
Has opened to the sun the curtains of disguise
That kept us in the dark, I advise you
That in my lands, there can be no summons
To a dueling-ground without my leave;
This I deny to you, so that time remains
For me to serve you . . .

ALFONSO: I don't accept
Hospitality or favors from the one
Who gives me pains. I come for Fernando;
To see him I was forced to come to Fez
Disguised like this; I came to speak to you, to put
An end, one way or the other, to the task
That brought me here. And if the greatest ill
Should happen, be advised, my lord,
That awaiting your response
Is all that holds me here.

KING: My response, King Alfonso, shall be complete
And brief: if you do not give me Ceuta,
Have no fear; you won't take him away.

ALFONSO: But I have come for him, and so I must
Take him away. If not, then prepare

For the war which I will wage. Ambassador,
Or whoever you are, we'll see each other
In the field. Today all Africa should tremble!
(HE exits.)

TARUDANTE: And now since I cannot achieve the exquisite
Refinement of serving you as your slave,
Beautiful Fénix, at least give me the pleasure
Of seeing myself at your feet. Give your hand
To one who offers you his soul.

FÉNIX: Your Highness, great lord, these kindnesses
And honors don't add anything to the esteem
That you know is yours already.

MULEY: *(Aside.)* To see this and not die—
What else can happen?

KING: Since your Highness came to Fez so
Unexpectedly, please pardon our lack
Of hospitality.

TARUDANTE: My absence from
My court cannot be more than momentary;
I must go, but I'll return with a great army,
That will make these empty deserts
Seem like cities filled with warriors.

KING: Then it's well that you prepare now
For the journey. And Fénix, it would
Make the city happy if you would come
To Fez. Muley.

MULEY: Great Lord.

KING: Prepare an escort
From our best soldiers, under your command,
To guard her safety until you can deliver
Her to her husband.

MULEY: *(Aside.)* My misfortune is complete.
This latest task was all I lacked.
Being absent, I cannot help Fernando;
He's lost even that small bit of hope.
(Exeunt omnes.)

A street in Fez.

(DON JUAN, BRITO, and other captives carry the INFANTE DON

FERNANDO in their arms. They also bring a mat on which they set him)

FERNANDO: Put me here so that I can better enjoy
  The light that Heaven sends. O, infinite,
  O sweet Lord, what thanks I should give you!
  When Job came to my state of being
  He cursed the day; but I will bless it
  For the grace that God has given us;
  It's clear that every rosy sunset
  And every ray of sunlight now must be
  A tongue of fire with which I praise
  And bless Him.

BRITO: Are you all right here, my lord?

FERNANDO: Better than I deserve to be, my friend.
  What mercies, Lord, have you shown me!
  When you finally brought me out
  From my dark dungeon, you gave me the sun
  To warm me. Lord, you are liberal with me.

FIRST CAPTIVE: Heaven knows we'd like to stay with you
  And keep you company, but now our work
  Awaits us.

FERNANDO: Good-bye, my sons.

SECOND CAPTIVE: What sorrow.

THIRD CAPTIVE: What fierce agony!

  (Exeunt CAPTIVES.)

FERNANDO: Will you two stay with me?

JUAN: I too must leave you.

FERNANDO: What will I do without your favor?

JUAN: My lord, I'll return as quickly as I can;
  I only go in search of something
  You might eat. After Muley left Fez,
  We've lacked the slightest shred
  Of human comfort. But, even so,
  I will go to find some food; although my quest
  Is doomed to fail, since no one gives me
  Anything, so as not to go against
  The King's command that you
  Are to have nothing, not even water.
  Our luck has fallen far to reach this level
  Of severity. But here come some people.

(Exit JUAN.)

FERNANDO: Oh, if my voice could only move someone
    To pity, so that thereby I might live
    Another instant in my suffering!
    (Enter the KING, TARUDANTE, FÉNIX, and CÉLIN.)

CÉLIN: Great Lord, along this street
    You're certain to encounter the Infante.
    Be forewarned.

FERNANDO: Give alms today to this poor man,
    Some sustenance at least. Observe that I
    Am a human being, starving,
    Perishing of hunger. Fellow men:
    Do you not feel my pain? Even a beast
    Shows sympathy for his fellow beast.

BRITO: Maybe this isn't the place to beg this way.

FERNANDO: How should I speak, then?

BRITO: Like this—Moors, have some compassion,
    And give this poor man something he might eat
    By the sacred old bones
    Of the great Prophet Muhammad.

KING: That he still has faith, being in this state,
    So miserable and so unfortunate,
    Offends me greatly, and insults me more!
    Master! Infante!

BRITO: The King is calling you.

FERNANDO: Calling me? Brito, you've been tricked. For I
    Am neither Prince nor Infante. I am
    Their corpse, that's true.
    And since I'm already in the earth,
    Although I was a Prince, was the Infante,
    Those are my names no longer.

KING: Well then: if you aren't the Infante,
    Answer me as Fernando.

FERNANDO: Now, although I'll have to rise up from the ground,
    I'll come to throw myself at your feet
    So I may kiss them.

KING: You make such a show of being constant
    That it oppresses me. Is this obedience
    Born of humility or valor?

FERNANDO: It shows

How much a slave owes to his master.
And since I am your slave, and in your presence,
I must take this time to speak to you,
My King and lord; please listen.
I called you King, and although you are
Of another law and faith, the deity of Kings
Is so august, so strong and absolute,
That it must engender a compassionate soul;
And thus, it follows that you must answer
The call of this generous blood with pity
And with wisdom; because even among
The wildest beasts this title holds such high
Authority that the law of nature
Brings obedience to bear.
We read in some less civilized republics
That the Lion is the King of Beasts,
And when he frowns, his mane becomes his crown;
He shows great pity, because he never
Makes a captive of his wounded prey.
The mighty eagle, crowned with feathered plumes
That the wind ruffles as he soars through the air,
Is emperor of all the birds that salute the sun;
And when a snake has sullied a pure spring
With its poisonous venom,
The eagle, with nobility and pity,
Will swoop down to drive away
Both snake and venom so that a man
Will not, for lack of knowing, drink his death.
So if among the wild beasts and birds,
The king shows his majesty in pity,
It would not be unjust to do the same
Here among men, my lord:
Being of a different law does not excuse you,
For cruelty's the same in every faith.
I do not want to gain your sympathy
With my sufferings and anguish
So that you will let me live,
I do not ask for that; I know well enough
That I must die from this infirmity
That chills my limbs and makes my blood run cold.

I know well enough that I am wounded
To my death, because I cannot speak
A word without my tongue becoming
A sharp sword that cuts me with each breath.
And finally I know too well
That I am mortal, and that no hour is sure;
And so one form is given,
With the same material and shape,
To the cradle and the grave.
When a man receives something
His natural response is to raise his hands
Together in this way; and when he wants
To throw something away, he uses
The same action, but he turns his hands downward,
Because in that way they discard
Whatever they were holding. So the world,
When we're born, as a sign that we are welcome,
Receives us in a cradle, and makes us safe
In open arms; but when, in fury or disdain,
It wants to throw us out, it puts its hands
Together once again and forms this same device:
A cradle when it's turned upwards to greet us,
Turned upside down becomes a tomb.
That's how close we live to our own death;
So bound together are they that when we're born
We lie in both our cradle and our grave.
What should one who hears this hope for?
What should one who knows this go to seek?
It's clear the answer is not life: no doubt
Of that; but death, yes, death; this I beg of you,
So that the heavens may fulfill
My desire to die for my faith; and if pity
Cannot conquer you, then be commanded
By your own severity. Are you a lion?
Then you should roar, and drive away all those
Who injure or offend you. Are you an eagle?
Then with your beak and claws you'll wound
Whoever disturbs your nest.
Because for me,
Although I suffer harsher torments,

Although I witness more severity,
Although I cry in deeper anguish,
Although I pass through countless miseries,
Although I find still more misfortunes,
Although I am afflicted with more hunger,
Although these clothes don't cover my poor flesh,
And although my realm is filth,
I must still be constant in my faith;
Because it is the sun that shines on me,
Because it is the light that guides me,
And I wear laurel for a crown.
You cannot triumph over the Church;
Over me, if you wish, you can triumph;
God will defend my cause, for I defend His.

KING: Is it possible that in such misery you can
Still take comfort in your boasting?
Your misfortunes are your own design: why condemn me?
They don't distress me, not being mine,
If, being yours, they do not cause you pain;
And since your death is at your own hand,
Not mine, don't look for any pity from me;
Take pity on yourself, Fernando; then
I will show you mine.
(The KING exits.)

FERNANDO: *(To TARUDANTE.)* My Lord, will your majesty protect me?

TARUDANTE: What misfortune! *(HE exits.)*

FERNANDO: *(To FÉNIX.)* Divinity must live within this soul of beauty.
My lady, please help me with the King.

FÉNIX: What an overwhelming sorrow!

FERNANDO: Will you not even look at me?

FÉNIX: What horror!

FERNANDO: You do the right thing after all; your eyes
Are not meant to look on suffering.

FÉNIX: What a pity! What dread I feel!

FERNANDO: Very well then. Even though you won't
Look at me, and your intention is
To leave me here, my lady, it is well
That you should understand no matter how
Beautiful you think you are, your life
Is not worth any more than mine.

FÉNIX: Your voice fills me with horror,
    Your breath wounds me.
    Leave me, man! What do you want
    From me? I cannot suffer any more.
    (SHE exits; enter DON JUAN with bread.)
JUAN: To get this bread I bring you now, I've had
    To run from several Moors who wounded me
    With blows, trying to take it back.
FERNANDO: Adam's inheritance.
JUAN: Take it.
FERNANDO: Loyal friend,
    You come too late. My sickness is now mortal.
JUAN: Heaven comfort me; my woes are overwhelming.
FERNANDO: What sickness isn't mortal, after all,
    If man himself is mortal, and in this
    Confused abyss his sickness always
    Kills him in the end?
    Man walks the hard earth without stopping,
    And with each step he takes, he treads
    On his own grave. What a sad law,
    What a hard sentence it is to know
    That in every single case
    Each step is one step closer to the end,
    And even God will not prevent
    That final step from being taken.
    Friends: I'm coming to my end;
    In your arms, please, carry me from here.
JUAN: In all my life, these will be the last bonds
    Of friendship.
FERNANDO: What I beg of you, noble Don Juan,
    Is that when I expire, you strip me naked.
    In the dungeon you will find my religious mantle;
    Dress me in it, and bury me like that,
    In full view, if the fierce King has softened
    His rage enough to allow me a grave;
    And leave a marker, since I hope that though
    I die a captive here today, I will
    Be ransomed when the sacred prayer is said
    For me upon the altar; I've given You,
    My God, so many churches, I am sure

That you will choose to give me one.
(THEY carry him out in their arms.)

A beach some distance from Fez. Night.

(Enter DON ALFONSO, ENRIQUE, and armed soldiers.)
ENRIQUE: My Lord, this place you chose
  To disembark is not a happy one,
  Because on one side a huge army comes,
  Marching like the wind in martial style,
  And their numbers seem to grow like hills
  Becoming mountains as they ride. Meanwhile
  Tarudante leads as many men, carrying his bride,
  The happy Infanta of Fez, toward Morocco . . .
  But listen—the armies' echoing voices tell the story.
ALFONSO: Enrique, this was no mistake,
  But rather fortunate, and this is why:
  If I had come to land at Fez, I would
  Have found both armies there; now, divided,
  I can defeat them both with lesser power;
  And so, before they can prepare, we'll sound
  The call to arms.
ENRIQUE: My lord, take heed; it's not
  The time yet for this battle.
ALFONSO: My wrath outruns all counsels.
  My vengeance will not wait one moment more;
  In my strong arms I hold the whip and scourge
  Of death for Africa.
ENRIQUE: See how the night already envelops
  The sun's bright chariot in concealing shadows.
ALFONSO: Then let us fight in darkness; my faith
  Is strong, and neither time nor enemy power
  Can weaken it. Fernando, I call on you
  To offer up your martyrdom to God:
  Then victory is certain, and mine will be
  The honor, yours the glory.
ENRIQUE: Your arrogant pride is a mistake.
FERNANDO: *(From within, a ghost.)* Attack, Alfonso!
  To war, to war!
ALFONSO: Fernando's voice! Do you hear it

Ripping through the sad, swift winds?

ENRIQUE: I do not know, but in those winds I also hear
Our enemy's trumpets sounding the alarm.

ALFONSO: Then let's attack, Enrique!
I heard Fernando's voice. There's no more doubt
That Heaven will help us win today.

(DON FERNANDO appears, in his religious cloak, carrying a lighted torch.)

FERNANDO: Indeed it will, since Heaven
Sees your faith, your zeal,
Today it will defend your cause.
To free me from my slavery is your aim,
Because in return for all the temples
That I gave to Him, God has offered me
One temple, and with this bright torch
Borrowed from the sunrise, I will go before
Your mighty army, lighting your way
So that today, great Alfonso, your desires
And your triumphs shall be equal when you
Come to Fez—not to be crowned there,
But to end my long night with your new dawn.

(HE exits.)

ENRIQUE: I must say, Alfonso, that I doubt
What I just saw.

ALFONSO: Not I—I believe it all;
And if the glory is to God, we will
No longer talk of war, but victory.

(THEY exit.)

Sounds of battle.
Inside the walls of Fez.

(Enter the KING and CÉLIN, and above the stage DON JUAN and a
CAPTIVE, and the INFANTE's coffin, of which we see nothing more than
the box itself.)

JUAN: Barbarian, tyrant, rejoice that here
You've taken the life of the best of men.

KING: And who are you?

JUAN: A man who, even though
You kill me, cannot leave Fernando,
And though my anguish makes me rabid,

I must be the faithful dog that stays beside him
Even in his death.

KING: Christians, here you see a template
To inform all future ages of my justice:
You cannot call it too severe when vengeance
Punishes those who insult royalty.
Let Alfonso come right now, in all
His arrogance, to free him from his servitude;
For even though I've lost all hopes
That Ceuta would be mine, his hopes of freedom
For the Prince are lost as well, and I am glad
To see him in this narrow cell. Even dead
He won't be free of my well-known severity;
And thus, I wish him to be placed where all
Who pass him by can see his shame.

JUAN: Soon enough you'll see your punishment,
Because by land and sea I now can see
The Christian standards coming.

KING: Let's go up on the walls to see what's happening.

JUAN: They're dragging down the banners, and the drums
Are out of time and tune; all the torches
And all the lights are dead; everywhere
Are signs of sadness.
Exeunt.

Outside the walls of Fez.

*(Drums sound mournfully. Enter DON ALFONSO and DON ENRIQUE,
along with all their soldiers bringing TARUDANTE, FÉNIX, and MULEY
as prisoners.)*

ALFONSO: Ah, to see those walls! Tell the King to come
And listen to me.
(The KING and CÉLIN enter onto the walls.)

KING: What do you want, valiant youth?

ALFONSO: That you hand the Infante over to me,
The Master Don Fernando, and for ransom
I will give you Tarudante and Fénix,
Who are here before you as my prisoners.
Choose what you wish: give me the Infante,
Or see the death of Fénix.

KING: What should I do, Célin,
    My friend, in such a great confusion?
    Fernando's dead, my daughter's in their power.
    How changeable is fortune's condition,
    To bring me to this state!
FÉNIX: What is this, my lord?
    Seeing my life in present danger,
    My honor assailed like this, can you doubt
    What your response must be?
    My life is in your hands,
    And you consent that I should be unjustly
    Bound in shackles? You were a King,
    But you've become a wild beast;
    Once father, you've become a serpent;
    And having been a judge, you're now my executioner;
    No longer King, nor judge, nor father.
KING: Fénix, I did not answer right away,
    Not because I wish your death; the Heavens
    Know I wish my own instead.
    Alfonso, you must also hear this news.
    When Fénix left, last evening,
    That sunset marked two deaths;
    The sun and the Infante both expired.
    His body rests in this plain and humble coffin.
    Now, give death to beautiful Fénix,
    And take vengeance for your own blood with mine.
FÉNIX: Now my hopes are dashed at every turn.
KING: I have no remedy; my life is over.
ENRIQUE: Heaven help me! What do I hear? How late,
    O heavens, how late has come this liberty!
ALFONSO: Don't say that; because if it was Fernando's ghost
    That told us before to free him from
    His slavery, he was speaking for his corpse.
    He said: for the many temples he has built,
    His body would enjoy one temple: that would be
    His ransom. King of Fez, so that
    You do not think that even in death Fernando
    Is worth less than this great beauty here,
    I offer her in exchange for his body.
    I ransom an unhappy corpse

With this image of divinity.

KING: What are you asking, invincible Alfonso?

ALFONSO: That these captives lower him down to us.

FÉNIX: I am the ransom of a dead man's life;
    So heaven exacts its tribute after all.

KING: Let down the coffin here beside the wall,
    And give it to them; to finish the exchange,
    I come to throw myself at your feet.
    (THEY lower the coffin with ropes beside the wall.)

ALFONSO: In my arms I receive you, divine Prince and martyr.

ENRIQUE: And I, dear brother, here make reverence.
    (Enter the KING, DON JUAN, and CAPTIVES.)

JUAN: Invincible Alfonso, give me your hand.

ALFONSO: Don Juan my friend, you've been a true caretaker
    For the Infante.

JUAN: Until his death
    I stayed with him; until I saw him free
    In life and death I had to be with him:
    Look where he lies.

ALFONSO: Uncle, give me your hand;
    For even though I came too late
    To free you, my great lord, from this danger,
    Now in death let friendship flow.
    A sovereign temple shall receive your blessed body.
    And to you, King, I deliver Tarudante
    And Fénix, asking only that she marry
    With Muley, in honor of the great friendship
    He showed to the Infante. Now, captives,
    Come and see your saint and bear him
    On your shoulders toward the armada.

KING: It's right that they should all accompany him.

ALFONSO: To the sound of sweet trumpets and of muted drums
    Let the army march in funeral formation,
    So to bring an end, begging pardon for all errors,
    To the Catholic Fernando,
    In his faith, the Constant Prince.

THE END

LIFE IS A DREAM

(La vida es sueño)

 1636

CHARACTERS

ROSAURA, A LADY

SEGISMUNDO, A PRINCE

CLOTALDO, AN OLD MAN

ESTRELLA, INFANTA

CLARÍN, A GRACIOSO OR COMIC SERVANT

BASILIO, KING

ASTOLFO, PRINCE

SOLDIERS, GUARDS, MUSICIANS

ACT ONE

A mountainside.

Enter ROSAURA in man's clothing, dressed for travel, from the top of a hill; while speaking the first few lines, she begins falling.

ROSAURA: Violent hippogriff,
 You run like the wind,
 Like lightning without thunder,
 Like a bird who's lost its feathers
 Or a fish without its scales
 Or, to be precise,
 A beast who's lost his wits.
 Where are you bolting
 In the tangled labyrinth
 Of these bare rocks,
 Throwing yourself this way and that?
 Stay here on this mountain,
 So the wild beasts can have their Phaeton,
 And so that I, blind and desperate,
 Traveling no farther
 Than fate already has compelled me,
 Might descend this tangled mountain's face,
 Whose frowning forehead
 Is scorched by the Sun.
 Poland, you receive this stranger badly,
 For her entrance on your soil is written
 All in blood, and pain marks her arrival
 Even though she's barely crossed your border.
 So that's the message my luck delivers;
 But after all, when did one unhappy person
 Ever find pity?
 (Enter CLARÍN, a gracioso.)
CLARÍN: Say two, and don't leave me
 Back at the Inn when you're complaining;
 For if we've both been forced
 To leave our native land
 To find adventures; and both of us,
 Between our various misfortunes, have come here;

And both of us have tumbled down the mountain,
Isn't it my right to feel bad
When I get included in the troubles,
But left out of the story?

ROSAURA: I didn't want to cast you
In the drama of my troubles, Clarín,
So as not to deprive you of
Your endless whining,
The source of your own comfort.
Because there's so much pleasure
In complaining, said the philosopher,
That in order to have something to complain about,
We should go looking for misfortunes.

CLARÍN: That philosopher was a drunken idiot;
Someone should slap him in the face
A thousand times; then he could complain
About how well or badly he'd been beaten.
But, what shall we do, my lady,
On foot, alone, and lost at this hour
On a deserted mountain
While the Sun departs for the far horizon?

ROSAURA: Who knows? It's strange beyond compare.
But if my eyes aren't suffering
From a fantastical illusion,
By the fearful light that the day still holds
It seems to me that I see a building.

CLARÍN: Either my desires are playing tricks on me
Or I have lost my senses.

ROSAURA: Between bare crags,
A little rustic palace lies
Mostly in the shadows.
The building's shape—or lack of it—
Is so rough that it looks more like
A boulder that has tumbled
From the summit, touched with sunlight,
To the foot of the mountain
Down here below, in shadow.

CLARÍN: Let's get up closer to it.
Instead of letting us stand around out here
So long, trying to look in,

It would better if whoever lives there
Would be kind enough
To invite us in for supper.
ROSAURA: The door is open, and deep within its center
It seems that night is born.
(A sound of chains.)
CLARÍN: Heavens! What's this I hear?
ROSAURA: I am frozen solid—fire and ice at once.
CLARÍN: It sounds like the rattle of a chain.
Strike me dead if it's not a galley-slave in pain;
My fear tells me that's what it is.
SEGISMUNDO: *(Within.)* Oh, my misery . . .
ROSAURA: What a sad voice!
Now I have new pains to struggle with.
CLARÍN: And don't forget new fears.
ROSAURA: Clarín!
CLARÍN: My lady!
ROSAURA: Let's flee the torments
Of this enchanted tower.
CLARÍN: I'm even too afraid
To flee, when it comes to that.
ROSAURA: Don't you see a flickering light,
A pale star, its dying breath expiring
In tremulous fainting spells,
Its pulsing heat and fading rays
Making this dark place
Even blacker with its doubtful light?
Yes—as it flickers
In the distance, I can just make out
A shadowy prison, serving as
The grave for a living corpse.
And what amazes me even more,
A man lies there dressed like a wild beast,
Burdened with imprisonment
With no companion other than that light.
Now since we cannot flee,
Let's listen to his troubles from here;
Let's find out what he says.
(SEGISMUNDO is discovered with a chain and the light, dressed in skins.)
SEGISMUNDO: Oh, my misery . . .

Heavens, hear me:
I am trying to conclude
What has brought me to this state;
What crime against you I've committed
By simply being born.
Although since I was born, I understand
I am a criminal, and you have cause enough
For the rigor of your justice,
Because the greatest crime of man is being born.
But I cannot sleep not knowing
How I have offended even more
(Leaving aside the crime of birth)
So that you punish me
More harshly than the others.
Weren't the others also born?
Well, if they were born,
What freedoms have they had
That I have never known?
The bird is born, and with its finery
That gives it perfect beauty,
It almost seems a flower made of feathers,
Or a winged bouquet,
When it flies so fleetly through the halls of air,
Ignoring the comforts of its nest
Which it leaves behind without a thought;
And I, who have more soul,
Have less liberty?
The brute is born, and with its hide
Painted all over with glorious spots,
Almost makes a picture of the stars
(thanks to the painter's skill);
Then mankind cruelly imprisons
And abuses it, teaches it cruelty,
Until it transforms into
A monster in its labyrinth;
And I, with better instinct,
Have less liberty?
The fish is born, not breathing,
A miscarriage of eggs and slime,
And scarcely does this vessel made of scales

Take one look upon the waves,
When it darts around everywhere,
Measuring the deep immensity
That makes the ocean cold;
And I, with more free will,
Have less liberty?
The stream is born, a snake
Unwinding itself among the flowers,
And scarcely does this silver serpent
Slide through the meadows
When music celebrates
This blessing from the heavens,
Which gives it majesty
As it breaks free from the open fields;
And I, who have more life,
Have less liberty?
Coming to this point my passion boils,
And I become an Etna, a volcano.
I want to tear my heart out
From within my breast.
What law, what justice or what reason
Denies to men that sweet privilege,
That fundamental right,
That God has given to a shining stream,
A fish, a brute, a bird?

ROSAURA: His arguments have made me
Feel both fear and pity.

SEGISMUNDO: Who's been listening to me?
Is it Clotaldo?

CLARÍN: Say yes.

ROSAURA: It's no one but a sad person
Who heard your melancholies
Here in these cold vaults.
(HE seizes HER.)

SEGISMUNDO: Then I will kill you,
Because no one must know that I know
That you know my weaknesses.
Simply because you heard me,
My strong arms have to tear you
Into pieces.

CLARÍN: I'm deaf, so I couldn't
    Have heard you.
ROSAURA: If you were born
    Human, it should be enough that I kneel
    At your feet for you to free me.
SEGISMUNDO: Your voice seems to soften me,
    Your presence interrupts me,
    And your regard disturbs me.
    Who are you? For although I know
    So little of the world,
    Since this tower was my cradle and my grave,
    And ever since my birth
    (If this counts as being born)
    I've only seen this rough desert
    Where I pass my days in misery,
    A living skeleton, one of the walking dead;
    And though I've never seen or spoken with
    Anyone, except with one man only
    Who pities my misfortunes here,
    From whom I learn the news
    Of heaven and Earth;
    As you grow more amazed,
    And call me a human monster,
    A marvel, a chimera, I will admit it's true:
    I am a man among the beasts,
    And a beast among men.
    Through all my grave misfortunes
    I have studied politics,
    Taught by the beasts,
    Advised by the birds;
    And I have measured circles
    In the subtle pathways of the stars.
    You, and you alone, have interrupted
    The passion of my rages,
    Given respite to my eyes,
    And wonder to my hearing.
    Each time I look at you
    I'm filled with greater admiration,
    And when I look at you again,
    I find I never want to stop.

I believe my eyes must have the dropsy,
For even when it's death to drink
They keep on drinking, and in the same way,
Seeing that this sight kills me
I'm dying to see more.
But let me look at you and die,
For I don't know, exhausted with devotion as I am,
If seeing you would kill me,
What not seeing you would do.
It would be worse than anger, sorrow, death;
It would be life. See how powerful you are!
Since giving life to one who suffers
Is just the same as killing one who's fortunate.

ROSAURA: I look at you and I'm amazed;
I listen to you in wonder.
I don't know what I should tell you,
Or what I can ask of you.
I'll only say that heaven has led me
To this place today for consolation,
If one who is unfortunate
Can be consoled by seeing
One whose fortune's even worse.
Stories tell of a wise man, who one day
Was so poor and miserable
That he subsisted only on
Some herbs that he had gathered.
"Will there ever be another," he said to himself,
"Poorer and sadder than I?"
And when he turned around,
He found his answer, in the sight
Of another wise man gathering
The leaves he threw away.
And so I lived, complaining of my fortune,
Until the day I wondered:
"Could there be even one
Other person in the world
Whose luck is worse than mine?"
And then I turned around and saw you.
Your passion gathers all my pains
And turns them into joys.

And if by any chance, my pains
Can lessen any part of yours,
Listen to them closely, and feel free
To take whatever is superfluous to me.
I am . . .
CLOTALDO: *(Within.)* Tower guards!
Asleep, or afraid, you've let
Two people past you, and now
They've broken into the prison!
ROSAURA: Here's more confusion!
SEGISMUNDO: This is Clotaldo, my jailer.
My bad fortune's not finished yet.
CLOTALDO: *(Within.)* Come here, be vigilant,
And either capture them, or kill them!
ALL: *(Within.)* Treason!
CLARÍN: You tower guards
Who allowed us to get in here,
Since there seems to be a choice,
Capturing us is easier.
(Enter CLOTALDO with a gun, and soldiers, all with faces covered.)
CLOTALDO: Cover your faces, everyone,
Because it is essential
That no one recognize us
While we're here.
CLARÍN: Are these masqueraders?
CLOTALDO: Now, ignorant, unhappy souls,
Who passed the boundary
Of this forbidden site
Against the King's decree
That no one dare
Investigate the prodigy
That lies among these crags:
Give up your arms and your lives,
Or this pistol, this metal snake
Will spit its penetrating venom
In two bullets, whose fire
Will shock the air.
SEGISMUNDO: My tyrant master, before
You hurt them, in God's name understand
That I will tear myself to pieces

In these chains, with my hands,
My teeth, against these rocks,
Before I will consent to their misfortune.
CLOTALDO: Since you know that your misfortunes,
Segismundo, are so great
That before you were born, you died
By heaven's decree; since you know
That this confinement is a bit
That checks your arrogant fury,
A rein that holds you back,
Why do you boast so proudly?
Close the door of this narrow cell,
And hide him in it.
(The SOLDIERS close the door and speak within.)
SEGISMUNDO: Oh, heavens!
You're wise to take away my freedom!
Because I would rise up against you,
A giant who would shatter the Sun
Into shards of fire, and over stone foundations
Would build up palaces of jasper.
CLOTALDO: To stop you from building them today,
Perhaps you'll have to suffer even more.
ROSAURA: Now that I see how much pride
Offends you, I would be remiss
Not to beg you humbly for my life
Which now lies at your feet.
May you be moved to pity me.
Your severity would be extreme
If neither pride nor humility
Could find favor with you.
CLARÍN: And if Humility and Pride
(Those characters we've all seen
In a thousand morality plays)
Don't move you, then let me,
Not too humble, not too proud,
But all mixed up between the two,
Beg you to protect us.
CLOTALDO: You there!
SOLDIERS: My lord!
CLOTALDO: Take away their arms, and cover

Their eyes, so that they cannot see
Where they are or how they got there.
ROSAURA: This is my sword, and you alone
Are worthy to receive it:
Because, when all is said and done
You are the leader here, and it
Will not be surrendered
To one of lesser stature.
CLARÍN: Mine is one of those that can be given
To the worst of you: here, you take it.
ROSAURA: And if I have to die, I wish
To offer you, believing in your pity,
A gift worthy of high esteem
By the master who will one day strap it on.
I charge you to guard it, because although I
Do not know what secret it carries,
I know that this golden sword
Contains great mysteries;
So great that, trusting only in its power,
I have come to Poland to avenge an injury.
CLOTALDO: *(Aside.)*   Sacred heavens!
What's this? Now my pains
And my confusions, my anxieties
And my burdens grow more grave.
(Aloud.)
Who gave this to you?
ROSAURA: A woman.
CLOTALDO: What is her name?
ROSAURA: That must remain a secret.
CLOTALDO: What were you implying just now?
Or do you really know
The secret of this sword?
ROSAURA: The one who gave it to me said: "Leave
For Poland, and by study, wit, or art
Make sure the nobles and the leaders
See you and this sword,
Because I know that one of them
Will favor and protect you."
But, in case he might be dead,
She did not wish to name him.

CLOTALDO: *(Aside.)* Heaven help me! What do I hear?
  I still don't know if this is truth
  Or merely an illusion.
  This sword is the one that I
  Left with the beautiful Violante
  As a signal that he who strapped it on
  Would find in me the pious love of
  A father for a son.
  But, what should I do—oh my—
  In such confusion,
  If the one who bears it to win my favor
  Wins his death instead,
  Since he arrives before me
  Already sentenced to die?
  This is my son, and all the signs
  Agree with the signals of my heart,
  Since as soon as I laid eyes on him
  My heart called out, I felt like wings
  Were beating inside of me,
  Struggling to break free;
  As when someone who is locked inside a house,
  Or in a prison, hears a noise out in the street,
  He rushes to the window; so my heart,
  Not knowing what is happening,
  Yet hearing some new noise,
  Goes to my eyes—the windows of the heart—
  To look outside. And then, seeing what it sees,
  It rushes out in tears.
  What should I do? Heaven help me!
  What should I do? Because to take him
  To the King is to take him
  To his death. But I cannot hide him
  From the King, if I obey
  My vow of loyalty.
  On one side, there is love itself,
  Love of my own flesh and blood.
  On the other side is loyalty.
  And they are tearing me apart.
  But why do I doubt what I should do?
  Loyalty to the King—doesn't that supercede

Both life and love?
So loyalty lives and love falters.
Beyond that, I now remember
What he said, that he came here
To avenge himself for an insult, and a man
Who is insulted is beneath contempt.
He is not my son, not my son,
Nor does he have my noble blood!
But if he has been through some peril,
From which nobody can escape,
Since honor is so fragile a material
That one bad blow can shatter it—
Even a touch of air can stain it—
What more can he do, what more,
With his nobility at stake,
Than to risk everything in a dangerous quest
To come here and redeem it?
He is my son. He has my blood.
What's more, he has great valor!
And thus between one doubt and another,
The most important measure
Is to tell the King
That this is my son,
And that he must kill him.
Perhaps some sort of pity
For my honor will move his mercy;
And if I am worthy to save my son's life,
I will help him to avenge his insult.
But if the King, keeping to his edict,
Puts him to death, he will die
Without knowing that I am his father.
(Aloud.)
Come with me, strangers.
Do not fear, not for a moment,
That you lack company in misfortunes;
For in this dreadful balance
Between life and death,
I don't know whose are greater.

In the palace.

(Enter on one side ASTOLFO accompanied by soldiers, and on the other, ESTRELLA with ladies. Music sounds.)

ASTOLFO: The moment your brilliance
    Shone forth its beaming rays
    Like comets, all the guns,
    All the trumpets, all the birds
    And all the fountains
    Joined in musical applause,
    Marveling at the celestial sight of you.
    Feathered trumpets, metal birds,
    All salute you: the guns as Queen;
    The birds as Aurora, beautiful dawn;
    The trumpets as Pallas Athena,
    And the flowers as their princess, Flora.
    For you are all of these and more,
    Bringing blazing day
    To conquer blackest night:
    You are Aurora in your joy,
    Flora in peace, Athena in war,
    And Queen of all my soul.

ESTRELLA: If what you speak has anything to do
    With how you act, you have done ill
    In speaking such fine courtesies
    When all your outward signs
    Are of martial power and the spoils of battle.
    To my mind, the flatteries you speak
    Do not support these warlike shows.
    You must know that it is baseness itself,
    The kind belonging only to a beast,
    To flatter with the mouth
    (The fount of trickery and malice)
    While with your deeds you make as if to kill.

ASTOLFO: You are very ill informed,
    Estrella, if you doubt the faith
    Of my fine words,
    And I beg of you to hear the case
    From me, to see if we agree.
    Eustorgio the Third, King of Poland, died,

And left Basilio as his heir,
Along with two daughters, of whom
You and I were born. Clorilene,
Your mother and my lady,
Who in a better empire now
Rests under a canopy of stars,
Was the elder, and you
Are her daughter. The younger,
My mother and your aunt,
The elegant Recisunda,
May God guard her a thousand years.
Married in Muscovy, and I was born to her.
As to the present problem:
Basilio, who now, my lady,
Begins to yield to Time's disdain,
And finds himself more inclined
Toward his studies than toward women,
Is growing old without an heir.
Now you and I aspire to this kingdom.
You have advanced the idea that you are
The daughter of the elder sister,
And thus Basilio's rightful successor;
I, that I was born male,
And although my mother was the younger,
I should be preferred over you.
We have told our uncle
Of our contrary intentions;
He responded that he wanted
To reconcile us, and we appointed
This place and day.
With this desire I left Muscovy;
And this same desire has brought me here;
That instead of making war on you,
You should conquer me.
Oh! May Love, wisest of the gods,
Bring the people (always the best astrologers)
Together with us today,
So that we may arrive at an arrangement
Whereby you will indeed be Queen—
But Queen in my heart and soul,

Wearing our uncle's crown,
And for your greater honor,
Ruling over the empire of my love.

ESTRELLA: To such generous courtesy
My heart must respond in kind,
Since I would wish the imperial monarchy
Were mine, only so that I could make it yours.
Yet as you speak of love, my heart
Suspects you are a bit ungrateful,
Since to every word you speak,
The portrait that you wear around your neck
Might object, and say you're lying.

ASTOLFO: I intend to satisfy you about that;
But the sound of trumpets leaves us no time,
Signalling the entrance of
The King and his retinue.

(Music sounds, and old KING BASILIO enters, with his train.)

ESTRELLA: Wise Thales,
ASTOLFO: Learned Euclid,
ESTRELLA: Who among the signs,
ASTOLFO: Among the stars,
ESTRELLA: Today governs,
ASTOLFO: Today resides,
ESTRELLA: Describing their pathways,
ASTOLFO: Measuring their very footprints,
ESTRELLA: Allow me like humble tendrils—
ASTOLFO: Allow me in tender embraces—
ESTRELLA: To be the ivy around this trunk,
ASTOLFO: To be seen begging at your feet.

BASILIO: Niece and nephew, give me your arms!
Now believe me when I tell you
That I will reward your loyalty
In such a way that no one will be angry.
Both of you will remain as equals.
And so, when I confess
That this exhausting weight
Has worn me out,
I ask on this occasion
Only silence, since the event
I will describe will stagger you.

You already know—be attentive,
Beloved niece and nephew,
Illustrious court of Poland,
Vassals, family, and friends.
You already know that
Through my studies I have earned
The surname Learnèd;
So, as proof against Time
And fickle Memory,
The brushes of Timantes and
The marbles of Lisipo
Around the world acclaim me
As Basilio the Great.
And you know that the sciences
I most esteem are subtle mathematics,
By which I steal from time and fame
The office of predicting each new day.
For when my tables reveal to me
The news of coming centuries,
I win respect from time,
Who can only show again
The things of which I've already spoken.
These snowy circles,
These canopies of glass
That the Sun's rays illuminate,
That the Moon's revolution divides;
The orbs of diamond, crystal globes
That the stars adorn, where signs abound,
Have been the primary study
Of my years, my sacred texts,
Where on diamond paper,
In sapphire notebooks,
In lines of gold and gorgeous characters
Heaven writes the story of our lives,
Whether adverse or benign.
I read these all so easily
That my spirit follows their swift movements
Along their paths and roads.
A plague on Heaven, then,
That my genius had to be

A comment in its margins
And an index to its pages!
Would that I had been
Their first victim, because to the unhappy,
Wisdom and merit can stab like a knife.
For knowledge cuts both ways,
And the man who knows too much
Can easily become his own murderer!
I say this to you, though you'll understand
Much better when you hear the story,
And I once more beg your silence
So you can wonder at it.
My wife bore me an unhappy son,
At whose birth the heavens
Purged themselves of all their prodigies.
Before he came into the light of day
From the living sepulcher of the womb,
(For birth and death are oddly similar),
His mother, often floating
Between reason and the deliriums
Of a dream, saw a vision of a monster
In the form of a man
Break through her entrails,
And stained with her blood,
He took her life, becoming at his birth
The human viper of the age.
The day of his birth arrived,
And, as if to confirm the prophecies
His horoscope revealed
The Sun, dyed red with his blood,
Entering into a vicious combat
With the Moon; the Earth
Was caught between them.
The two divine lamps
Fought a battle, not with arms,
But all with light
This was the greatest, most horrendous
Eclipse that the Sun
Has ever suffered since it wept
Blood for the death of Christ.

Seeing the Earth assailed on every side
By fire from the heavens,
The people all concluded
That this must be the end,
The final paroxysm.
The heavens darkened, buildings shook,
The clouds rained down stones,
The rivers ran with blood.
Under this deadly sign of misery
Was Segismundo born, giving notice
Of his true condition,
Since he caused his mother's death,
And his cataclysmic birth seemed to cry out:
"I am a man, since right now I begin
To repay kindness with evil."
I, attending to my studies,
See many indications, unmistakable,
That Segismundo would grow to be
The crudest man,
The cruelest Prince,
The most impious monarch,
Under whose reign the land would break apart
And soon become a school for treason,
An academy for vice;
And that he, carried away by his fury,
Would come at last to set his feet upon me,
And I would see myself a subject,
Begging at his feet:
(The anguish that it costs to say this!)
The white hairs of my head
Making a carpet for him to tread upon.
Who could ignore these warnings,
Especially when you've seen them
Revealed to you in your own study?
So, giving credit to the fates,
I determined to lock up
The beast that had been born,
To see if a sage's wisdom could exert
Dominion over the stars.
It was published that the infant

Was born dead, and, forewarned,
I ordered a tower to be built
Among the crags and cliffs
Of these mountains, where light
Can barely find its way,
And to defend and mark the entrance,
Placed rustic obelisks.
This is the reason that the area
Is so strictly prohibited to all,
With grave penalties for trespassing
Made known by public edicts.
There Segismundo lives,
Miserable, poor, and captive,
Where only Clotaldo has seen and spoken with him:
He has taught him in the sciences,
Instructed him in Catholic law,
And is the only witness of his miseries.
Here are three things to consider, Poland:
First, that I so esteem you
That I want to free you
From the oppression of a tyrant King,
Since a benign and kindly ruler
Would never put his empire in such danger.
Now for the second point to ponder:
Christian charity forbids me
To deprive my own flesh and blood
Of the rights that he was given,
Both human and divine,
Since no law has decreed
That to save another
From a tyrant's cruelty
I can become one.
Must I commit a tyrant's crimes
To stop my son from doing so,
Supposing that he is indeed a tyrant?
The third and last is this:
I would like to test
Whether it may have been an error
To give such easy credit
To predictions and foreseen events;

For although his tendencies
May lead him toward the abyss.
Perhaps they will not conquer him;
Because the coldest fate,
The most violent inclination,
The most ferocious planet,
May only work their influence
On free will; they cannot force it.
And so, between one cause and another,
Weighing each question with great care,
I foresaw a remedy so brilliant
That it will leave you speechless.
Without his knowing that he is my son
And your king, Segismundo,
(For that has been his name)
I plan to place him on my throne tomorrow,
Taking my place completely,
Where he will govern and command you,
And all you subjects
Will swear obedience to him.
With this bold stroke I accomplish
Three things, corresponding to the three
Concerns that I have told you.
The first is this: if he turns out to be
Prudent, sensible, and benevolent,
Giving the lie to all the signs
That spoke of these disasters,
You will enjoy your natural
Prince, who has been courtier
Of the mountains, neighbor of the beasts.
The second is: that if he proves, as feared,
Arrogant, cruel, impudent, and reckless,
Giving free rein to all his vices,
I will have piously complied
With all my obligations,
And later, in dispossessing him
I will act as an invincible King,
His return to prison being
Not cruelty, but punishment.
Now for my third and final argument.

If the Prince turns out to be
What I have said to you,
Because I love my people so profoundly
I will give you Kings more worthy
Of the crown and scepter;
My niece and nephew,
Who, by joining the rights of both in one,
Confirmed in the faith by marriage,
Will achieve what they have long deserved.
This as King I command you,
This as father I beg you,
This as sage I implore you,
This as ancient I tell you.
And if, as Spanish Seneca said,
A King's a humble slave to his republic,
Then as a slave I plead for this with you.

ASTOLFO: If it falls on me to respond
As the one who, in effect, has been
The most interested party here,
In the name of all I say:
Let Segismundo appear,
Since it's enough that he's your son.

ALL: Give us our Prince!
We already ask him to be King.

BASILIO: Vassals, I thank you for this courtesy,
And I esteem you for it.
Accompany my two Atlases
To their rooms; tomorrow
You will see him.

ALL: Long live Great King Basilio!
(Exeunt omnes. Before the KING exits, enter CLOTALDO, ROSAURA, and CLARÍN, and they detain the KING.)

CLOTALDO: May I speak with you?

BASILIO: Oh, Clotaldo!
You are very welcome.

CLOTALDO: Although kneeling at your feet
Has always been a welcome duty, lord,
This time a sad, cold fate
Disrupts our customary style.

BASILIO: What's the matter?

CLOTALDO: A terrible misfortune,
     My lord, that should have been
     A cause for joy.
BASILIO: Continue.
CLOTALDO: This handsome young man,
     Brave or careless, it doesn't matter,
     Entered the tower, sire,
     And there has seen the Prince.
     And he is . . .
BASILIO: Forget your cares, Clotaldo.
     If this had been another day,
     I confess that I would been enraged;
     But I have just revealed the secret,
     And it's not important that he knows it,
     Since I have announced it to the court.
     See me later, because I have
     Many things to tell you,
     And there is much that you must do for me;
     For you will have to be, I'm warning you,
     The instrument of the greatest event
     The world has ever seen.
     And for these prisoners, so that
     You do not think that I am punishing
     Your carelessness, I pardon them.
     (HE exits.)
CLOTALDO: May you live a thousand centuries!
     (Aside.)
     Heaven has improved our luck.
     Now I don't have to say that he's my son.
     (Aloud.)
     Wandering foreigners, you are free.
ROSAURA: I'm kneeling before you in great gratitude.
CLARÍN: And I'm reeling; one letter
     More or less doesn't matter among friends.
ROSAURA: You have given me my life, my lord,
     And since I live on your account,
     I will be your slave forever.
CLOTALDO: Not life; that I cannot give you,
     Because a well-born man,
     If he is insulted, has no life;

And if indeed you've come here
As you said, to avenge an insult,
I have not given you life,
Because you did not have it when you came.
An infamous life, you know, is no life at all.
(Aside.)
That should spur him on.
ROSAURA: I admit I do not have it,
Although I have received it from you;
But when I take my vengeance
I will leave my honor so clean,
That later on, my life,
Outrunning all the dangers that beset it,
Will be worthy of your gift.
CLOTALDO: Take back this burnished sword
That you brought with you, because I know
That once it's tinted by your enemy's blood
Your life will be your own again;
Because any blade of steel that was mine
(I speak of that one instant, that brief moment
That I had it in my power)
Will know how to avenge you.
ROSAURA: In your name I strap it on a second time,
And on it, swear my vengeance,
No matter how much stronger
My enemy may be.
CLOTALDO: Is he that strong?
ROSAURA: So powerful I dare not tell you,
Not because I do not trust
Your prudence in great affairs,
But only so you will not withdraw
Your favor, which I wonder at.
CLOTALDO: You would better win my help by telling me;
Because that would allow me to avoid
Giving comfort to your enemy by mistake.
(Aside.)
Oh, if I only knew who it is!
ROSAURA: So that you do not think that I esteem
Your confidence so little,
Know that my adversary is

No less than Astolfo, Duke of Muscovy.

CLOTALDO: *(Aside.)* I can scarce hold back
The pain, for the truth
Is worse than I imagined.
(Aloud.)
Let's examine the case more closely.
If you were born a Muscovite,
He who is your natural lord
Cannot, in truth, insult you;
So return home to your country,
And leave behind this burning spirit
That propels you.

ROSAURA: And yet I know
That even though he is my Prince,
He could and did insult me.

CLOTALDO: He could not,
Even if he rudely struck your face.

ROSAURA: My injury was greater.

CLOTALDO: Tell it now, since you cannot
Say anything worse than I imagine.

ROSAURA: Indeed I'll tell you;
But I don't know how.
Since I hold you in such high regard,
And feel such affection, veneration,
And respect for you,
How do I dare to tell you
That this external dress
Conceals an enigma, since it is not what
It appears to be? Consider in full knowledge
Whether Astolfo can insult me
If I am not who I seem to be,
And he is married to Estrella.
I have said enough.
(Exeunt ROSAURA and CLARÍN.)

CLOTALDO: Listen, look, stop!
What kind of confused labyrinth
Is this, when reason
Cannot find the thread?
It's my honor that's insulted,
The enemy is powerful,

I a vassal, she a woman.
Heaven, find the way; and yet
I no longer know if it is capable.
But in this turbulent abyss,
The entire sky's a portent
And the whole world's a prodigy.

END OF ACT ONE

ACT TWO

The palace.

(Enter KING BASILIO and CLOTALDO.)

CLOTALDO: Everything has been done
    As you commanded.
BASILIO: Tell me,
    Clotaldo, how it went.
CLOTALDO: It went, my lord, like this.
    The tranquilizing drink
    That you ordered made,
    Whose strong power
    Steals away the faculty of
    Human discourse, leaving
    A man a living corpse;
    This drink compounded
    Of opium, poppy, and henbane
    I took to Segismundo's
    Narrow cell; I spoke with him a while
    Of the world of humane letters
    That nature has taught him
    From the textbook of the mountains
    And the sky, in whose divine academy
    He learned the rhetoric
    Of the birds and the beasts.
    In order to lift his spirit more
    Toward the enterprise you seek,
    I took for a theme the quickness
    Of a majestic eagle,
    Which, spurning the mere regions
    Of the wind and air, shot quickly up,
    Toward the higher realm of fire,
    A feathered beam of light
    Or a comet set free from its track.
    I praised its lofty flight,
    Saying: "after all, you are the queen
    Of the birds, and thus, it's only right
    That you should be preferred above all others."

Nothing more was necessary;
He began to speak of majesty
With ambition and great pride;
Because, it seems, his blood
Incites him, encouraging great thoughts.
He said: "So even in the chattering republic
Of the birds, there's one
To whom the others swear obedience?
When I arrive at this conclusion,
My misfortunes console me;
Because at least if I am
A subject, I must be one by force;
Because I would not voluntarily submit
To any other man."
Seeing him now enflamed
With this idea, the root of all his pain,
I had him drink
The potion, and scarcely
Did the liquor pass his lips
When he lapsed into a dream.
A cold sweat ran all through
His limbs, so that if I didn't know
His death was only feigned,
I would doubt that he still lived.
Right then, the people you assigned
To transport him arrived,
And placing him in a coach
They brought him to your room,
Which had been prepared
With majesty and grandeur
Worthy of his person.
They laid him in your bed,
Where, once the potion's lethargy
Had lost its force, they began
To serve him just as they serve you,
According to your orders.
And if my obedience to you in this
Obliges you to offer any small reward,
All I can beg (pardoning my ignorance)
Is that you tell me: what is your intention

In bringing Segismundo to the palace
In this manner?
BASILIO: Clotaldo, this doubt you have
Is very just, and I will satisfy it.
As you well know, my son
Is under the influence of his stars,
Which threaten a thousand tragedies.
I wish to find out whether heaven
(Which never lies, and which has given us
So many demonstrations of his cruelty)
May yet mitigate or temper
His fate, and if his valor triumphs
Over destiny, perhaps
The judgment of the heavens
May be withdrawn.
Can man prevail over the stars?
This I wish to test
By bringing him here,
Where he will know he is my son,
And he will have to prove his gifts.
If generosity conquers him,
He'll reign; but if he shows
His nature to be cruel and tyrannous,
He goes back to his chains.
Now you will ask me,
Why, for the sake of this experiment,
Was it important to have him brought here
Sleeping in this fashion?
And I want to satisfy you
By giving you a full response.
If he discovered that he is my son
Today, and tomorrow saw himself
A second time reduced
To his imprisonment and misery,
It's certain that he would despair
Of his condition;
For, knowing who he is,
What consolation would he have?
This way the door is open
To convince him that it was a dream.

I will achieve two things thereby:
First, a better window on his nature,
Since when he awakens, he will behave
Exactly as his instincts prompt him.
The second is his consolation;
Although he'll feel the power of being obeyed,
And afterwards returned to prison,
He will be able to perceive it as a dream.
And he'll do well to understand this,
Because in the world, Clotaldo,
All of us who live are dreaming.

CLOTALDO: I do not lack for reasons
To argue against this course,
But it's too late. The signs suggest
He has awakened and is on his way.

BASILIO: I will withdraw.
You, as his tutor, stay,
And let the truth deliver him
From all the confusions
That afflict his reason.

CLOTALDO: I have your permission, then,
To tell him everything?

BASILIO: Yes;
For it may be that, if the danger's known,
It may be more easily defeated.
    (The KING exits and CLARÍN enters.)

CLARÍN: The price of admission to this show
Apparently is four blows to the head
From a red-bearded guardsman.
But I have to see what's happening;
And the best seat in the house
Is often the one that a clever fellow
Finds by slipping past the ticket-seller.
One way or another, you can always
Get a look if you're shameless enough.

CLOTALDO: This is Clarín, the servant
Of that (oh, heavens!) that
Woman who deals in misfortunes,
Carrying my injury here to Poland.
Clarín, what's new?

CLARÍN: What's new,
     My lord, is that your great clemency,
     And your promise to help avenge
     Rosaura's honor, has prompted her
     To dress more like herself.
CLOTALDO: And that is well, so that she does not appear
     Unseemly.
CLARÍN: And also, by changing her name,
     And sensibly borrowing your niece's,
     Today her honor grows so much
     That she has won a place in the palace
     As a lady in waiting of the singular Estrella.
CLOTALDO: I'm glad that for this once at least,
     She gains honor on my account.
CLARÍN: And also, that she is hoping
     That soon the time may come
     For you to aid in the restoration
     Of her honor.
CLOTALDO: That hope's a wise precaution;
     Because finally, time must
     Be the one to take care of these things.
CLARÍN: And also, that since she seems to be your niece,
     She's being given gifts, treated like a queen,
     While I, the one who came here with her,
     I'm dying of hunger
     And no one pays me any mind.
     But nevertheless I am Clarín;
     My name, you know, means Trumpet.
     And if this Clarín blows,
     It will trumpet everything right
     To the King, to Astolfo and Estrella;
     Because a Trumpet and a Servant
     Are two things that don't keep
     Secrets very well;
     And it might come to be,
     If you force me to break my silence,
     That I will sing this little wake-up song:
     The trumpet that sounds to greet the dawn
     Sometimes keeps blowing on and on.
CLOTALDO: Your complaint is well founded.

I will see that you are satisfied,
And meanwhile be my servant.
CLARÍN: But here comes Segismundo.
*(Enter musicians, singing, and servants in the process of dressing
SEGISMUNDO, who enters as if astonished.)*
SEGISMUNDO: Heaven help me! What am I looking at?
Heaven help me! What do I see?
I wonder at it, yet it does not frighten me.
I believe it, but only long enough to doubt it.
I, in a glorious palace?
I, surrounded by soft cloth and brocade?
I, attended by servants
So magnificent and brilliant?
I, awakening from sleep
In such an excellent bed?
I, among so many people
Who serve me as I dress?
Am I dreaming? That is an illusion,
Since I know quite well that I'm awake.
Am I not Segismundo? If I'm dreaming,
Give me, Heavens, disillusionment.
Tell me what could have happened
In my fantasies, while I slept,
That brought me here
To see this gorgeous place.
But be that as it may,
Who wants to think about that now?
I wish to be served, and served right away,
And let come whatever comes.
SECOND SERVANT: How melancholy he is!
FIRST SERVANT: Well, with all that's happened to him,
Who wouldn't be?
CLARÍN: Not me.
SECOND SERVANT: Why don't you speak to him?
FIRST SERVANT: Shall we have them sing again?
SEGISMUNDO: No,
I don't want them to sing any more.
FIRST SERVANT: Since you are so bewildered,
I only wished to entertain you.
SEGISMUNDO: I don't need the entertainment

Of your voices for my sorrows;
Military music is all
That my ear has ever enjoyed.
CLOTALDO: Your Highness, great lord,
Give me your hand to kiss,
For I must be the first to offer you
My honor and obedience.
SEGISMUNDO: *(Aside.)* Clotaldo: but how can it be
That the man who treated me so badly
In my prison cell now treats me
With respect? What is happening to me?
CLOTALDO: In the deep confusion
That your new state causes you,
Your thoughts and reason
Will suffer a thousand doubts;
But now I want to free you
From them all (if that can be).
You must know, my lord,
That you are the hereditary prince
Of Poland. If you've been
Withdrawn from the world and hidden,
It has been at the insistence of
A merciless fate
That predicts a thousand tragedies
In this kingdom, when
The sovereign laurel
Crowns your august brow.
But, trusting in your care and your discretion,
Which can overcome the stars,
Because it's possible for a
Generous man to conquer them,
We have brought you to the palace
From the tower where you lived,
While sleep held
Your spirit subdued.
Your father, my lord the king
Will come to see you, and from him you'll know,
Segismundo, all the rest.
SEGISMUNDO: Well—you vile, infamous man, you traitor!
What more do I have to know,

Understanding who I really am,
To show my pride and power
From this day on?
How have you done such treason
To your country, that you hid me away,
That you denied to me,
Against right and reason,
My proper state?

CLOTALDO: Oh, unhappy me!

SEGISMUNDO: You were a traitor against the law,
A flatterer to the King,
And cruel to me;
And thus the King, the law, and I,
Among all these fierce misfortunes,
Add one more: we sentence you to death.

SECOND SERVANT: My lord!

SEGISMUNDO: Let no one
Hinder me; that's useless.
And in the name of God,
If one of you gets in my way,
I'll throw you out the window.

FIRST SERVANT: Flee, Clotaldo.

CLOTALDO: Alas for you,
You show such arrogance,
And you don't even know that you are dreaming!
(HE exits.)

SECOND SERVANT: Be aware . . .

SEGISMUNDO: Get out of here.

SECOND SERVANT: . . . that he was obeying his King.

SEGISMUNDO: In a case where the law is unjust,
He does not have to obey the King,
And besides, I was his Prince.

SECOND SERVANT: He's not supposed to question a command.

SEGISMUNDO: I suspect that something's wrong with you,
Since you insist on talking back to me.

CLARÍN: The prince is speaking very right,
And you are doing very wrong.

SECOND SERVANT: Who gave you equal license?

CLARÍN: I took it for myself.

SEGISMUNDO: Who are you,

Tell me?

CLARÍN: A meddler,
And the captain of that company,
Because I am the biggest
Busybody you've ever seen.

SEGISMUNDO: In this strange new world
You are the only thing that pleases me.

CLARÍN: Sire, I am a great pleaser
Of all the Segismundos.

(Enter ASTOLFO.)

ASTOLFO: The day is suddenly brighter
By a thousandfold, dear Prince,
Because you show us all
The true sun of Poland, and fill
The near and far horizons
With your radiance, rising
Like the Sun behind the mountains.
So rise; and as your coming was delayed,
So let the laurel that crowns your brows
Last long, and wither late.

SEGISMUNDO: God save you.

ASTOLFO: That you did not know me
Is the only thing that excuses you
For not honoring me more. I am
Astolfo, duke of Muscovy,
And your cousin;
The two of us are equals.

SEGISMUNDO: I said God save you—
Doesn't that show proper courtesy?
But now I see you boast of who you are
And complain about my lack of courtesy,
So the next time that you see me
I will tell God not to save you.

SECOND SERVANT: Your Highness must consider
That since he was born in the mountains
He's behaved this way with everyone.
Astolfo, sire, prefers . . .

SEGISMUNDO: He tires me out, the way he came
To speak with me so gravely, and then the first
Thing he did was put on his hat.

SECOND SERVANT: He is a grandee.

SEGISMUNDO: I am even greater.

SECOND SERVANT: And so, between you two
>   There should be more respect
>   Than among the rest.

SEGISMUNDO: And who
>   Set you on to me?
>   *(Enter ESTRELLA.)*

ESTRELLA: Your Highness, Sire, must be
>   A thousand times welcome
>   To this throne which gratefully
>   Receives you and desires you;
>   Where, in spite of all your past illusions,
>   You will live august and eminent,
>   And your life will be measured
>   In centuries, not in years.

SEGISMUNDO: You, tell me now, who is
>   This sovereign beauty?
>   Who is this human goddess,
>   At whose divine feet
>   The sky lays down its radiance?
>   Who is this beautiful woman?

CLARÍN: It is, my lord, your cousin Estrella.

SEGISMUNDO: Named for a star, but so much
>   Better you had said "the Sun."
>   Even though your great good wishes
>   Are well-intended, since I have risen so far,
>   Only the sight of you just now
>   Gives me reason to accept them.
>   And so, having come upon
>   A blessing that I don't deserve,
>   I thank you for your wishes,
>   Estrella, you who could replace the dawn,
>   And bring a brighter beauty to
>   To the morning light.
>   What's left for the Sun to do,
>   If you rise with the day?
>   Let me kiss your hand,
>   In whose cup of snow
>   The wind drinks innocence.

ESTRELLA: Be a more gallant courtier.

ASTOLFO: *(Aside.)* If he takes her hand, I'm lost.

SECOND SERVANT: *(Aside.)* I see Astolfo's problem,
>   And I will intercede.
>   *(Aloud.)*
>   Be mindful, sire, that it is not
>   Right to be so forward,
>   And Astolfo being . . .

SEGISMUNDO: Didn't I tell you
>   Not to interfere with me?

SECOND SERVANT: I'm saying what is right.

SEGISMUNDO: You're saying things that just enrage me.
>   Nothing looks right to me
>   That goes against my pleasure.

SECOND SERVANT: But, sire, I have heard
>   From you that when the cause is right,
>   It's good to serve it.

SEGISMUNDO: You've also heard me say
>   That I'll throw whoever makes me mad
>   Off of a balcony.

SECOND SERVANT: With men like me that can't be done.

SEGISMUNDO: No? By God, I'll prove it can!
>   *(SEGISMUNDO grabs HIM in his arms, and exits; everyone follows, then reenters.)*

ASTOLFO: What have I just seen?

ESTRELLA: Everyone, go help!
>   *(SHE exits.)*

SEGISMUNDO: *(Reentering.)* He fell from the balcony to the sea;
>   By God, it seems it could be done!

ASTOLFO: You need to measure your violent
>   Impulses with more caution,
>   Since the distance between men and wild beasts
>   Is the same as between a mountain and a palace.

SEGISMUNDO: And you should watch yourself: if you keep giving
>   Your pious speeches so severely,
>   Perhaps one day you'll find you lack
>   A head to hang your hat on.
>   *(ASTOLFO exits; enter the KING.)*

BASILIO: What has happened?

SEGISMUNDO: Nothing happened;

I threw a man who bored me
From that balcony.

CLARÍN: Be advised that he's the King.

BASILIO: Already on the first day you arrive,
Your coming here has cost a life?

SEGISMUNDO: He told me it could not
Be done, and I won the bet.

BASILIO: It grieves me greatly, Prince,
That I came here to see you,
Believing that I'd find you well-controlled,
Triumphing over your stars, your fate.
Instead I see in you such rage,
And the first thing you accomplish,
On the occasion of your freedom,
Is an act of murder.
How can I approach you now with love?
How can I open my arms to you,
If I've been shown that your embrace is fatal?
Who could look upon
The naked knife that has just killed
And not be struck with fear?
Who comes across the bloody place
Where another man was murdered,
And does not feel revulsion?
So, seeing you now this way,
As nothing but an instrument of death,
I must withdraw; and though with love I thought
To hold you in my arms,
I must forego that thought,
Because I fear your touch.

SEGISMUNDO: Without your embraces I will remain
Just like I've been until today;
For with a father who practices
Such severity against me,
Who with cruel intentions
Sent me from his side,
Raised me like a beast,
Treats me like a monster,
Seeks my death,
It doesn't matter much

That you withhold your arms,
When you've already taken
My humanity from me.

BASILIO: By God and Heaven, would
    That I had never given that to you;
    Then I would never have heard your voice
    Or seen your rashness.

SEGISMUNDO: If you hadn't given it to me,
    I'd have no complaint against you;
    But once it's given, yes, I will complain
    For having lost it;
    For although giving
    Is the noblest and most singular action,
    The greatest baseness is to give
    And then to take the gift away.

BASILIO: This is how you thank me
    For your transformation
    From a poor and humble prisoner
    Into a prince!

SEGISMUNDO: But what
    Do I have to thank you for?
    If you're old and failing, tyrant,
    Dying even, what are you giving me?
    Do you give me more than what is mine?
    You are my father and my King;
    So all this grandeur Nature gives me
    By the rights of your own laws.
    I'm not obliged to you,
    And I can call you to account
    For all the years you've stolen
    My liberty, life, and honor from me;
    And so you should thank me
    That I don't charge you for it,
    Since you're in debt to me.

BASILIO: You are barbarous and rude:
    You bear out heaven's word;
    And seeing you like this,
    To that same heaven I appeal,
    To behold your pride and vanity.
    Although you now know who you are,

And are without illusions,
And though you see yourself in such a state
Where you are lord of all,
Look well to my advice:
Be humble and tender,
Because it might be that you are dreaming,
Although you feel that you're awake.
(The KING exits.)

SEGISMUNDO: Might it be that I am dreaming,
Although I feel that I'm awake?
I am not dreaming, since I can feel and know
What I have been and what I am.
And though you might regret your actions,
There's nothing you can do about it now.
I know who I am, and you cannot steal
My birthright from me twice.
You saw me first defeated and imprisoned,
But that was only possible because
I did not know who and what I was.
But now I've learned. I know I am
A compound creature, man and beast.
(Enter ROSAURA, as a woman.)

ROSAURA: *(Aside.)* I come in search of Estrella,
And in great fear of finding Astolfo;
Since Clotaldo wishes me to conceal
Myself from him, for honor's sake.
I trust Clotaldo and his plan;
Besides I owe him for the help he's given
To save my life and honor.

CLARÍN: Of everything you've seen today,
What have you admired the most?

SEGISMUNDO: My life has been so singular
That nothing can astonish me.
But if I had to admire
Something in the world,
It would be woman's beauty.
I read once, in a book that I'd been given,
That God gave his greatest care
To man, creating in him a little world.
But now I suspect it's really woman,

Since she is a little heaven;
And embodies much more beauty
Than a man, as far above him in beauty
As heaven is from Earth;
And even moreso if it's this one that I see.

ROSAURA: *(Aside.)* The prince is here; I'll withdraw.

SEGISMUNDO: Listen, woman, stop.

Do not join sunset and sunrise in an instant
By fleeing so quickly away;
Because in joining sunrise and sunset,
Warm light and cold shadow,
You will without a doubt cut short the day.
(Aside.)
But what is this I see?

ROSAURA: *(Aside.)* I see this—and I don't know
Whether to believe or doubt it.

SEGISMUNDO: *(Aside.)* I have seen this beauty somewhere else.

ROSAURA: *(Aside.)* I've seen this royalty confined
In a narrow prison cell.

SEGISMUNDO: *(Aside.)* Now I've found my life.
(Aloud.)
Woman, since that name
Is the highest compliment a man can speak,
Who are you? Without my seeing you,
You already owe me adoration;
And that's my luck. But my faith
Persuades me that I've seen you once before.
Beautiful woman—who are you?

ROSAURA: *(Aside.)* I must pretend.
(Aloud.)
I am an unhappy lady
In Estrella's service.

SEGISMUNDO: Don't say that; say you are the Sun,
By whose fire that other star lives,
Since it takes its splendor from your rays.
In the kingdom of perfumes,
I noticed that the rose presides,
A goddess among the common flowers;
She became their empress by being the most beautiful.
I saw among the gems

That the learned academy of mines
Prefers the diamond,
The most brilliant, and so the emperor of stones.
In the beautiful but turbulent
Republic of the stars, I first observed
The morning star is king.
Among the perfect spheres we call the planets,
I saw the Sun calling them all to court,
Ruling as the oracle of day.
So then: How, if in the world of flowers, stars,
Stones, and planets, the most beautiful
Are always of the highest rank,
Have you been serving one less beautiful,
Since you are the equal,
In your beauty and your loveliness,
Of the Sun, the morning star, the diamond, and the rose?
(Enter CLOTALDO.)

CLOTALDO: *(Aside.)* Segismundo's my responsibility,
Because I brought him up.
But what do I see here?

ROSAURA: I have great reverence for your favor,
But the rhetoric of silence must be my response.
When reason finds itself so sluggish,
The one who speaks best, sire,
Is the one who best keeps silent.

SEGISMUNDO: Wait—you needn't go.
Why do you want to leave my feelings
In the dark this way?

ROSAURA: I beg this license of Your Highness.

SEGISMUNDO: To leave so quickly, so abruptly,
Is not to beg that license, but to take it.

ROSAURA: Well, if you will not give it, I hope to take it.

SEGISMUNDO: You change my courtesy to ugliness.
Resistance is a venom to my patience.

ROSAURA: Still, even when that venom,
Full of fury, severity, and rage,
Has poisoned your patience,
It could not, would not dare
To conquer your respect for me.

SEGISMUNDO: Just to see if I can do it,

You'll make me try to shake my fear of beauty,
Because I always find myself inclined
To conquer the impossible. Today I threw
A man off of a balcony because he said
I couldn't do it;
And so, if only to see what's possible,
It would be just as easy
To throw your honor out the window.
CLOTALDO: *(Aside.)* He's losing his control.
Heavens, what am I to do when
Mad desire and lust
Put my honor at risk a second time?
ROSAURA: Your tyranny in this unhappy kingdom,
The hideous scandals, treasons, crimes, and deaths
Were all foretold, and now I see
That prophecy was not in vain.
But after all, how should a man behave
If all that's human in him is the name,
And he was born among the beasts,
Growing arrogant and cruel by example?
SEGISMUNDO: I showed my utmost courtesy to you
To prevent you from insulting me this way,
Thinking I would win you;
But if I am what you've been saying,
Then by God! I'll give you reason enough to say it.
Hey there! Leave us alone, and lock
That door, let no one enter.
(Exit CLARÍN.)
ROSAURA: *(Aside.)*   I'm dead.
(Aloud.)
Take care . . .
SEGISMUNDO: I am a tyrant,
And now no matter how you struggle
You cannot stop me.
CLOTALDO: *(Aside.)* This is the critical moment!
I'll interrupt him, even if he kills me.
Sire, listen, look . . .
SEGISMUNDO: Old man! This is the second time
You've made me mad today.
Are you crazy? Or demented? Does the power

Of my rage mean nothing to you?
Why have you come in here?
CLOTALDO: The fury of your voice
Called me here to tell you
That you ought to be more peaceful
If you wish to reign.
And just because you see yourself
As lord of everything right now,
You shouldn't dare to be so cruel:
Since after all, this may be just a dream.
SEGISMUNDO: You drive me to insanity
When you talk of dreams and disillusionment.
Let's test if this is real or a dream
By killing you.
(As HE goes to draw his dagger, CLOTALDO grabs it and kneels.)
CLOTALDO: This is the only way
To save my life.
SEGISMUNDO: Hands off my blade. You're shameless.
CLOTALDO: Until someone comes
And checks your wrath,
I must not let go of it.
ROSAURA: Oh, heavens!
SEGISMUNDO: Let go, I say,
Decrepit, crazy, barbarous enemy,
Or this is how we'll go about it—
(THEY fight.)
I'll kill you now with my bare hands.
ROSAURA: Everyone, quickly, help,
He's killing Clotaldo!
(SHE exits; enter ASTOLFO, at the same time as CLOTALDO falls at his feet, and ASTOLFO interposes himself.)
ASTOLFO: But, what is this,
Generous Prince? Will you stain such brilliant steel
With an old man's icy blood?
Return that shining blade to its sheath.
SEGISMUNDO: As soon as I see it colored red
By his infamous blood.
ASTOLFO: Now he
Has taken sanctuary at my feet;
That should do some good.

SEGISMUNDO: If you'd like to do some good,
    Try dying. With you out of the way
    I'll be able to take my full revenge.
ASTOLFO: I will defend my life,
    And the honor of his majesty . . .
    (THEY draw their swords, and enter KING BASILIO and ESTRELLA.)
CLOTALDO: Don't hurt him, my lord.
BASILIO: What, swords drawn here?
ESTRELLA: *(Aside.)* Astolfo is enraged!
BASILIO: Now, what has happened here?
ASTOLFO: Nothing, sire, since you have arrived.
    (THEY sheathe their swords.)
SEGISMUNDO: Much, sire, even though you're here;
    I have tried to kill this old man.
BASILIO: Had you no respect
    For these white hairs?
CLOTALDO: My lord, you see, they're mine;
    And so they're not important.
SEGISMUNDO: A vain desire,
    Wishing me to respect his white hair;
    It's possible that we all might see
    Some other mane of snow
    Trampled under my feet some day;
    Because I'm still not avenged
    For the unjust way I was brought up.
    (HE exits.)
BASILIO: Before you see that, you'll go back to sleep
    Where you'll believe that everything
    That's happened was a dream.
    (Exeunt the KING and CLOTALDO. ESTRELLA and ASTOLFO remain.)
ASTOLFO: Fate never seems to lie
    When it speaks of misfortunes,
    As certain of evils
    As it is doubtful of blessings!
    What a good astrologer he would be
    Who always announced
    Disastrous results, since there's no doubt
    That those predictions would always be true!
    Comparing me and Segismundo
    Can confirm this, Estrella,

Since fate gave the two of us
Such different signs.
In him, he predicted arrogance,
Misfortune, death, and in every way
He told the truth.
It has all come to pass.
But for me, the prediction was good fortune,
Blessings, victories, and applause.
The astrologer spoke well and he spoke ill;
Because the only certain thing
Since the dawn of your great radiance
Is that fate has signaled favor for me
And delivered only your disdain.

ESTRELLA: I don't suspect the truth of these fine phrases;
But I suggest they're for another lady,
Whose portrait, hanging
From your neck, you wore
When you arrived to see me;
And since that's the case, Astolfo, these flatteries
Are hers and hers alone.
Hurry to her so she can reward you;
Because in the court of love,
Flatteries and vows
Will not advance your cause
When they're made in service
Of other ladies, other kings.
(Enter ROSAURA, to the side.)

ROSAURA: *(Aside.)* Thank God, my miseries are at an end,
Since seeing this, there's nothing left
For me to fear!

ASTOLFO: I'll make that portrait disappear
So that my breast has room
For the image of your beauty.
When Estrella rises, there's no place
For shadows, just as the Sun
Makes the stars recede.
I'll go and bring it to you.
(Aside.)
Pardon this injury, beautiful Rosaura,
But this is all the faith

That men and women keep
When they're apart.
(HE exits.)
ROSAURA: *(Aside.)* I didn't hear a word,
Since I was fearful that they'd see me.
ESTRELLA: Astrea.
ROSAURA: My lady.
ESTRELLA: I'm glad you've come,
Because I have a secret to confide
And you're the only one I trust with it.
ROSAURA: You honor, my lady, whoever serves you.
ESTRELLA: In the short time, Astrea,
That I have known you,
You have won the keys to my heart.
Therefore, I dare to confide in you
Something that so many times I've hidden
From myself.
ROSAURA: I am your slave.
ESTRELLA: So, to tell you in brief,
My cousin Astolfo
Is supposed to marry me,
That is, if fortune wishes
To undo a heavy weight
Of ill-starred luck with one
Great stroke of happiness.
It bothers me that the first day we met,
He wore around his neck
The portrait of a lady.
I spoke to him about it courteously;
He is gallant, and loves me well;
So he went for it, and will return here shortly.
It will embarrass me a great deal
If he has to give it to me.
Stay here, and when he comes
Tell him I have asked you to receive it.
I'll say no more to you.
You are discreet and beautiful;
You'll understand what love is.
(SHE exits.)
ROSAURA: I wish I didn't understand!

Heaven help me!
Who else is prudent enough, or clever enough,
To give me good advice
In this impossible situation?
Will there ever be another soul
Lashed with more misfortunes,
Surrounded by more sorrows?
Reason cannot rescue me
From this confusion,
And consolation seems a distant dream.
Since my fate first started to go astray,
Nothing has happened to me
That hasn't been a disaster,
One leading to another,
Creating their own heirs.
They spring up like Phoenix,
The next one born from the ashes of the last.
A wise man said that troubles
Were like cowards, since it seemed
They never went abroad alone;
I say that they are valiant,
Because they're always moving forward,
And they never turn their backs.
I say this, since throughout my life
I've never been without them,
And they will never rest until they see me,
Wounded by fortune, in the arms of death.
Alas for me! What should I do
Right here, right now?
If I say who I am, Clotaldo,
To whom I owe my life,
Would be offended with me,
Since he tells me that staying silent
Is the best hope for gaining back my honor.
If I must not tell Astolfo who I am
And he comes to see me,
How can I conceal myself?
My voice, my tongue, my eyes
Might try to fool him,
But my soul will tell him that they're lying.

What shall I do? Why should I try to reason
What to do, if it's evident
That the more I prepare,
The more I study and think,
When the moment arrives
My pain will do whatever pleases it?
For no one has dominion over pain.
And since my soul doesn't dare determine
What to do, let sorrow
Find its bitter end today, let
Pain reach its extreme, and let's be done
With doubts and appearances
At last; but until then,
Help me, heavens, help me!
(Enter ASTOLFO with the portrait.)
ASTOLFO: Here, my lady, is the portrait;
    But—oh my God!
ROSAURA: What shocks
    Your Highness? What do you wonder at?
ASTOLFO: At hearing you, Rosaura, and seeing you.
ROSAURA: I, Rosaura? You must be deceived,
    Your Highness, if you take me for
    Another lady; since I
    Am Astrea, and my humility
    Does not merit the great compliment
    Of causing you this upset.
ASTOLFO: Rosaura, enough with the deception,
    Because the soul never lies;
    And although I may regard you as Astrea,
    As Rosaura I love you.
ROSAURA: I do not understand Your Highness,
    And so I don't know how to answer.
    All that I will say
    Is that Estrella (who could as well be
    Venus) commanded me
    To wait for you in this place,
    And on her part to ask you
    For that portrait; a sensible request.
    And then I am to bring it to her.
    Estrella wishes it so,

And even if it's dangerous for me,
I'll do it for Estrella.

ASTOLFO: Try as hard as you can,
Rosaura, but you are a
Terrible deceiver. Tell your eyes
To tune their music and be in concert
With your voice; because an instrument
That's playing in two keys
Will always sound distempered.
You should try to harmonize the lies
You speak with the truth of what we feel.

ROSAURA: I tell you that I'm only waiting
For the portrait.

ASTOLFO: Since you wish
To carry out the trick to the finish,
I'll respond to you in kind.
Astrea, please say to the Infanta
That so highly do I value her
That when she asks me for a portrait,
It seems like much too small a thing
To give her. And so,
Because of my great esteem for her,
I send her the original.
And you may bring it to her,
Since you carry it with you as yourself.

ROSAURA: When a proud and valiant man decides
To undertake an enterprise,
He won't return without the thing he seeks,
No matter what he's offered in its place,
Even if its value is far greater.
He'd feel spurned and foolish.
I come for a portrait,
And although I may carry an original
That's worth far more, I don't wish to be spurned.
And so, Your Highness, give me back that portrait,
Since without it I must not return.

ASTOLFO: Well if I won't give it to you,
How are you going to get it?

ROSAURA: Like this. Let it go, ingrate.

ASTOLFO: It's no use.

ROSAURA: By God, this portrait will not end up
    In the hands of another woman.
ASTOLFO: You are a terror.
ROSAURA: And you are treacherous.
ASTOLFO: Enough now, my Rosaura.
ROSAURA: Yours, villain? You lie.
    (Enter ESTRELLA.)
ESTRELLA: Astrea, Astolfo, what is this?
ASTOLFO: *(Aside.)* Estrella!
ROSAURA: *(Aside.)*   Now give me,
    Love, the genius and the wit
    To get my portrait back.
    (Aloud.)
    If you wish to know what's happening,
    My lady, I will tell you.
ASTOLFO: What are you playing at?
ROSAURA: You ordered me to wait
    Here for Astolfo, and to ask him
    For a portrait that he promised you.
    I remained alone, and as you know how
    Some thoughts bring others so easily to mind,
    Seeing that you spoke of portraits,
    The memory of that reminded me
    That I had one of mine
    In my sleeve. I wished to look at it,
    Because a person alone
    Diverts herself with crazy things.
    It fell from my hand
    To the floor. Astolfo, coming back
    To give you a portrait of some other woman,
    Picked it up, and so unruly
    Is he that, instead of giving one, he wants
    To take the other. Since he refused
    To give mine back to me,
    I tried to get it from him
    First with pleadings and persuasions,
    Then angrily and impatiently as you saw.
    The one he has in his hand is mine;
    You will see if there's a likeness.
ESTRELLA: Let go of the portrait, Astolfo.

(SHE takes it from HIM.)

ASTOLFO: Madam . . .

ESTRELLA: The painting
Is not unkind to the reality.

ROSAURA: Is it not mine?

ESTRELLA: There can be no doubt.

ROSAURA: Now tell him to give you the other one.

ESTRELLA: Take your portrait, and go.

ROSAURA: *(Aside.)* I have got my portrait back,
Now come what may.
(SHE exits.)

ESTRELLA: Give me that portrait of yours,
The one I asked for; for even though I do not plan
To see you or talk to you again,
I cannot stand the thought that you should have it,
If only because I so foolishly
Asked it of you.

ASTOLFO: *(Aside.)*
How can I
Get out of this?
(Aloud.)
Although I would wish, beautiful Estrella,
To serve you and obey you,
I will not be able to give you the picture
That you ask of me, because . . .

ESTRELLA: You are
A crude and ill-bred lover.
I don't want you to give it to me;
Because I really do not wish
To be reminded that I ever asked for it.
(SHE exits.)

ASTOLFO: Hear, listen, look, consider!
Heaven help me, Rosaura!
And tell me how and why
You've come to Poland
To ruin me, and ruin yourself!
(HE exits.)

The Tower.

(SEGISMUNDO is discovered, as at first, with skins and chains, sleeping on the ground. Enter CLOTALDO, CLARÍN, and two SERVANTS.)

CLOTALDO: Leave him here.
  For today his pride ends
  Where it began.

FIRST SERVANT: Just as before,
  I'll chain him to the rocks again.

CLARÍN: Don't ever wake up fully,
  Segismundo, to see yourself
  Lost, your luck changed,
  Your glory feigned,
  A shadow of life,
  A candle flame of death.

CLOTALDO: For someone who knows how to discourse
  Like this, it's a good idea to prepare
  A room where he can have
  Plenty of space to argue.
  Here—seize this one
  And lock him in that cell.

CLARÍN: Why me?

CLOTALDO: Because a big-voiced trumpet like you,
  Who knows secrets, must be guarded
  In a prison where he can't sound off.

CLARÍN: Did I, by any chance, offer
  To kill my father? No.
  Did I throw that little Icarus
  Off the balcony?
  Do I die, and then get resurrected?
  Am I dreaming now, or sleeping? So why
  Do they lock me up?

CLOTALDO: Like I said, you are a trumpet.

CLARÍN: What if I tell you that I'll be
  A cornet instead, and never blow a note,
  Since that's an ugly instrument.
  (THEY carry HIM away; enter KING BASILIO, masked.)

BASILIO: Clotaldo?

CLOTALDO: Sire, your Majesty
  Comes here like this?

BASILIO: A foolish curiosity to see
How Segismundo is has brought me here.
CLOTALDO: Look at him there, reduced
To a miserable state.
BASILIO: Oh, unhappy Prince,
Born at a sad hour!
Wake him up, now that
The opium he drank
Has made him lose his vigor.
CLOTALDO: He's restless, sire,
And speaking.
BASILIO: What will he dream of
Now? Let us listen.
SEGISMUNDO: *(In his sleep.)* A compassionate Prince is one
Who punishes tyrants.
Let Clotaldo die at my hands,
Let my father kiss my feet.
CLOTALDO: He threatens me with death.
BASILIO: And me with cruelty and insult.
CLOTALDO: He intends to take my life.
BASILIO: His plan is to subdue me at his feet.
SEGISMUNDO: *(In his sleep.)* Let my unequaled valor take the stage
Of the great theater of the world:
So that my vengeance squares
With my humiliation,
Let them see the triumph
Of Prince Segismundo over his father.
(HE awakens.)
But—alas!—where am I?
BASILIO: *(To CLOTALDO.)* He must not see me.
Now you know what you must do.
I'll listen to you from over there.
(HE withdraws.)
SEGISMUNDO: Is this me? Do I really see myself
In this condition now,
In prison, and in chains?
Aren't you my tomb,
My tower? Yes. Heaven help me,
What things have I been dreaming!
CLOTALDO: *(Aside.)* It's now my role to play make believe.

SEGISMUNDO: Is it time to wake up?

CLOTALDO: Yes, it's time to wake up.
    Would you spend the whole day
    Sleeping? Since I
    Followed the eagle's flight
    As it slowly flew out of sight,
    And you remained here,
    You haven't been awake at all?

SEGISMUNDO: No,
    And I'm not awake right now;
    Because according to what I understand,
    Clotaldo, I'm still sleeping,
    And I think I am not greatly deceived.
    Because if I have been dreaming
    What I saw so vividly and certainly,
    What I'm seeing now would be uncertain;
    And it doesn't matter that I'm exhausted,
    Since I understand that, being asleep,
    I dreamed I was awake.

CLOTALDO: Tell me what you dreamed.

SEGISMUNDO: Supposing that it was a dream.
    I will not tell you what I dreamt;
    What I saw, Clotaldo, yes.
    I awoke, and saw myself
    (what cruelty that flattery was!)
    In a bed that could have been,
    With all its hues and colors,
    A bed of flowers
    Woven by the spring.
    There a thousand nobles, bowing
    At my feet, called me their Prince,
    And served me fine things, jewels, and clothing.
    My feelings then—calm and tranquil—
    You changed to joy,
    By telling me my good fortune;
    That I was the Prince of Poland.

CLOTALDO: I assume I had a good reward.

SEGISMUNDO: Not so good; for being a traitor,
    I tried to kill you twice.

CLOTALDO: Such severity with me?

SEGISMUNDO: I was the lord of all,
    And I took revenge on all of them.
    I loved one woman only,
    I still believe that was true;
    All the rest is gone,
    And only that remains.
    (The KING exits.)
CLOTALDO: *(Aside.)* The King is touched
    By what he's heard.
    (Aloud.)
    Since we were talking
    About that eagle when you fell asleep,
    Your dreams have been of empire;
    But in those dreams, it would be well
    From this day on to honor the one
    Who brought you up so carefully,
    Segismundo; since even in dreams
    You shouldn't forget to do what's right.
    (HE exits.)
SEGISMUNDO: That's true; so let's restrain
    This wild beast's nature,
    This fury, this ambition
    In case sometime we dream again.
    And indeed we will, since we find ourselves
    In such a singular world,
    That to live is just to dream,
    And experience teaches me
    That the man who lives, dreams
    What he is until he awakens.
    The king dreams that he is king, and lives
    With this illusion, commanding,
    Governing, disposing.
    And all the loud applause that he receives
    Is merely lent to him, written on the wind,
    And death transforms it soon enough
    To ashes—a powerful misfortune!
    Who would want to reign,
    Seeing that one has to wake up
    To the dream of death!
    The rich man dreams his riches,

That only offer him more cares;
The poor man dreams he suffers
His misery and poverty;
He dreams—the one who is beginning to thrive,
He dreams—the one who toils and tries,
He dreams—the one who injures and offends;
And finally, in this world,
Everyone dreams the thing they are,
Though no one understands this.
I dream that I am here
Weighed down and shackled by these chains,
And I dreamed that in another state,
I saw myself much happier.
What is life? A frenzy.
What is life? An illusion,
A shadow, a fiction.
The greatest good is smaller than it seems,
Since all life is a dream,
And even dreams themselves are only dreams.

END OF ACT TWO

ACT THREE

The Tower.

(Enter CLARÍN.)

CLARÍN: Because of what I know,
    I'm a prisoner in an enchanted tower.
    What will they do to me
    For what I don't know,
    If they've practically killed me for what I do?
    On top of it all, why should I
    Have to suffer this living death
    On an empty stomach?
    I feel sorry for myself.
    Everyone will say: "that, I believe."
    And so they should believe it;
    Because this silence doesn't fit the name Clarín.
    I can't keep quiet.
    Keeping me company
    Here, if I've got this right,
    Are spiders and rats.
    Look what sweet little songbirds they are!
    My poor head still aches
    From my dreams last night,
    Which featured the sound of
    A thousand shawms and trumpets,
    A strange, illusory procession
    With crosses and flagellants; and of these,
    Some are rising, others falling,
    Some are fainting when they see
    The blood that others spill.
    But actually, truth to tell,
    I'm faint with hunger,
    Since I find myself in prison,
    Where now every day
    I study the philosophy of the Empty Plato
    And at night I recite the story
    Of the Lost Supper.
    If silence is a saintly virtue,

Then in the new calendar,
Saint Secret is the one for me,
Because I fast for him without a break;
Although I guess this punishment I suffer
Is well deserved,
Since a silent servant
Is a sacrilegious sinner.
(A noise of drums and people offstage.)

FIRST SOLDIER: This is his tower.
Break the door down;
Everyone in.

CLARÍN: By God!
I'm sure they're looking for me,
Since they say this is my tower.
What will they want of me?
(Enter those SOLDIERS who can.)

FIRST SOLDIER: Go inside.

SECOND SOLDIER: Here he is.

CLARÍN: No, he isn't.

ALL: Sire . . .

CLARÍN: Are they all drunk?

SECOND SOLDIER: You are our prince;
We do not want and will not accept
Anyone but our natural lord.
No foreign princes here.
Give us your feet to kiss.

ALL: Long live our great Prince!

CLARÍN: *(Aside.)* Good God, they mean it!
Is it the custom in this kingdom
To seize someone one day
And make him Prince, and later
Put him back in the tower? Yes,
It must be, since I see it happen
Every day. So I'll play my part.

SOLDIERS: Give us your feet.

CLARÍN: I can't,
Because they're quite necessary
To me, and it would be a shame
To have a footless prince.

SECOND SOLDIER: We have all told your father

That we recognize you alone
As our prince, and not
The one from Muscovy.

CLARÍN: Have you lost
Your respect for my father?
You're all a bunch of riffraff.

FIRST SOLDIER: It was the loyalty in our hearts.

CLARÍN: Oh, if it was loyalty, I pardon you.

SECOND SOLDIER: Come out and take back your kingdom.
Viva Segismundo!

ALL: Viva!

CLARÍN: *(Aside.)* Did they say Segismundo? All right.
Apparently they call all their
Counterfeit princes Segismundos.
(Enter SEGISMUNDO.)

SEGISMUNDO: Who calls the name of Segismundo here?

CLARÍN: *(Aside.)* I'm guessing my career is over.

SECOND SOLDIER: Who is Segismundo?

SEGISMUNDO: I am.

SECOND SOLDIER: Well, how come you were impudent and stupid
Enough to play Segismundo?

CLARÍN: I, Segismundo? I deny it.
It was you who
Segismundized me; so
The only stupidity is yours.

FIRST SOLDIER: Great prince Segismundo!
Your father, King Basilio,
Fearing that the heavens
Would fulfill a prophecy
That you must conquer him,
Is trying to steal your rightful power
And give it to Astolfo, duke of Muscovy.
The people, now aware of this,
And that they have a natural king,
Don't want a foreigner
To rule over them.
And so, bravely challenging
That merciless fate,
They have sought you out
In your prison tower. We've come

In force to free you,
Strengthening your arms
And helping you restore
Your imperial crown and scepter
By tearing them from the tyrant's grasp.
Leave, then; for just outside
An army of the people
Calls for you. They cry out for
Your liberty: listen to their voices.

VOICES: Viva Segismundo! Viva!

SEGISMUNDO: Once again, heavens,
You'd have me dream of grandeurs
That time must take away?
Once again you'd have me see,
In shadowy glimpses,
My majesty disappearing in the wind?
Once again you'd show me
Disillusionment, and have me risk
Believing I was once again alive?
It must not be. It must not be.
I will not see myself once more
A subject to my fate.
And since I know
That all life is a dream,
I command you shadows now
To leave me. Stop pretending
To my dead senses that you have
A body and a voice.
I do not want false majesty,
No more illusions
That must vanish at the slightest puff of air.
I understand you now. I understand.
And I know that you play this way
With everyone who sleeps.
But for me, no more pretending.
Now that I am undeceived,
I know quite well that life's a dream.

SECOND SOLDIER: If you think we are deceiving you,
Turn your eyes toward that mountain there—
You see your people waiting to obey you.

SEGISMUNDO: I've seen this once before,
    So clearly and distinctly, just like now,
    And it proved to be a dream.
FIRST SOLDIER: Great happenings, my lord,
    Always are foretold by omens.
    And that's what it would be,
    If you dreamed it first.
SEGISMUNDO: You're right, it was an omen;
    And just in case it's true,
    Since life is so short,
    Let's dream, my soul, let's dream
    Again; but this time, let me wake
    From my sweet pleasure
    Into a better moment.
    Keeping this in mind,
    My disenchantment will be easier to take;
    It's possible to make a jest of danger
    When you meet it well-prepared.
    Now: knowing that even when it seems
    The strongest, all power is held on loan,
    And must at last be paid back to its owner,
    We can and will dare everything.
    Vassals, I thank you
    For your loyalty; and I will use
    My strength and skill to free you
    From foreign slavery.
    Sound the call to arms.
    You'll quickly see my valor show itself.
    I will take arms against my father
    And tear the truth from the heavens;
    Soon I'll see him at my feet.
    (Aside.)
    But what if I wake up
    Before it happens? It might be
    Better not to speak of it, in case
    I'm not meant to succeed.
ALL: Viva Segismundo! Viva!
    (Enter CLOTALDO.)
CLOTALDO: In heaven's name, what is this uproar?
SEGISMUNDO: Clotaldo.

CLOTALDO: My lord . . .
   (Aside.)
   Perhaps he'll try his cruelty out on me.
CLARÍN: *(Aside.)* I bet he throws him off the mountain.
   (HE exits.)
CLOTALDO: I come to kneel before you,
   Knowing now that I must die.
SEGISMUNDO: Get up,
   Get up, father, from the ground,
   For you must be my North Star, my guide
   In whom I have the utmost trust;
   I know now that I owe you a great deal
   For raising me so loyally.
   Give me your arms.
CLOTALDO: What are you saying?
SEGISMUNDO: That I am dreaming, and I want to do
   Some good. Because one should not forget
   To do good, even in dreams.
CLOTALDO: Well, my lord, if doing good
   Is now your motto, it's certain
   That I won't offend you if I
   Ask you to do some good today.
   Must you make war upon your father?
   I cannot advise you, nor help you
   Against my King.
   I'm here at your feet;
   Kill me.
SEGISMUNDO: Villain, Traitor, ingrate!
   (Aside.)
   But—stop. I must control myself,
   Since I still don't know if I'm awake.
   (Aloud.)
   Clotaldo, I envy
   Your valor, and I thank you for it.
   Go now and serve the King,
   And we'll see each other in the field.
   You there, sound the call to arms.
CLOTALDO: I kiss your feet a thousand times.
   (HE exits.)
SEGISMUNDO: Fortune, we go to reign again;

If I am sleeping, do not awaken me,
And if this is real, you must not let me sleep.
But, whether real or a dream,
Doing good is the important thing.
If this is real, then we'll do good
For its own sake;
If not, to win some friends
Against the time when we awaken.
(THEY exit, sounding arms.)

The Palace.

(Enter KING BASILIO and ASTOLFO.)
BASILIO: Astolfo—can prudence ever check
 The fury of an unbridled horse?
 Can one man stop the current of a river
 That rushes, proud and headlong, to the sea?
 Who can bravely keep a boulder
 From breaking off a mountain peak?
 All these would seem easy to accomplish
 Compared to reining in the people,
 Proud and reckless.
 The instant that some rumor starts to fly
 That someone's up, or someone's down,
 You hear the mountains echoing,
 Some crying "Astolfo" and others "Segismundo."
 The royal throne, reduced now
 To a secondary role,
 Becomes a theater of death
 Where unlucky fate puts on its tragedies.
ASTOLFO: My lord, I beg you to withhold for now
 The happiness and pleasure
 That your loving hand has promised me.
 For if Poland (which I aspire to command)
 Resists obeying me,
 It's telling me I must deserve it first.
 Give me a horse, and I will rush to battle,
 Hurling bolts of lightning,
 Exulting in the thunder.
 (HE exits.)

BASILIO: There's no remedy for the inevitable;
    The future that was foretold
    Is fraught with danger.
    One can't defend against a certainty,
    For the more one tries to avoid it,
    The more one brings it on.
    The law is hard, relentless!
    Whoever thinks they're fleeing danger
    Runs to meet it,
    Just as I, by trying too hard
    To save my people,
    Have destroyed my country, and myself.
    (Enter ESTRELLA.)
ESTRELLA: Great lord! The tumult spreads
    From one faction to another,
    Chaos running through the streets and plazas.
    You must make an appearance, lord,
    And face this down, or you will see
    Your kingdom swim in waves of scarlet.
    Everything points toward destruction
    And toward tragedy.
    So great is the ruin of your empire,
    That the Sun itself is troubled
    And the wind is stifled;
    The stones rise up in pyramids,
    The flowers circle into funeral wreaths;
    Each building is a haughty sepulcher,
    Each soldier a living skeleton.
    (Enter CLOTALDO.)
CLOTALDO: Thank God that I have reached your feet alive!
BASILIO: Clotaldo, what's happening with Segismundo?
CLOTALDO: A mob, like a blind-drunk monster,
    Breached the tower, and from its depths
    Released the Prince, who as soon
    And he saw his rank restored again,
    Showed his valor, saying proudly
    That he would tear the truth from heaven.
BASILIO: Give me a horse. I must go myself
    To conquer my ungrateful son
    And defend my crown;

Where science failed, let steel triumph.
(HE exits.)
ESTRELLA: Then I will be Bellona
And ride beside the royal sun.
I hope to elevate my name with yours;
So now my wings must take me to the battle.
(SHE exits, and the call to arms sounds.)
(Enter ROSAURA, who detains CLOTALDO.)
ROSAURA: Although your valor calls you
Urgently away, I beg you, listen to me;
I know that war is everywhere.
You know that I arrived in Poland
Poor, humble, and unfortunate,
And assisted by your valor,
In you I found pity.
You ordered me (oh heavens!)
To live in the palace in disguise,
Concealing my jealousies,
And hiding from Astolfo. Finally
He saw me, and so grossly does he trample on
My honor that, after seeing me, he still
Talks with Estrella in the garden
Every night. I've taken the key to it,
And I can make it possible
For you to enter there
And put an end to all my cares.
You will restore my honor,
Since you are resolved
To avenge me with his death.
CLOTALDO: It's true I was inclined,
Rosaura, from the moment I first saw you
To do for you whatever was in my power.
My first idea was to have you
Change your clothing,
So that, if you met Astolfo,
He would see you as yourself,
And he would have to take
Your anger seriously,
Since it comes from wounded honor.
At the same time I was planning

To avenge your loss,
Even if it meant killing Astolfo.
That's how much your honor means to me.
I must have been delirious,
Thinking, well, he's not my King,
He doesn't frighten me, and so
I thought to kill him
When Segismundo tried to
Do the same to me, and then
Astolfo came on the scene,
Ignoring his own danger,
And made, in my defense,
A show of recklessness
That far surpasses simple courage.
So, how can I now,
With my soul full of gratitude to him,
Kill the man who gave me life?
And thus, between you two I must divide
My affection and my care.
Seeing that I've given life to you,
And from him I have received it,
I don't know whom to help;
The one who owes her life to me
Or the one to whom I owe my life.
ROSAURA: I don't have to remind you
What a noble action giving is,
And what baseness to receive.
If we agree on that,
You need not be grateful to him.
If he's the one who gave you life,
And you gave life to me,
It's very clear he forced you into
An ignoble action by receiving life
From him; while I, accepting life
From you, have caused you to be
Generous and noble.
Therefore he has offended you;
And you're obliged to me,
Since you've given to me
What you have received from him.

And so you should assist
My honor in this great danger,
Since I have shown you how much better
It is to give than to receive.
CLOTALDO: Although nobility favors giving,
Gratitude resides on the part
Of the receiver;
Since I've known the joy of giving,
I have the reputation of a generous man.
Let me also be accounted as
A grateful one, since I maintain
There's equal honor
In giving and receiving.
ROSAURA: From you I received my life,
And you told me that
A life insulted was no life at all.
I have received nothing from you;
Since the life your hand gave back to me
Was not life after all.
And if you seem to favor
Generosity over gratitude
(as I heard you say just now)
Then I hope you'll give me life,
Since you have not done it yet.
Since giving makes you greater,
Be generous first; you can be
Grateful afterwards.
CLOTALDO: Conquered by your argument,
I will be generous first.
Rosaura, I will give you
All my fortune, and in a convent
You will find your sanctuary.
With the kingdom so divided,
I cannot, as a nobleman, be a traitor
And add to its misfortunes
By carrying out your plan.
In selecting this remedy
I am loyal to the king,
Generous to you,
Grateful to Astolfo;

So I offer you this path,
And it can be our secret now and always.
God knows I could do no more,
Even if I were your father.

ROSAURA: If you were my father,
I would endure this injury;
But since you're not, I won't.

CLOTALDO: Well, what do you plan to do?

ROSAURA: Kill the Duke.

CLOTALDO: A woman
Who has never known her father
Can have such courage?

ROSAURA: Yes.

CLOTALDO: Who spurs you on?

ROSAURA: My reputation.

CLOTALDO: Look at Astolfo and you must see . . .

ROSAURA: All my honor trampled on.

CLOTALDO: . . . your King, and Estrella's husband.

ROSAURA: In God's name that will never be!

CLOTALDO: This is madness.

ROSAURA: I see that.

CLOTALDO: Then conquer it.

ROSAURA: I can't.

CLOTALDO: Then you'll lose . . .

ROSAURA: I know . . . .

CLOTALDO: . . . your life and honor.

ROSAURA: Yes.

CLOTALDO: What are you seeking?

ROSAURA: My death.

CLOTALDO: This is only spite!

ROSAURA: It's honor.

CLOTALDO: It's absurdity.

ROSAURA: It's courage.

CLOTALDO: It's a frenzy.

ROSAURA: Rage, fury!

CLOTALDO: Can't you find a way to soften
Your blind passion?

ROSAURA: No.

CLOTALDO: Who is there to help you?

ROSAURA: Just myself.

CLOTALDO: There's no remedy?
ROSAURA: No remedy.
CLOTALDO: Think carefully, if there's another way . . .
ROSAURA: Another way to lose myself.
    (SHE exits.)
CLOTALDO: Daughter, wait! If you're going to lose yourself,
    Let's lose everything together.
    (HE exits.)

A field.

(Sounds of martial music, and enter, marching, SOLDIERS, CLARÍN,
and SEGISMUNDO, dressed in skins.)
SEGISMUNDO: If Ancient Rome, at her imperial height,
    Could see me on this day,
    Oh, how she would rejoice
    At the wonder of this rare occasion:
    A wild beast as leader of great armies,
    For whose high aspirations
    The firmament itself would be
    A minor conquest!
    But let's not fly that high,
    My spirit. Let's not overreach
    And make this fragile moment vanish,
    In case I have to wake up to the anguish
    Of having gained it
    Only to have lost it.
    So, the less it means to me,
    The less regret I'll feel if it goes.
    (A trumpet, within.)
CLARÍN: A proud, swift steed
    (Excuse me, but I have to do some touch-ups
    When I tell a story),
    Whose body is a map of all the Earth,
    With fire in his soul,
    His foam the sea, his breath the air,
    A chaos of confusion,
    Since in his soul, foam, body, spirit,
    A monster of fire, Earth, sea, and wind,
    His color, dappled grey,

And ridden to the purpose
By one who puts the spur to him,
Instead of running, flies,
And brings here to your presence
A graceful woman.

SEGISMUNDO: Her light blinds me.

CLARÍN: By God, it's Rosaura!

(HE exits.)

SEGISMUNDO: Heaven has restored her to me.

(Enter ROSAURA, dressed in loose peasant clothing, with a sword and dagger.)

ROSAURA: Generous Segismundo,
Whose majesty rises like the day,
Just as your heroic deeds
Break forth from your
Long night of shadows;
Just so may you dawn upon the world,
A shining sun of Poland,
And, as well, on this unhappy woman,
Who throws herself at your feet today,
Trusting that being a woman, and unhappy,
Is enough to win the help of one
Who boasts he's valiant.
Three times already
You have looked upon me in surprise,
And three times you have not known who I am,
Since three times you have seen me
In different form and dress.
The first time you believed
I was a man, in that terrible prison
Where your life made my misfortunes
Seem like nothing.
The second time you admired me
As a woman, when the pomp
Of your majesty was a dream,
A fantasy, a shadow.
The third time is today, and now
I'm of two species, since
Along with my woman's clothing
I bear the weapons of a man.

And so that your compassion
Might dispose you more to help me,
Please listen to my tragic fortune.
I was born in Muscovy,
The daughter of a noble mother
Whose beauty matched her sorrows,
Both being great.
A traitor cast his eyes
On her, a traitor whom I will not name
Since I did not know him,
But who must have had great valor;
My own informs me of it.
Being his offspring, I'm sorry now
I wasn't born a pagan,
So I could fool myself
Into believing he was some god
Who in a metamorphosis became
A shower of gold, a swan, a bull,
For Danae, Leda, and Europa.
I guess my wandering story has revealed
How my mother, more beautiful
Than any other woman,
But unhappy like us all,
Was seduced by amorous lies,
And her own naïve faith
In that foolish word, that vain promise
Of marriage; how it won her over
So completely that still today
The thought of it overwhelms her.
After his tyrannical conquest,
He left behind his sword.
It's right here, in its sheath,
But I will bare it
Before my story's over.
So I was born from this, this ill-tied knot
Which neither binds nor punishes,
This marriage or this crime,
It's all one thing. And I was like
A portrait or a copy of my mother,
Not of her beauty,

But of her fortunes and her life;
And now I don't need to tell you
That as her unlucky heiress
I've run into her same fate.
The most that I can tell you
Of myself is to name the lord who robbed
The trophy of my honor.
Astolfo . . . oh, alas! Just saying that,
My heart becomes enraged,
Reacting to the enemy's name.
Astolfo was the ungrateful lord
Who, forgetting all our shared delights,
(Since a love that's past
Is all too soon erased from memory),
Came to Poland to marry Estrella,
Who was the rising star to my sunset.
Offended, tricked, outraged,
I remained, disturbed,
My feelings dead; I kept my pains in secret,
Until one time, alone
With Violante, my mother—oh heavens!—
She broke open the prison of silence,
And the captive troops
Stormed out of my breast together.
It did not embarrass me
To tell her of them;
Somehow, knowing that your confessor
Has made the same mistakes as you have
Makes the telling easier
And the truth pours out.
And so at times a bad example
Is good for something. Finally, she heard
My troubles sympathetically, and wished
To console me with her own.
How easily the judge who's been delinquent
Gives a pardon!
And learning a lesson from herself,
Having left the restoration of her honor
To the futility of idleness and time
She was not about to let me do the same.

Her best counsel was to follow him,
Find him, and with prodigious kindness
Oblige him to repay the debt of honor.
And so that I could travel in greater safety
She advised that I should dress in men's attire.
She took down this ancient sword,
The one I'm wearing. Now is the time
To reveal this blade, as I promised.
Then, trusting in its signs,
She told me, "Leave for Poland,
And make sure the greatest nobles
See this steel that adorns you;
For in one of them
Your fortunes will find pity and some comfort."
So I arrived in Poland.
We'll skip the story, since it's not important
And you already know it,
Of how a wild horse that threw me
Brought me to your cave, where
You were so stunned to see me.
We'll also skip the part wherein Clotaldo
Took my part so passionately,
Begged the King for my life,
And the King did spare me, and also how
When Clotaldo found out who I am
He persuaded me to put on my own clothing,
And to serve Estrella, where
Ingeniously I interfered with Astolfo's courtship
And marriage plans.
We'll skip right over how you saw me
Once again confused, and now in
Woman's dress, a change that
Quite confounded you;
And we'll move on to Clotaldo, who,
Persuaded that the most important thing
Is that Astolfo and the beautiful Estrella
Should marry and reign together,
Told me, against my honor, to drop my claim.
Seeing that you, valiant Segismundo,
Are bent today on taking vengeance,

Since heaven wishes you to break
These prison bars, where you've suffered
Like a beast in chains,
And as you take up arms against your country
And your father,
I come to help you, joining
Diana's robes with Athena's armor,
Dressed in cloth and steel.
So, great leader,
For both of us it is important
To disrupt these wedding plans;
For me so that the man who's called my husband
Does not marry,
And for you, to stop them
From joining their two states,
Uniting their powers
To put our victory in doubt.
As woman, I come to beg you
To help restore my honor,
And as man, I come to stir you up
And help you win your crown.
As woman, I come to seek your pity
And as man, I come to serve you
By fighting on your side.
As woman, I come so that you'll help me
In my injury and anguish,
And as man, I come to aid you
With my body and my steel.
And so, consider that if today
You fall in love with me as woman,
As a man I'll kill you
To defend my honor.
In this conquest of love, I have to be
A woman to tell you my complaints,
And a man to gain my honor back.
SEGISMUNDO: *(Aside.)* Heavens, if it's true that I am dreaming,
Suspend my memory,
For it's not possible to hold
So many things in one dream.
God help me! How can I escape all this,

Or else find some way not to think about it?
Has there ever been so doubtful a condition,
Or one so painful?
If I only dreamed that grandeur
That I saw before, how can
This woman now recall it so precisely?
It had to be the truth; I did not dream.
And if it was the truth, here's more confusion,
How can my life be called
A dream? So—are glories
So similar to dreams
That the true ones are
Taken for falsehoods,
And the falsified for true?
Is there so little difference between them
That what you see and what you love
Must constantly be questioned:
Lies or truth? Is the copy
So like to the original
That there always must be doubt
Of which is which?
If this is so, and one must see
Greatness, power, majesty, and pomp
Disappearing into shadows,
We should learn to take advantage
Of this little time we have,
Since all there is to be enjoyed
Must be enjoyed between our dreams.
Rosaura is in my power,
My soul adores her beauty.
So let's enjoy the moment.
Love breaks the laws of chivalry and trust
By which she's lying at my feet.
This is a dream; and since it is,
Let's dream of great good fortune now,
For afterwards the sorrow always comes.
But now my reason
Begins to doubt itself.
If this is all a dream, pure vainglory,
Who would trade that for divine glory?

What remembered blessing
Does not seem like a dream?
Who has had great happiness
Who hasn't said, in thinking back on it,
"That was such a lovely dream"?
Then perhaps my disillusionment
Begins right here; if I know
That pleasure is just a beautiful flame
That turns to ashes
Whenever there's a puff of wind,
Let us turn to the eternal;
Where fame is longer-living,
Where happiness does not sleep
Nor greatness rest.
Rosaura's lost her honor;
And a prince's task consists of
Giving honor, not of taking it.
By God! I must restore her honor
Before I win my crown.
Her attraction's overpowering,
So I must fly.
(Aloud.)
Sound the call to arms,
For today I must give battle,
Before black shadows
Bury the rays of gold
Deep within the dark green waves.
ROSAURA: My lord, why are you leaving like this?
Don't my care and anguish
Deserve a single word?
How it is possible, my lord,
That you neither look at me nor listen to me?
Won't you even turn and face me?
SEGISMUNDO: Rosaura, your honor demands
That my compassion for you
Must seem like cruelty right now.
My voice cannot answer you, not yet,
Because my honor must respond;
I do not speak to you, because my deeds
Must speak for me;

I do not look at you, because it's necessary,
In this extremely painful moment,
That he who must look after your honor
Must not look upon your beauty.
(THEY exit.)

ROSAURA: *(Aside.)* Heavens, what are these enigmas?
After so many troubles,
Still I'm left to doubt
These equivocal replies!
(Enter CLARÍN.)

CLARÍN: My lady, is this a good time to see you?

ROSAURA: Oh, Clarín! Where have you been?

CLARÍN: Locked up in a tower,
Dealing for my death in a deck of cards,
And wondering whether the next card would be it;
I was playing *quínola* and the face card
That came up turned out to be
My life; and still I was
About ready to explode.

ROSAURA: Why?

CLARÍN: Because I know the secret
Of who you are, and, in fact,
(Sound of drums within.)
Clotaldo . . . but, what noise is this?

ROSAURA: What can it be?

CLARÍN: It can only mean
That the beleaguered palace
Has finally sent out its forces
To conquer Segismundo's army.

ROSAURA: Then why am I being a coward,
Not rushing to his side
In this great scandal of a world,
So lawless, so disorderly, so cruel?
(SHE exits.)

SOME VOICES: Long live our invincible King!

OTHERS: Long live our liberty!

CLARÍN: Long live liberty and the King!
May they both live very happily,
And it doesn't matter to me who wins,
As long as when it's over, I'm welcomed back.

I've decided to play Nero,
Who didn't let things bother him too much,
And stay a bit removed from the day's confusion.
I won't let this battle bother me!
From my hiding place,
I'll be able to see the whole party.
I've got a secret spot among these rocks.
So now death won't find me, and I can say
That I don't care two figs about it.
(CLARÍN hides himself. A noise of battle.)
(Enter the KING, CLOTALDO, and ASTOLFO, fleeing.)

BASILIO: Is there an unhappier king,
A more persecuted father?

CLOTALDO: And your defeated army
Retreats without rule or order.

ASTOLFO: The victorious traitors remain.

BASILIO: In such battles, those who win are loyal,
The defeated are the traitors.
Therefore let us flee, Clotaldo,
From the cruel, inhuman
Wrath of a tyrant son.
(Shots offstage, and CLARÍN falls, wounded, from where he is.)

CLARÍN: Heaven help me!

ASTOLFO: Who is this
Unhappy soldier, fallen at our feet
All stained with blood?

CLARÍN: Just an unfortunate man,
Who found death by trying to avoid it.
Fleeing from it, I ran right into it,
Since death knows all the secret places.
From this the argument is clear
That he who tries the hardest
To run away from death
Is the one who meets it first.
And so, turn back, turn back
To the bloody combat now;
For between the blades and bullets
There's greater safety for you
Than in a well-armed fortress;
There is no safe pathway that will take you

Through the forces of destiny
And around your merciless fate.
And thus, although you try to free
Yourself from death by fleeing,
See this: that you will die
If it is God's will you die.
(HE falls offstage.)
BASILIO: See this: that you will die
If it is God's will you die.
Oh heavens, how well this corpse,
Speaking through the mouth of a wound,
Persuades us of our error,
Of our ignorance, toward
A better understanding.
A bloody tongue, a dying voice
Can unleash great wisdom, teaching us
That all of man's precautions
Are in vain as long as they are set
Against a higher power and purpose!
So I, to free my country
From death and treachery,
Came to inflict on it the very things
That I was trying to avoid.
CLOTALDO: Although fate, sire, knows
All roads, and finds
Whomever it looks for among
The rocks and in the thickets,
It is not a Christian judgment to say
There is no remedy.
There is; and the prudent man
Can win a victory over fate.
And if you're not exempt
(As no man is) from punishment,
Go to where you may be saved.
ASTOLFO: Clotaldo, sire, speaks to you
As a prudent man
Whose age brings great experience,
And I as a valiant youth.
Among the folds and branches
Of this mountain there is a horse,

A swift one, born of the wind;
    Take him and fly, and I meanwhile
    Will safeguard your retreat.
BASILIO: If it is God's will that I should die,
    Or if death awaits me here,
    I want to meet it face-to-face.
    (Sound of arms, and enter SEGISMUNDO and his whole company.)
SOLDIER: The king is hiding somewhere
    In the tangles of this mountain.
SEGISMUNDO: Follow him,
    And search these trees
    Trunk by trunk and branch by branch.
CLOTALDO: Flee, sire!
BASILIO: Why?
ASTOLFO: What are you doing?
BASILIO: Astolfo, step aside.
CLOTALDO: My lord, what are you doing?
BASILIO: Something, Clotaldo, that I need to do.
    If you are looking for me,
    Here I am, prince, at your feet;
    Let this be a white carpet for you,
    This snowy hair of mine.
    Step on my neck, and make a footprint
    On my crown; drag down
    My dignity and my respect;
    Take vengeance on my honor;
    Make me serve you as a slave.
    Thus, fate receives its tribute,
    And in spite of all my care,
    Heaven fulfills its word.
SEGISMUNDO: Illustrious court of Poland,
    You who have been witnesses
    To so many wonders, listen,
    For your Prince is speaking to you.
    What heaven has determined never lies.
    What is written by God's finger
    On a blue tablet, with ciphers and engravings
    In decorated golden letters,
    Never can deceive.
    Lying and deception enter in

When someone tries to understand them,
Penetrate their meaning,
And use them to do ill.
My father, this man here,
To check the cruelty
Of my condition, raised me as
A human beast; so brutal
Was my upbringing that if I
Had been born docile, humble,
With my gallant nobility
And brave nature intact,
It would have been enough, that way of life,
To make me bestial.
What a fine design that was!
If they said to any man:
"Some inhuman beast
Is going to kill you" would he choose
To wake the beast
While he was sleeping?
If they told him: "This sword
You're wearing must be the one
To slay you," what wise man
Would take it out
And place it at his breast?
If they told him: "The seas
Must be your grave,
Your tombstone made of foam"
He would not do well to go to sea,
When, in storm, it throws up whitecaps
And angry crystal mountains.
The same thing has happened
To one who, because he feared a wild beast
Was threatening him, awakened it;
Fearing a certain sword,
Unsheathed it; and put out
To sea in a wild storm.
And even if (listen to me)
My rage were a sleeping beast,
My fury a sheathed sword,
My severity a quiet, calm sea,

Fortune cannot be conquered
By injustice or by vengeance;
If anything they incite it more.
And thus, whoever wants to triumph
Over fortune must do so
With prudence and with temperance.
Not until harm comes
Can the one who has foreseen it
Mount a good defense against it,
Hoping to preserve himself; although
With humility, he can (and this is clear)
Protect himself from it, he still must wait
Until it finds him in the moment of his peril,
Because there is no way to stop it.
Let this rare spectacle
Serve as an example, this strange
Wonder, this horror,
This prodigy; since nothing
Is more spectacular than this:
In spite of all precautions,
My father kneels at my feet,
A king's white hair my carpet.
It was heaven's sentence;
No matter how much he wanted to divert it,
He could not. And shall I,
His inferior in age,
In valor, and in knowledge,
Conquer it instead? Sire, rise,
Give me your hand; for now
That heaven undeceives you
About your errors, I humbly offer you
My neck. Take your vengeance;
I kneel at your feet.
BASILIO: Son, because this noble action
Gives you a second birth
Deep within my heart, you are the Prince.
The laurel and the palm
Belong to you. You have conquered;
Your own deeds crown you.
ALL: Viva Segismundo! Viva!

SEGISMUNDO: Since my valor hopes
    To win great victories,
    Today the greatest one
    Must be over myself.
    Therefore: Astolfo,
    Give your hand to Rosaura,
    Since you know it is your debt
    Of honor. I've promised to recover it.
ASTOLFO: Although it's true I owe her
    Certain obligations, take note
    That she does not know who she is;
    And it is baseness and infamy
    For me to marry a woman . . .
CLOTALDO: Enough; wait; stop.
    Rosaura is as noble
    As you, Astolfo, and my sword
    Will defend her in the field;
    She is my daughter, and that's enough.
ASTOLFO: What are you saying?
CLOTALDO: That until I saw her
    Nobly and honorably married,
    I did not wish to reveal this.
    The story's very long;
    But in the end, she is my daughter.
ASTOLFO: Since this is so, I will
    Fulfill my word.
SEGISMUNDO: So that Estrella
    Is not left disconsolate,
    Seeing that she has lost a prince
    Of such valor and fame,
    With my own hand I
    Will join you to a husband
    Whose merits and whose fortune,
    If they don't exceed, at least they equal his.
    Give me your hand.
ESTRELLA: I gain
    By this good fortune.
SEGISMUNDO: For Clotaldo, who loyally
    Served my father, my arms await,
    To do whatever favors he might ask.

FIRST SOLDIER: If this is how you honor one
     Who fought against you,
     How about me, who caused
     The uproar in the kingdom,
     And freed you from the prison tower?
     What will you give me?
SEGISMUNDO: The tower in return;
     And so you won't escape
     From there until your death,
     You must be closely guarded;
     For the traitor is no longer needed
     When the treason's past.
BASILIO: Your wisdom amazes us all.
ASTOLFO: What a transformation!
ROSAURA: What discretion, and what prudence!
SEGISMUNDO: Why are you amazed? What surprises you,
     If my master was a dream,
     And I am anxious, ever fearful
     That I must wake up and find myself
     Locked up again in prison?
     And even were this not to be,
     The dream of it alone would be enough.
     I've come to understand, you see,
     That all of human happiness,
     In the end, passes like a dream.
     And now I wish to take advantage
     Of the short time that remains to me,
     To ask a generous pardon for our faults,
     Because for such noble hearts as these,
     That's the proper thing to do.

END OF *LIFE IS A DREAM*

THE GREAT THEATER
OF THE WORLD

(El gran teatro del mundo)

⊷ 1648 ⊶

CHARACTERS

THE AUTHOR
THE WORLD
THE KING
DISCRETION
THE LAW OF GRACE
BEAUTY
THE RICH MAN
THE WORKER
THE BEGGAR
A CHILD
A VOICE*

MUSICAL ACCOMPANIMENT

*Note: In the text, A VOICE is identified as VOICES, reflecting choices made in various productions of this translation.

ACT ONE

(Enter THE AUTHOR wearing a starry robe and a hat with rays of light that resemble a crown, like that seen around the head of the infant Jesus.)

AUTHOR: O, for a lovely scene to hide this architecture!
    Between the shadows here in front
    And the distant background view,
    Let's have a sky that steals its luster from the stars,
    And here on Earth, some lovely flowers
    That vie with them in number and in brilliance,
    At least until they wither and expire,
    Like the living things they are,
    Like humankind itself.
    Whatever I imagine, let me see it:
    For this Earth's a great battlefield too,
    A battlefield of the elements,
    Where mountains, lightning, wind, and water fight;
    Where eagles struggle and surge like ships in a stormy sea—
    And in the ocean, now and then, we'll see
    Squadrons of fish flying from wave to wave;
    And thunderbolts so bright that blind men see
    Their flaming fury;
    We'll see mountains filled with men and beasts
    Bearing witness to this everlasting war,
    This monster of fire and air, of water and Earth.
    Now that's a better scene.
    What should I call you—you ever-changing vision,
    Woven from every thread the universe can offer?
    You're the greatest prodigy ever created,
    You have no equal—so what to call you?
    How about The World—born like the Phoenix
    Out of your own ashes. Yes, The World.
    (Enter THE WORLD from a different door.)
WORLD: Who's calling?
    Who calls me from the rock-hard center
    Of the globe where I've been hiding?
    Who pulls me out from deep within myself—?
    Who's calling?
AUTHOR: Your Author calls—

And all it took to summon you
Was one sigh of my breath, one wave of my hand—
That's what took you from your primal chaos,
Gave you form.
WORLD: But—what do you want from me?
AUTHOR: I'm your author, and you're my creation.
Today I'm thinking of a project I want done,
And you're the one I want to do it.
I want to stage a festival in honor of my powers.
Nature's always celebrating me
With dazzling shows of sound and light,
But I'm in search of something different:
A simple comedy of human life.
Ages ago I cast mankind to be
My company, and they're the ones who'll act
In this great theater of the world.
I'll give a part to each one that appears.
And your role will be just as crucial,
Preparing all the wonders of the stage—
The costumes, scenery, props, the lights and sound—
You'll be in charge of everything behind the scenes.
I'll write the play.
Mankind will form the company of Actors.
WORLD: My generous Author, whose every breath's
Obeyed by everyone, you may indeed
Call me the *Great Theater of the World,*
Because upon my stage mankind will act,
And each one finds in me the things they need
To do their work—especially that crucial skill
Of following directions without the need for praise.
Since it's obvious that even though the hard work's mine,
The glory is all yours. And now to work:
It's always better not to see
The stage before the play begins, so I've arranged
A black curtain to hide the scene.
Because as you know better than anyone,
It's Chaos back there until everything is set.
They'll all be running around in a fog until
I light the stage and chase away the mist.
I'll use two lamps—

One is the divine lantern of the day,
And the other one lights up the night,
Along with those thousand little diamonds
That sparkle across the face of night and lend a hand.
In the first act, when everything's still simple,
Innocent, and governed only by
The great law of nature, the first light of the first day
Will reveal a garden that's so beautiful
That you'll begin to wonder how nature knew
Enough to make such graceful works without
Even having a degree in art.
All the flowers, in or out of season, will burst forth
To see the Dawn. The trees will be filled with tasty fruit,
And none of it yet poisoned by that envious snake.
A thousand brilliant crystals will break themselves apart,
Flying up toward the still-dark sky
So that the Dawn can cry them down as tiny dewdrops.
To ensure abundance in this human heaven,
I'll see that it's provided well with virgin fields.
And wherever we need a mountain or a valley,
A mountain or a valley there shall be;
And rivers, wise and vigorous, digging their way
Through the Earth in all directions, carrying their waters
To the wild arms of the sea.
So there it is—Scene One—
There's not a single building yet, but in an instant
You will see republics, cities, palaces revealed.
And that will be Scene Two.
And when all the walking wears the mountains down
And the air grows tired of bearing all the birds,
I'll change the scene completely:
A raging flood will cover all the world.
Everyone will drown.
And yet amid the ocean's rise and fall
A ship will come, heaving blindly,
Its belly pregnant with mankind,
With birds and beasts. When Heaven signals peace,
A rainbow of three colors will appear
And the waves will take their proper places once again,
Gently caressing the edges of the Earth,

Which once again reveals its true face,
Its fresh and newborn face, no longer wan and withered.
And so the First Act ends. Now the Second Act begins:
The act of the Commandments.
Here I'll show great things:
The flight of the Hebrews headlong out of Egypt
Through the crystal waters of the Red Sea;
The waves will rise on either side so that
Everyone will see the miracle I've made.
And then with two great pillars of fire I'll light
The desert all the way into the Promised Land.
Moses will catch a wind-swift cloud to reach
A mighty mountain where he will receive
The Laws. And then this second act will end
In a terrible eclipse. The Sun will seem
To flicker and almost die. Darkness and smoke.
A final paroxysm. The blue Earth staggers.
Latitude and longitude tumble and are lost.
The mountains shake. The walls collapse,
Leaving all the transitory troubles
Of this world in ruins.
Now let's hear a bit about the Third Act:
The Law of Grace, we'll call it, and we'll see
Portents great and small, which happily
I don't have to spend much time describing here.
And so: three acts, three laws.
The Law of Nature, The Law of the Commandments,
And the Law of Grace. To end our revels
The whole great scene and all its apparatus
Will dissolve in one pure flame, one ray of light:
Because light's the kind of theme our Author
Really likes. Wait! What am I saying?
Imagining it, I tremble, I am shaken;
We must delay this scene, this horrible end
So future centuries will never see it!
Now mankind will see prodigious things
Presented in three acts, and none of them
Will lack a thing through any fault of mine.
I've prepared the theater so well
That everything is here and ready now.

To make an entrance or an exit, see
How I've provided for two doors,
The only doors we need:
One is the Cradle, the other is the Grave.
As to the costumes, everything's in order:
To make a King, royal purples and stately laurel;
For a valiant Captain, dress him in his armor,
Courage, and his victories. A scholar?
Books, scholastic robes; the cleric, dressed
In his devotions. Insults for the criminal,
Due honors to the noble; and for the masses,
Their right and proper liberties. To the worker,
Who has to labor for a living
(Thanks to that fool Adam's little slip),
I'll give him simple tools. As for the one
Who has to play the Lady, I'll adorn her
With those perfections that are sweet poison
To so many. Only the poor will not be dressed—
That part calls for nakedness.
And now no one can complain that they
Didn't have the proper things to play their roles—
If they slip up, the fault will not be mine.
And since the stage is ready, Come on, mortals!
Come and get your costumes on, each one of you,
So that you can act in our Great Theater of the World!
(Exit THE WORLD.)
AUTHOR: Mortals—even though you're not yet born
I'll call you mortals, because I see you just as clearly
As if you were already here; and though
You cannot hear my voice, I ask you now
To enter: for it's time to cast the play.
(Enter the ACTORS who will become RICH MAN, KING, WORKER,
BEGGAR, BEAUTY, DISCRETION, and a CHILD.)
KING: Author! Here we are, obedient to your will.
We have no soul, no feeling,
No power, life, or reason;
We don't know who we are.
We're all unformed before you.
We are the dust at your feet.
Breathe on this dust, and let us act our parts.

BEAUTY: We exist in your mind only—we do not touch or feel,
  Nor can we enjoy what's good or bad;
  But, if we're going to represent
  The world, please tell us who we're playing.
  We won't turn down our roles—because we can't.
WORKER: My sovereign author, now that I can see
  Just who you are, I'm here at your command.
  You made me after all, with your own hand.
  And since it's plain to see that God knows all,
  Whatever part you give me, if I mess it up
  No need to run to God about it, no,
  Just bring your criticism straight to me.
AUTHOR: I know that if the choice were left to you,
  No one would want the parts where feeling pain
  Or suffering is required; everyone
  Would choose those roles where power and command
  Come into play—it's strange they never notice
  That these roles are just a part to play,
  Not life itself.
  Now—it's time to cast the show. I know well
  Which part each one of you is suited for;
  And here are my selections. You—the King.
  (AUTHOR gives each one a paper.)
KING: I am honored.
AUTHOR: A lady, who stands for all that's beautiful
  In humankind, for you.
BEAUTY: What luck!
AUTHOR: You'll play the rich man, a powerful part.
RICH MAN: The Sun is shining on me, too!
AUTHOR: You must play the Worker.
WORKER: Is that a job or a free ride?
AUTHOR: A job, and lots of hard and grueling work.
WORKER: Oh, in that case I have to say I'd be
  A lousy worker.
  In Heaven's name . . . your name, that is . . .
  Even though I'm a son of Adam,
  Please don't give me all this work to do—
  How about giving me lots of stuff instead?
  I see myself in no uncertain terms
  As a member of the leisure class.

No good at digging, and even worse at farming.
If my opinion counts for anything
Let me say a big "No thanks"—
All right, in front of such a mighty author,
I guess "No thanks" won't do—so let me say
That I will be—by far—the worst actor in the play.
You're very smart, it's clear, and so
You've given me a job that fits my talents.
You'll just have to ignore my little trials.
When I need wool to keep me warm
You give me snow:
But you are just, and so I can't complain;
And if you'll pardon me, my Lord,
I'll play my part real slow—
Don't want to get worn out before the end.

AUTHOR: You'll play discretion.

DISCRETION: It's my lucky day.

AUTHOR: Your part is difficult—the Beggar's role.

BEGGAR: What kind of part is that?

AUTHOR: *(To the CHILD.)* Your part is to die before you're born.

CHILD: That won't be hard to memorize.

AUTHOR: Thus I guarantee that all of life
    Is represented in our play.
    My justice is universal, and I know
    That my casting is appropriate.

BEGGAR: If I could get another role, I'd do it;
    If I dared, I'd fire myself today
    From this life that you've chosen to give me;
    But since I can't recast myself, although
    I wish I were that bold, I'll take the part.
    But just consider for a moment, Lord—
    Hear what the one who plays the beggar has to say:
    Mine's the worst role in the play, because
    For me it has to be a tragedy,
    While the others get to play romance or comedy.
    When you handed me this part,
    Didn't I get a soul the same as his?
    Or hers? Equal feelings? Equal being?
    So why is my role so different?
    If I was made from different clay, if you

Had dressed my soul up differently, put in
Less life, or fewer feelings—
Please forgive me now, but it looks cruel
To give a bigger part to one whose being's
No better than my own.

AUTHOR: In this production, the one who plays
The Beggar well—with feeling, soul, and drive—
Pleases me as much as he who plays
The King: both parts are leading roles.
Do your work well, and think about the fact
That when payday comes, you'll be his equal.
Although, being poor, you'll be in pain,
In my book it's a better part than his,
If you play it well. And at the end
Everyone will get the salary they've earned;
You see, every role can be a winner here,
For all of human life's a play,
And what matters is how well you act it.
When the comedy is finished,
Those who've played their parts without mistakes
Will join me at my side in a great banquet
And there, everyone will be equal.

BEAUTY: But tell us, Lord, what's the title of this famous play?

AUTHOR: *Do Good, for God Is God.*

KING: This play is so mysterious that I think
We dare not make mistakes—

RICH MAN: And so it's vital
We rehearse before we do another thing.

DISCRETION: But how can we rehearse unless we find
Our light, our soul, our being,—which we lack
Because we've done no action yet?

BEGGAR: Well, how are you supposed
To do a play without rehearsal?

WORKER: I'm with the Beggar, I feel the same way.
That makes sense, I guess, since a Beggar
And a Worker are pretty much the same.
But listen—even a well-known play goes flat
When the actors have no chance to brush it up—
If we don't rehearse this brand-new work,
How will we get it right?

AUTHOR: The time has come to let you know
    That heaven is the only critic, judge,
    And audience for this show—
    And you only get one chance to play it right—
    This business of being born and dying.
BEAUTY: But—how are we supposed to know
    Our entrances and exits—who's calling "places"?
AUTHOR: I'm not going to tell you even that—
    Just be ready at all times to play your part,
    And I'll call for you when it's all over.
BEGGAR: What if I go blank, forget my lines?
AUTHOR: Suspecting that might happen now and then
    I've engaged a prompter to correct
    Whoever strays too far from the script
    Whether you're the Beggar or the King.
    So let's not have any more complaints.
    And now: you have Free Will to act—
    The theater is ready—
    Begin to measure out the course
    Of all your lives from birth to death.
DISCRETION: What are we waiting for?
ALL: Let's go and start the show:
    Do Good, for God Is God!
    (As THEY begin to leave, enter THE WORLD, who stops them.)
WORLD: Now everything's in order to present
    This play that brings humanity to life.
KING: I'd like some laurel sprigs and purples.
WORLD: Why that?
KING: *(Showing HIM his part.)*
    Because that's what's written here
    In my character description.
WORLD: And here they are, all ready for you.
BEAUTY: For me, some hints of jasmine, rose, carnation.
    Leaf by leaf and ray by ray,
    All the light of day,
    All the flowers of May
    Will be awakened from their slumbers
    And they'll flock to me, and the poor Sun
    Will suffer mortal envy just from looking at me.
    And if the silly sunflower were to try

To outshine me, he'd quickly find
I have my own sunflower called the Sun!
WORLD: Hmmm—you're just an actress—
How did you get to be so vain?
BEAUTY: That's the basis of my part.
WORLD: And what's your part again?
BEAUTY: Human beauty.
WORLD: We'll daub you with crystal, carmine, snow, and garnet
Set off by shadows, so your highlights glow more brightly.
(Gives her a bouquet.)
BEAUTY: I'm a prodigal of colors!
Carpet me with flowers—let my crystals
Serve me as a mirror!
(Exits.)
RICH MAN: Give me my riches, my fortune and my joy—
Because my prosperous life begins today.
WORLD: For you I'll break my insides into stones;
From my breast I'll tear out all the silver,
All the gold, that like a miser I've been
Hiding deep within me.
(Gives him jewels and/or rich coins.)
RICH MAN: I'm drowning under all these riches—
But I'm proud of them, make no mistake!
DISCRETION: Now for my part in today's play—
All I ask is a simple plot of land
On which to live.
WORLD: And what's your part?
DISCRETION: Discretion.
WORLD: Your role requires little: only fasting
And continuous prayer. Discretion, here's your gown.
(Gives a religious habit.)
DISCRETION: It wouldn't be discreet to ask for more.
(Exits)
WORLD: *(To the CHILD.)* Why don't you ask for anything to help
You play your part?
CHILD: 'Cause I don't need a thing for the amount
Of living that I'm going to do.
Without being born, I have to die.
I'll only be in you, World, long enough
To pass from one dark place to another,

And all you have to give me is a grave.

WORLD: You—with the rough edges—What do you want?

WORKER: What I told him before.

WORLD: Aaagh—Let me at least acquaint you with your part.

WORKER: Aaagh—I'm telling you I don't want to.

WORLD: If you're going to be like that, go right ahead—
You'll have to fight for every scrap of bread
Just like a brute.

WORKER: That's my tough luck.

WORLD: Here, take this hoe.

WORKER: Adam's inheritance. Mr. Father Adam,
You could have played it smarter. 'Cause you knew
What was in store. Your woman didn't pass
Her test—but no, you had to eat that fruit
She handed you—now that was not too swift.
But like a star-crossed lover you just did
Exactly what she asked of you—so I
Can play my part as badly as you played yours.
(Exits.)

BEGGAR: I've seen you hand out happiness, and blessings,
Joys and fortunes. I know that's not for me.
Give me my griefs, my pains, and my bad luck.
I'm not like the others. I don't want purples and laurels;
No bouquets, no gold or silver neither.
Just my rags.

WORLD: Which part is yours?

BEGGAR: My part's affliction, anguish, misery, sadness,
Wounds, bad luck, the passion of pain, compassion too;
Suffering, sighs, and moans, and begging:
Never having anything to give,
Always holding out my hand
To ask for everything.
Being scorned and shunned, insulted, pitied;
Feeling shame, and nakedness, and filth—
Tears, distress, hunger, thirst, and hardship.
This is the vile necessity of being poor.

WORLD: You're right. The one who plays the beggar's part
Gets nothing from the world—but let me think—
Yes, take off these clothes. To play your part
As written, your only costume is yourself.

(Undresses BEGGAR.)

    I have to do this—it's my job. Perhaps
    Later on you can beg yourself some rags.
BEGGAR: When all is said and done, this sad old world
    Gives more to those who already have plenty—
    And takes the clothing off the backs of those
    Who haven't got a stitch.
WORLD: Now our theater is well provided
    With all the various states of humankind:
    Here we have a King, with his far-flung empire;
    Beauty that makes the senses lose their reason;
    Power that commands applause;
    Needy beggars, hungry workers, the devout,
    The whole cast is assembled.
    In order that they have the means to play
    Their proper parts today, I've given them
    A stage, costumes, props, and furnished them,
    As appropriate, with pleasure or with pain—
    Now—divine Author, come out to see the show
    That your cast, mankind, is ready to put on!
    Open up the center of the Earth,
    So you can take your seat right in the middle
    Of the action!
    (Music plays; two globes open at the same time: in one, a glorious throne, on
    which sits the AUTHOR; the other should contain two doors, one of which is
    painted with the image of a cradle, and on the other, a coffin.)
AUTHOR: This show is being staged to celebrate
    My greatness, so I'll sit here on this throne
    Where it is always day, and watch my company perform.
    Look to your parts, mankind—
    You enter the stage by way of a cradle
    And leave it by a grave.
    Your Author's watching you from here above:
    The best seat in the house.
    (Enter DISCRETION with an instrument, and sings, joined by the
    VOICES.)
DISCRETION: *Earth and heaven, Praise the Lord;*
    Sun and Moon and stars;
    (VOICES join in.)
    Praise him, flowers that make the soil

A coat of many-colored hues;
Praise him, light, fire, and ice
Praise him, frost and dew;
Winter and summer, spring and fall
And whatever is beneath this earthly veil,
Praise him, one and all.
(Exit DISCRETION.)

AUTHOR: Nothing is more pleasing to my ears
Than the sound of faithful souls singing
The hymn that Daniel sang to calm the rage
Of Nebuchadnezzar.

WORLD: Who's going to give the prologue today?
But here, responding to your voice, appears
The Law of Grace.
(The Law of GRACE appears above, with a document in hand, over the place
where the WORLD was standing.)

GRACE: I, the Law of Grace, will introduce
Your festival today. But first, some business.
In order to help those who lose their words,
I have the text of our great play right here.
But all you really need to know is found
In these two simple verses:
(Sings.)
Love your neighbor as yourself,
And do good, for God is God.

WORLD: Now that the prologue's done, the Law of Grace
Will stay with us as prompter; she wanted more,
But there are no parts left, because
I'm playing myself. But I'll be quiet now,
Because the show is starting.
(Enter BEAUTY and DISCRETION through the cradle-door.)

BEAUTY: Come help me take the measure of these fields
That sing the happy song of May, and hear
The sweet flattery of the Sun; because
That's all that matters here, those two—
The Sun, the land; the light, the blossoms;
Each adds a splash of color to the picture.

DISCRETION: You know that I don't like to leave my house
And escape my peaceful prison, where all is quiet.

BEAUTY: Is everything austerity with you?

All rigor? Self-denial? Can't you have
One day of pleasure? Tell me, Lord, why grow
The flowers, if not to please our senses with their scents?
Why make the birds, which sing their flattering phrases
Like feathered mandolins, if we are not
Supposed to hear them? What is clothing for
If not to tempt our touch with silky softness?
Why does fruit taste sweet unless it serves
To ripen some good plot of yours? In short:
Why did God make mountains, valleys, sky,
If our eyes weren't meant to see them? Now it seems
Like sheer ingratitude not to enjoy
All these earthly wonders, born of heaven.

DISCRETION: To enjoy them by admiring them is just,
And offering thanks and praise is proper.
But to enjoy these beauties for bad ends is wrong
Or to admire the art without remembering
The Artist. I don't have to leave my house;
I chose this life to bury myself away;
That's why I'm called Discretion.
(Goes apart somewhat.)

BEAUTY: For that matter, I am Beauty. My only job
Is to be seen—oh yes, and see.

WORLD: It didn't take long for Beauty and Discretion
To figure one another out.

BEAUTY: Just as you hide your loveliness from view,
My beauty will weave nets and snares to catch
The fleetest, most elusive prey: the heart.

WORLD: Of these two actors, one's performing perfectly;
The other's off her text a bit.

DISCRETION: How can I better use my skill to serve the play?

BEAUTY: How can I make the most of my great beauty?

GRACE: *(Sings.) Do good, for God is God.*

WORLD: I don't think Beauty heard the prompt.
(Enter the RICH MAN.)

RICH MAN: Heaven has given me riches of power and property
And so I'm determined to spend them on constant delight.
Nothing pleases me unless I hunger for it;
And whatever I hunger for, I have:
See how my table overflows; let Venus

Come adorn my bed; and in conclusion,
Gluttony, envy, idleness, ambition
Are the masters of my soul today.
(Enter the WORKER.)

WORKER: Does anyone here work as hard as I do?
I break the breast of the Earth that gave me life,
Because that's the only way I earn my food.
I'm the Prime Minister of plows; but I don't see
A penny of the profits they produce.
My weapons are a sickle and a hoe:
My battle's with my livestock, and the soil.
In April and May I have a lust for rain—
And if the water lets me down, I'm poor again.
If anything I plant should have the luck
To grow, why then the tax-collector's got me
In his sights. I'll tell you what: because
I work and sweat, the people who depend
On what I grow will have to pay the price
I want to charge. And if it doesn't rain
(When I beg God for drought and famine), then
My granary will make me rich! I'll be
The greediest man for miles hereabouts,
And everyone will need me, I'll grow fat,
And then—what should I do?

GRACE: *(Sings.)* *Do good, for God is God.*

DISCRETION: Why didn't he hear the prompter?

WORKER: I happen to be a little deaf sometimes.

WORLD: Well, at least his behavior is consistent.

WORKER: Even if I seem to be resistant.
(Enter the BEGGAR.)

BEGGAR: Of all who live on Earth, whose misery
Is worse than mine? This ground's my feather bed,
The sky's my only shelter, so I have
No place to hide from frost and heat.
Hunger and thirst as well—Lord, give me patience!

RICH MAN: Now what can I do to show off my riches?

BEGGAR: And what can I do to endure my misfortunes?

GRACE: *(Sings.)*
Do good, for God is God.

BEGGAR: Oh, how that voice consoles me!

RICH MAN: Oh, how it tires me out!

DISCRETION: The King is coming to walk these gardens.

RICH MAN: I feel a powerful ambition to be
    Inferior to no one! None at all!

BEAUTY: I'll place myself in front of him to see
    If my beauty can make him fall in love with me.

WORKER: I'll stay behind; I don't want him to notice me
    And say—"well, there's a worker—and here I've got
    A brand new tax for him to pay." You see,
    I don't want any more favors.
    (Enter THE KING.)

KING: This world's not so grand, now that I see it.
    In my empire the narrowest spits of land
    Contain whole provinces the size of this
    Inferior corner of creation.
    I am the absolute lord, the supreme master
    Of everything surrounded by the sea
    And lit by Sun. My imperial vassals bow
    Before me wherever I go. So tell me:
    What should I be doing in the world?

GRACE: *(Sings.) Do good, for God is God.*

WORLD: You're prompting each one better
    Than the one before.

BEGGAR: I look out from deep within my misery—
    And what's before my eyes? What do I see?
    Unhappily enough, the happiness
    Of others. The King, great lord, enjoys
    His majesty, not comprehending that
    I need him; Beauty pays attention only
    To herself, she doesn't know that there is pain
    And deprivation in the world; and there's
    Discretion, always occupied in prayer,
    Who serves God well, it's true, but always serves
    In comfort. Then the worker: he comes home
    From laboring in his field dead tired, and then
    He finds an honest table set for him,
    Not opulent, but ample. The rich man
    Has everything he wants, twice over. I—
    I, alone in all the world, need everything,
    And so I come to everyone for help,

Not because I want to, understand:
Because I need to. Because they can all
Live just fine without me but I can't
Live even for a day without their help.
I'll beg from Beauty. In the name of God,
Can you spare some alms?

BEAUTY: Oh fountains! Yes, you fountains over there,
Since you're my mirrors of the moment, tell me—
Which dress do you like better on me?
And what about my hair? Straight? Curls?

BEGGAR: Don't you see me?

WORLD: Don't you see your begging is in vain?
Why should she take care of you,
Who is so careless of herself?

BEGGAR: I'll try the rich man. Sir, since you
Have so much more than you must need,
Please give me something.

RICH MAN: Aren't there other doors for you to knock on?
How dare you dare to be where I am.
You should get no closer than the threshold
Of the outer hallway—you should not
Under any circumstance be here. Where *I* am.

BEGGAR: Please don't treat me so unkindly.

RICH MAN: Get out of here, rude beggar. Now.

BEGGAR: You've got so much—enough for every pleasure—
Can't you spare a little?

RICH MAN: No!

WORLD: The parable's still with us—of Lazarus
And the man of Avarice.

BEGGAR: Now my necessity's so great, it drives
Me mad, deprives me of my reason, makes
Me flout the law and beg from the King.
Alms, sir? Alms?

KING: Ah yes. For things like this
I have my Ministry of Alms, Aid, Comfort,
And Assistance. Go see them. Good-bye.

WORLD: A King will always cleanse his conscience
By passing on a problem to a Minister.

BEGGAR: Mr. Worker? Since you receive God's blessing
In the sprouting of your seeds, I guess

In my great need I turn to you.

WORKER: If God
Did bless me, the blessing's cost me plenty
Of plowing, sowing seeds, and sweat to
Make a penny from it. Tell me:
Aren't you ashamed to beg from me?
Why don't you get a service job? And if
You need a meal, here—take this hoe
And earn one for yourself—or dig one up.

BEGGAR: In this particular play today I have
The beggar's part, and not the worker's.

WORKER: Well, my friend, I don't suppose our author
Demands that you do absolutely nothing else
Than beg. You don't have to be useless.
Sweat and toil are in the script whenever you are poor.

BEGGAR: In the name of God, you're hard on me, my brother.

WORKER: And for your part, you're demanding quite a bit.

BEGGAR: At least give me some comfort.

DISCRETION: *(Gives bread.)* Here, take this, and pardon me.

WORKER: Oh, a bit of bread. Well, sister, now
I see we're in your debt as well.
There's trouble when Religion gives you bread.

DISCRETION: Oh, my lord.

KING: What's going on?

WORKER: Some trouble
That Religion's poking into.
(DISCRETION begins to fall; the KING offers his arm.)

KING: I'm here to help you.

DISCRETION: That's good. No one else can offer us the kind
Of help that you can.

AUTHOR: I could certainly correct all these
Mistakes I'm seeing here, but then what good
Would free will be? I've given it to each
Of them, to see what choices they will make
In working out the action of the play.
That's my project. Improvisation is
The order of the day. At least for now.
When things get too confusing,
I'll simply have my prompter call:

GRACE: *(Sings.) Do good, for God is God.*

(Speaks.)
To each one for himself, and all together,
My voice has given warning;
If anyone goes far astray,
The fault will be their own.
(Sings.)
Love your neighbor as yourself,
Do good, for God is God.
KING: All right—supposing life's indeed a play,
And that we're all together on this journey,
Let's make the road a little easier
With some pleasant conversation.
BEAUTY: This world wouldn't be much fun without
That kind of thing—so—what should we say?
RICH MAN: Let's have each one tell a story.
DISCRETION: That might go on too long—a better plan
Might be for each of us to speak about
The things that we imagine—or we dream.
KING: I see my empires spread before me,
My majesty, my glory, and my greatness,
In forms so rich and various that nature
Herself must clear some space for them.
I have tall castles, beauty is my servant.
In my great kingdom, some are humble,
Others rich, according to their destiny.
To rule this many-headed monster properly,
I'll need some help from Heaven.
Give me wisdom to rule well, for it's
Impossible to tame this creature
With an ordinary collar, or a yoke.
WORLD: He asks for wisdom, just like Solomon,
To govern well.
(Sad VOICES sing within, from the side of the stage where the coffin is.)
VOICES: *King of a fallen empire, cease,*
O cease your mad ambition,
For in this theater of the world,
Your part is finished.
KING: A sad song tells me that my part is all played out.
As soon as I heard it, I seemed to lose my sense
Of direction, even my reason.

Since my part is finished, I want to leave the stage,
But where should I go?
Over there where I came in, I see
My cradle, and—oh my!—I can't go back that way.
That road is blocked. However I might try
I can't take even one step toward my cradle—
All of them are toward the grave!
A river might try to flee its destiny, the sea,
But it always will become the sea again;
The mist that rises from the river (oh my God!)
Becomes the river once again at last.
So man, born from the earth, back to the earth
Must always go, cannot remain what he once was—
What confusion! If my part's over,
Supreme and divine Author, please forgive
My errors, because I'm truly repentant.
(Exits through the coffin door, as everyone will have to do.)
WORLD: The King concluded his part well,
    Begging for forgiveness.
BEAUTY: Now the King's without his servants, pomp, and honor.
WORKER: As long as it rains on the fields in May,
    We're better off—see what I mean?—
    With good weather and without a King.
DISCRETION: All in all, it's a great pity.
BEAUTY: And very confusing.
    What are we supposed to do without him?
RICH MAN: Let's get back to our conversation.
    Tell us what you're imagining.
BEAUTY: I'm imagining myself.
WORLD: Imagine that. How quickly those
    Who are left alive find consolation!
WORKER: Even more so when the dead one
    Leaves them lots of land.
BEAUTY: I see my pure and lovely beauty, nothing else.
    And I don't envy the King a single triumph
    Because I think my beauty guarantees
    An ever-greater empire for me.
    If the King enslaves men's lives, their souls are mine.
    Beauty rules over hearts, and so
    I must conclude that mine's the greater empire.

The philosophers call man a "little world";
My empire of men is built to straddle Earth
And heaven—so to honor my divinity
The same folks who call man a "little world"
Should call a lovely woman a "little heaven."

WORLD: Apparently she's not acquainted with Ezekiel,
Who says that beauty's lost when pride's excessive.

VOICES: *(Singing.)*
All of human beauty, added up,
Amounts to one small flower.
Wither now and fade away,
Because the sunset
Of your radiant dawn has come.

BEAUTY: A sad song's singing of beauty's passing.
Don't die—please don't die. Come back
To that first light of dawn when you were born!
But—oh my—there's no rose, white or red,
That doesn't wilt and droop a little bit
In the harsh light of the day's flatteries.
And flowers don't shrink back into the bud.
But, what does it matter that the flowers of the dawn
Fade in the flattering golden sunlight?
What comparison is there between those flowers and me?
No, I am a flower whose beauty lasts much longer,
And if I saw the Sun at my beginning,
That doesn't mean the Sun will see my end.
If I'm eternal, why must I die?
What can you tell me, voices?

VOICES: *(Singing.) In your soul you are eternal,*
But your body is a temporary flower.

BEAUTY: I cannot argue. I entered through that cradle
And I go toward that grave.
It grieves me greatly
That I didn't play my part more perfectly.
(Exits.)

WORLD: She played it well, because she ended in repentance.

RICH MAN: Now Beauty lacks her gems and her adornment;
Her youthful bloom is gone.

WORKER: If we're not lacking bread and wine and meat
For Easter, why then, I won't miss Beauty.

DISCRETION: Still, all in all, it's a great sadness.
BEGGAR: And worthy of compassion. What should we do?
RICH MAN: Let's get back to our conversation.
WORKER: I stared down heat and cold, in every season,
　　With all the anxious care that goes along
　　With working in the fields; but now I find
　　I didn't cultivate my soul so carefully,
　　Just left it to fend for itself.
　　The fault was this: With each new harvest
　　I gave thanks to the fields from which I got
　　The grain, and not to God who gave it
　　In the first place.
WORLD: Acknowledging your debt is one step closer
　　To being truly grateful.
BEGGAR: I'm starting to like this fellow, even though
　　A while ago I couldn't stand him.
VOICES: *(Singing.)*
　　Worker, you've arrived
　　At the fatal end of all your labors;
　　Now you're bound for other fields.
　　But where? God knows!
WORKER: Voices, can this sentence be appealed?
　　Let me appeal it, please; let me take it
　　To a higher court. Don't let me die
　　Right now. The season's wrong; if nothing else,
　　My fields are still full of crops. And also,
　　Like you said, I'm not such a good worker—
　　My vines will tell you that, because the weeds
　　Have grown so tall that you can't tell the cornfields
　　From the vineyards. My neighbor's wheat grows huge
　　And everyone admires it, while mine is dwarfish,
　　Barely sprouting from the ground. So you might say,
　　It's time for me to die, since all my fields
　　Are dying; but here's my answer:
　　I want to leave something behind me when I go.
　　How will I be judged if I leave nothing?
　　Well, I guess this isn't a time for thankfulness,
　　Over there are voices telling me I'm dead,
　　And there the grave's mouth yawns to drag me in.
　　One more thing: if I haven't played my part

According to the contract, well, it pains me
That I feel no pain for feeling nothing painful
About that.
(Exits.)
WORLD: At first I judged
This worker to be a little crude,
But his ending made me notice my own ignorance.
The worker ended well!
RICH MAN: He's finished now with hoes and ploughs,
Dirt, exhaustion, sweat.
BEGGAR: And he leaves us feeling quite distressed.
DISCRETION: What a shame!
BEGGAR: What grief!
DISCRETION: What tears!
BEGGAR: What confusion!
DISCRETION: What should we do?
RICH MAN: Let's keep our conversation going;
And, to do my share, I'll tell you what I'm thinking.
Who wouldn't be amazed to learn that life's a flower,
Born in dawn's first light, and dying
With the dusk? If life's appointment is so
Brief, we should enjoy it for the little time
We have. I say we worship our stomachs like gods.
Let us eat, let us drink today, for tomorrow we shall die!
WORLD: Well, that's a sort of pagan proposition—
At least that's what Isaiah said.
DISCRETION: Who's going next?
BEGGAR: I'll go.
Perish the day I came into this world.
Perish the frozen night on which I was
Conceived to suffer this much pain.
Don't let the pure light of the Sun
Reach down into this darkening fog where I'm
Condemned to live—let everything be shadow,
Let no light in to challenge the hard oppression
Of the darkness.
Let night be eternal, terrifying all the lands;
And so they'll never get a glimpse of Heaven,
Let everything be cloaked in dark and fog,
Let the red glow of morning dissolve

Into a day that has no dawning,
A night that shows no Moon and stars.
The reason I'm not even more upset is this:
I could despair to see myself like this,
But then I figure I was born in sin.

WORLD: The signs of desperation have deceived you;
The sinner Job also cursed the day—until he saw the light.

VOICES: *(Singing.)*
There are many blessings in this world,
And many too are pains;
It's time to take a good account of both.

RICH MAN: Oh my God!

BEGGAR: What new happiness is this?

RICH MAN: Doesn't this song that calls us make you tremble?

BEGGAR: Yes.

RICH MAN: Don't you want to flee?

BEGGAR: No—it feels natural to tremble
When your soul fears God, for being God.
Besides, it would be vain to flee.
The King and Beauty couldn't do it—
What chance does the Beggar have?
In any case, my pain ends with my life.
And so I offer up a thousand thanks.

RICH MAN: Aren't you sorry to leave the stage?

BEGGAR: No, I never really liked it, so I
Leave it with a peaceful heart.

RICH MAN: I'm hanged—
My heart can't live without my property.

BEGGAR: What joy awaits.

RICH MAN: What sorrow!

BEGGAR: What a comfort!

RICH MAN: What affliction!

BEGGAR: What a blessing!

RICH MAN: What misery!

BEGGAR: What good luck!

RICH MAN: What an ending!
(THEY exit.)

WORLD: The Beggar and the Rich Man seem to differ
In their approach to Death.

DISCRETION: It seems that I'm the only one

Remaining in the play.

WORLD: Well, faith's the thing that sticks to me the most.

DISCRETION: Although that's true, I'm sure—
That faith can never die, I can—
Because I'm not Faith itself, I'm not Religion,
But just someone who chose that path.
And before the voices call for me,
I'll call myself toward the grave, and shut
My life away so as to bring an end
To our play for the moment—since I know
Our Author will write it all again tomorrow.
Let's hope that in tomorrow's comedy,
Everyone avoids the errors that they made today.
(The Globe of the Earth closes.)

AUTHOR: I offered punishment or reward to those
Who played their parts in worse or better style,
And now they'll see exactly what I meant by that.
(The Celestial Globe closes, with the AUTHOR inside.)

WORLD: Well—the play was awfully short!
But then the play of human life is never long;
The more so when you realize it all comes down
To just an entrance and an exit!
I can report they've left the theater now,
Reduced to their essential matter.
As dust they'll scatter, just as they arrived.
Now as a good stage manager, my job
Is to make sure I get back everything I gave them.
I'll station myself right here in this door,
To make sure my ghosts have not contrived
To steal any props or little scraps of costume.
As dust they'll scatter, just as they arrived.
(Enter the KING.)
Tell me, what part did you play?
You're the first one to come back.

KING: What's this—does the World forget me so quickly?
I've only just departed.

WORLD: The World, I'm afraid, has indeed forgotten you.

KING: We stood right there; right there, you gave me
All the gold the Sun could offer—there you
Dressed me in light and splendor, and the arms

Of dawn cradled me as I was born,
Until at last I came to lie in the arms of night.
Upon this stage I ruled, judged, commanded,
Reigned over lands without number;
There I found, inherited, acquired a royal
Store of memories; I had brave and loyal subjects
By the score; many victories were mine;
And I wrote the histories that made them famous.
I gave my favorites jewels, gold, and more;
And under rich embroidered tapestries,
I dressed in purples, clutched my scepters, wore
My laurels.

WORLD: Well, it's time to leave it all behind,
Take off the crown, your majesty is gone,
Get rid of it, it's lost, forgotten.
(The KING takes off his gear.)
Give back the trappings of your life.
The purple that you crowed about will soon
Be dressing someone else. You'll find
You're done with clutching scepters, wearing laurels.

KING: Didn't you give me all those ornaments?
Why are you taking back what you gave?

WORLD: Because they weren't a gift, no, they were lent
To you so you could play your part.

KING: What's left to me for having been the King?

WORLD: Only this: a punishment or a reward.
Our Author will decide which one, according
To how well you played your part. Don't look at me,
As I suspect you are, to know how well you did:
Just make sure I get back everything I gave you.
(Enter BEAUTY.)

WORLD: What did you play?

BEAUTY: Elegance and Beauty.

WORLD: What was it that I gave you?

BEAUTY: Beauty, simply perfect beauty.

WORLD: Well, where is it?

BEAUTY: It remained behind—in the grave.

WORLD: Great Nature herself is all amazed
To see how short a time beauty lasts.

It seems to end almost before it begins.
But even if I wanted to preserve it, I'm not able.
Now see, the King has left his majesty with me;
His luster and his greatness hang right here.
But real Beauty cannot be acquired;
It breathes its final breath and it's expired.
Look in this mirror.
BEAUTY: I've seen myself already.
WORLD: Where's your loveliness now? The graceful gowns
I lent you for your role? I'd like them back.
BEAUTY: The grave consumed them all.
There I lost my jasmine and my corals;
There my roses vanished; there my ivories
And my crystals all were shattered.
My plans and proclamations were erased,
Not that it mattered.
There I lost my colors and my rings,
All my sunlit splendor was eclipsed;
Down there you cannot find
Even the merest shadows of these things.
(Enter the WORKER.)
WORLD: Hey, rascal—what was your part?
WORKER: If I'm a rascal it's because you made me one,
So it shouldn't surprise you.
I'm the laborer, the farming kind.
The one with blisters on his hand from cutting grain.
The kind the courtiers call all sorts of names
To put us down. The kind—although it pains
Me even more to say it—that's always being called
By name—"Hey You!" "Yes, You!" or sometimes just a "Hey!"
But never "Sir" or "Friend" or even "Mister."
WORLD: Well, let's have what I gave you.
WORKER: You—what did you ever give me?
WORLD: I gave you a hoe.
WORKER: Oh, what a thing of beauty, what a treasure
That turned out to be!
WORLD: For good or ill, that's what you got.
WORKER: It would break the strongest heart to know
That no matter how you covet it, you can't

Even take along your hoe when you
Depart this awful world.
(Enter the RICH MAN and the BEGGAR.)
WORLD: Who's coming now?
RICH MAN: One who never wanted to leave you.
BEGGAR: And one who didn't want to stay.
WORLD: Why are you two taking
Such divergent points of view?
RICH MAN: Because I was rich and powerful.
BEGGAR: Because I was poor and miserable.
WORLD: Give me back your jewels.
(RICH MAN takes them off.)
BEGGAR: Now look—I'm lucky I don't have to feel
So bad about leaving the world.
(Enter the CHILD.)
WORLD: You came to the theater to play a part—
Why didn't you appear?
CHILD: Before my life began it ended in the grave.
There I leave behind everything you gave.
(Enter DISCRETION.)
WORLD: When you were among the living,
What did you ask for?
DISCRETION: I asked for religion and obedience,
Discipline and abstinence.
WORLD: Well, leave them in my hands; and I'll make sure
No one steals your coat of arms.
DISCRETION: I don't think so; sacrifices, love, and prayers
Don't remain back in the world—I have to take them with me.
WORLD: You're right.
Your good works cannot be taken from you—
They're all that you can carry from the world.
KING: If only I hadn't ruled so many kingdoms!
BEAUTY: If only I hadn't desired so much beauty!
RICH MAN: If only I hadn't had so many riches!
WORKER: If only I'd worked harder!
BEGGAR: If only I had suffered more quietly!
WORLD: Too late! It shouldn't surprise you that your
Ledger's closed and done with after death.
Now that I've reclaimed great majesties,

Erased beauty's perfections, exploded vanities,
Made hoes and scepters equal, it's time to go
Directly to the Theater of Truths—
For this has been the Theater of Fictions.
KING: Why did you welcome us so differently
From how you say good-bye?
WORLD: Let me tell you why.
When somebody has something welcome
To receive, he holds his hands like this;
When it's something that he'd just as soon avoid,
He throws his hands up just like this;
And it's the same way with the world—
When it's your luck to be born, the cradle
Opens to receive you; and this same cradle,
Turning once again, becomes your tomb.
So the cradle bids you welcome, the tomb says farewell.
BEGGAR: Well, since this world is such a tyrant,
Throwing us out from deep within as soon
As we arrive, let's go to this grand dinner party
That our Author has offered us, where we'll receive
Our just rewards.
KING: You dare insult my power, by going in front?
Have you so quickly forgotten the days
When you were my vassal, you miserable beggar?
BEGGAR: You're done with that part, and now we're all equal.
All dressed in the costume of the grave.
What we were before doesn't matter now.
RICH MAN: How can you forget that yesterday
You begged for alms from me?
BEGGAR: How can you forget
That you didn't give me any?
BEAUTY: I'm more beautiful than all of you
And better off than most—don't forget that.
DISCRETION: In terms of wardrobe, now we're all the same—
A shroud is a great equalizer.
RICH MAN: Are you cutting in front of me, rascal?
WORKER: Put aside your crazy ambitions—
You're dead! You are a shadow,
Even though you used to shine

Just like the Sun.

RICH MAN: I don't know why I feel like such a coward
     When I imagine that I'll see the Author now.

BEGGAR: Author of the heavens and the Earth,
     Now your whole company of actors
     Who played this little comedy of human life,
     Has come for the great dinner party that you offered us.
     Open up the curtains of your canopied throne.
     (While MUSIC plays, the Celestial Globe is once again revealed, and within
     it a table with chalice and Host; the AUTHOR is seated there. Enter there,
     THE WORLD.)

AUTHOR: This table, where I have the bread
     That Heaven adores and even Hell respects,
     Awaits you; but now it's time to learn
     Who will rise to dine with me.
     Those who didn't play their parts in such a way
     As to save themselves—with knowledge and remembrance
     Of the good that's always present,
     Even in the midst of suffering—
     Must leave my company.
     Now Beggar and Discretion, rise.
     Come, and take your place in glory.
     (THEY rise and join the AUTHOR.)

BEGGAR: How blessed I am! Who ever has endured
     More pain and anguish—but pain, endured for God,
     Becomes glorious!

DISCRETION: And I, who made so many penitential acts,
     Am blessed a thousand times, ending at this table.
     Here, even crying a confession is a blessed state.

KING: What about me, Lord?
     I know I acted rather pompously,
     But somewhere in amongst the grandeur
     Didn't I beg for pardon?
     Well, why don't you pardon me?

AUTHOR: Beauty and Power: what to do with them?
     Even though they suffered from vainglory,
     At least they had the good sense to lament it—
     They will ascend, but not right now—
     Likewise with the worker, who even though

He didn't help the beggar, it was not
For lack of wanting to do good—he had
The best intentions, and he seemed to be
Attempting to help you help yourself.

WORKER: That was my intention—that she leave bad company behind.

AUTHOR: And for this, you'll be rewarded.
Despite the errors of your ways,
Because you begged for mercy for your sins,
You three—Beauty, King, and Worker—will spend
Some time in Purgatory before you dine with me.

DISCRETION: Divine Author—in the middle of my anguish,
The King offered me his hand—and now,
I must give him mine.

(SHE gives her hand to the KING, and HE ascends to the table.)

AUTHOR: And I hereby remit the punishment,
Because this gentle soul speaks for you;
The centuries fly by, time runs, your sentence
Is expired.

CHILD: If I made no mistakes in playing my part,
Why don't you reward me, Great Lord?

AUTHOR: Because you did no action in the world;
So now you receive neither reward nor punishment.
You'll go into that darkened place, feeling nothing,
Until finally, in time, you are born into sin.

CHILD: Now, fearful night, like a dream, takes me blindly,
Feeling no pain and experiencing no glory.

RICH MAN: If Beauty and the King, with all their vanity,
Just cried a bit for mercy and—surprise!—
They were forgiven—if the worker, whose
Whining and complaining could wring tears
From hardest rock—if they're now trembling
In the powerful presence of the Author—
Well, it's time I got there too, because
There's nowhere else to hide from your stern judgment.
Author!

AUTHOR: Why do you call me that?
Even though I am your Author,
You're better off not naming me.
You should fear to say my name.

You are not permitted to remain in my company.
I expel you from it. Descend!
Descend to where your ambitions will be met
For all eternity with pain and anguish.
RICH MAN: Oh my God! In fire I fall, dragging my shadow
So huge and fearsome that it blocks me from myself,
And hard rocks hem me in on every side,
Down, down into this dark cave.
DISCRETION: I have infinite glory.
BEAUTY: I hope to have such blessing.
WORKER: Beauty, when it comes to hope,
You don't hold a candle to me.
RICH MAN: I have no hope, for all eternity.
CHILD: And never any glory now for me.
AUTHOR: You've seen four ways of ending:
The Beggar, the King, the Rich Man, and the Child.
Just one pertains to each of you.
One life, one death.
So to conclude:
Rise, now, Beauty. Worker, rise.
Come joyously to this mysterious table,
Because now, in return for all your labors
You deserve a share of glory.
(THEY go up to the table.)
BEAUTY: What good fortune!
WORKER: What solace!
RICH MAN: What misfortune!
KING: What a victory!
RICH MAN: What pain!
DISCRETION: What relief!
BEGGAR: What sweetness!
RICH MAN: What a poison!
CHILD: All this glory, all this pain;
And none of it for me.
AUTHOR: Sweet voices ring out,
In Hell, in Heaven, and on Earth,
All at once sweet voices ring out
In praise and harmony.
(Shawms play, and many VOICES sing the "Tantum Ergo" of St. Thomas Aquinas, composed for Vespers during the Corpus Christi festival.)

WORLD: Our play is over. Since we've shown you all
    Of life itself, from A to Z, with punishment
    And pardon all on view,
    I hope it's not too much to ask
    A pardon, here and now,
    From all of you.

THE END OF THE GREAT THEATER OF THE WORLD

Only about one-eighth of Calderón's body of work is readily available in English, and much of that will only suit the diligent student with no intention toward theatrical production. Translations into English saw an industrious beginning in the nineteenth century, took a pause while naturalism asserted its brief reign, and gained momentum once again beginning in the 1950s thanks to notable efforts over the last several decades by Edwin Honig, Roy Campbell, the team of Kenneth Muir and Ann L. Mackenzie, Gwynne Edwards, and Adrian Mitchell, among others. In order to create a context for the present volume of translations, it might be useful to spend a moment with several of the more significant existing English versions, past and present.

Nineteenth Century Beginnings

If arguments about translation strategy tend still to be framed in the tension between the "letter" and the "spirit" of the original, with "fidelity" the goal of both camps, in the second half of the nineteenth century two translators, Denis Florence Mac Carthy and Edward FitzGerald, stake out positions at the opposite extremes of the question. Mac Carthy heroically attempts to match Calderón's original metrical schemes. The result is a sometimes breathtakingly complex perturbation of an idea to fit a meter or place a rhyme. One marvels at the effort with affectionate and admiring despair, as in this speech from the first act of *The Constant Prince (El príncipe constante)*:

PHENIX
Ah! No more can gladden me
Sunny shores, or dark projections,
Where in emulous reflections

Blend the rival land and sea;
When, alike in charms and powers,
Where the woods and waves are meeting—
Flowers with foam are seen competing—
Sparkling foam with snow-white flowers;[1]

Remarkably, rhyme for rhyme (the scheme is a-b-b-a) and, somewhat less precisely, beat for beat, Mac Carthy reproduces his source. Calderón's lines are more varied in stress and rhythm than the matching English tetrameters, though Mac Carthy is just as strict in syllabic count. For a while, and in the proper context (as above, a beautiful lady musing on the waning power of nature's beauty to soothe her pain), such profusion of rhyme and strongly accented meter can serve a literary purpose without becoming too annoying.

When, however, the subject turns more serious, Calderón, like Shakespeare, often "opens up" the form, and Mac Carthy has difficulty adapting his music to the more direct and urgent speech that the dramatic situation demands. In the following passage from the second act, the Moorish general, Muley, wracked with remorse at the treatment his friend Fernando (the Constant Prince) has suffered as a prisoner, tells him of a plan he has devised for his escape. To create this new tonality Calderón uses assonance (repetition of vowel sounds without matching consonants, e.g., "wine" and "high" as opposed to "wine" and "fine") or what we might call "slant rhyme" (a loose variation of assonance) more often than true rhyme. He also employs a more varied meter, still on the baseline of the predominant octosyllable but with great freedom in both rhythm and syllabic count. Mac Carthy attempts to respond to this as well, but the effect seems forced and the diction mechanical:

MULEY
I know not how first to speak of,
How to think of, such a crime!—
How to tell the pain I've suffered
From this fickle frown of Time!
For this ruin, this injustice!
This dark boon that Fortune grants,
This, the world's most sad example, —
This inconstancy of chance!
But I run some risk if people
See me speaking here to thee,
For, without respect to treat you
Is the King's proclaimed decree;[2]

In the end, Mac Carthy's always diligent and occasionally inspired work is to be admired from a distance, on a library shelf; it cannot be expected (and was probably not intended) to serve in a theatrical context, but it remains a fascinating object lesson in the perils of a translation strategy that tries to be too faithful to one aspect of the source at the expense of nearly all others.

Edward FitzGerald openly substitutes his own poetic and dramatic judgment for Calderón's, hoping to improve on the latter's "bombast . . . conceits . . . violations of the probable . . . repetitions . . . so much, in short, that is not Calderón's own better self, but concession to private haste and public taste."[3] FitzGerald's *Life Is A Dream* is so far removed (and, would he say, improved?) from *La vida es sueño* that he titles it (slightly misquoting Prospero's great utterance) *Such Stuff As Dreams Are Made Of.* The cadences of Segismundo's final speech—which is almost four times as long in FitzGerald as in the original—swell to a crescendo of romantic vibrato that Calderón would likely not recognize:

> . . . And, whether wake or dreaming, this I know,
> How dream-wise human glories come and go;
> Whose momentary tenure not to break,
> Walking as one who knows he soon may wake
> So fairly carry the full cup, so well
> Disorder'd insolence and passion quell,
> That there be nothing after to upbraid
> Dreamer or doer in the part he play'd,
> Whether To-morrow's dawn shall break the spell,
> Or the Last Trumpet of the eternal Day,
> When Dreaming with the Night shall pass away.[4]

There is a certain grand energy, a nineteenth-century sort of brass-band confidence in rhythm, rhyme, and big effects in both Mac Carthy and FitzGerald's work that aligns them much more closely with their particular time than with Calderón's (as we currently understand it) or our own. This temporal dissonance makes us realize that even if these older versions had found the artful combination of fidelity to the source text and beauty in the target language that characterizes a successful translation, they would not now be useful as production texts for the contemporary theater. Even the reader has to pause from time to time to perform, as it were, an act of translating the translation. Obviously a stage production leaves no time for this kind of secondary translation to occur.

Modern Translations

It is always dangerous (and perhaps a bit ungracious) to suggest deficiencies in other translations by way of making a case for one's own, and yet it is a procedure that seems to tempt most practitioners. I admire and have learned from each of the translators cited below; still there are a few things that can be said about the current state of Calderón in English that may help explain his lack of exposure on the American stage.

Edwin Honig is a gifted poet and a keen reader of Calderón's imagery, and his texts are very beautiful, as the following excerpt from Act Three of *Life Is a Dream (La vida es sueño)* demonstrates. Here Segismundo wonders if his pending liberation from his tower prison is just another illusion:

> Heavenly God, do you wish me
> once again to dream of grandeur
> which time must rip asunder?
> Do you wish me once again
> to glimpse half-lit among the shadows
> that pomp and majesty
> which vanish with the wind?
>   . . .
> Knowing as I do that life's a dream,
> I say to you, be gone and leave me,
> vague shadows, who now pretend
> these dead senses have a voice
> and body, when the truth is they are
> voiceless and incorporeal.
> Because I'm through with blown-up majesty,
> I'm through with pompous fantasies
> and with all illusions scattered
> by the smallest puff of wind,
> like the flowering almond tree
> surrendering without the slightest
> warning to the dawn's first passing breeze,
> which dulls and withers the fine
> rose-lit beauty of its frilly blossoms.[5]

I quote this passage at some length because it is characteristic of what is, in my judgment, the best sustained attempt to date to capture Calderón in English. The verse flows easily from three to four to five beat lines, responding to (but not, thankfully, *matching*) the variety in the original prosody. There is just enough assonance (and occasionally a true rhyme, though always separated by several lines) to remind the ear that there is musical value to the speech. Yet accomplished as Honig's texts invariably are, they too often err, in my judgment, on the side of poetic diction rather than theatrical energy. They remain a superb *reader's* Calderón (even better than Roy Campbell's widely anthologized version of *Life Is A Dream*) but place certain obstacles, born of their very virtues, in the way of satisfactory production.

The team of Kenneth Muir and Ann L. Mackenzie strike a reasonable balance between accuracy and speakability, but seem to me to suffer from predictability. They develop a reliable iambic pentameter line and hew to it faithfully, thus negating a major feature of Golden Age dramatic poetry—its remarkable variety of meter, line length, and rhyme scheme—resulting in a curiously flat tone. The rhythmic insistence of the following passage from *Mañanas de Abril y Mayo (Mornings of April and May)* offers an example:

JUAN
I'm not afraid of death and therefore do not
Protect my life; and since misfortunes long
Companioned me, I now have ceased to fear them.
You know already of my luckless love
Since you're a neighbor of Doña Ana de Lara,
That divine lady with a glorious mind
And crowned with beauty. I was happy then.
I lived exulting in my lofty hopes
Proud of her favor . . . [6]

Clear, readable, and accurate, this language nevertheless does not leap off the page, and misses some of the verbal variety, energy, and sense of forward motion that characterizes much of Spanish Golden Age drama.

The translator Nicholas G. Round cautions against a too-faithful adoption of the English iambic pentameter despite (or perhaps because of) its familiarity through the works of Shakespeare: "Sooner or later . . . it becomes apparent that the translator who is trying to sound like Shakespeare is not Shakespeare after all, and the wages of pastiche is loss of credibility as speech."[7] I would not accuse Muir and Mackenzie of "trying to sound like Shakespeare," and in fact I have resorted to a similar verse form in various passages of these translations. Round's general point, however, is an important one. It helps explain why, even though the Muir/Mackenzie translations do make fine study texts and are without doubt a valuable resource, by and large they lack the "credibility as speech" that would stimulate successful production.

Adrian Mitchell, like Honig an excellent poet, goes out of his way to be stageworthy, with the result that his texts are so free that he quite correctly calls them adaptations, not translations. His version of *The Great Theatre of the World*, for example, interpolates songs and eliminates two characters entirely, cutting or reassigning their lines and functions.[8] Perhaps to capture the allegorical feeling of the original, Mitchell relies heavily on rhyme, including extended passages of couplets that end up sounding quite a bit like a modernized English mystery play:

BEGGAR
This Beggar role, well I realize
That it seems right and proper in your eyes,
But if you didn't mind, sir, on the whole,
I'd rather swap it for another role.
All right, Lord, since I have to play
The beggar, there's one more thing to say.
Why, Lord, did it have to be me?
For the others this play's a comedy
But for me it's a bloody tragedy.[9]

At first glance this simple, singsong, highly actable verse seems to point the reader to an appropriately analogous (and perhaps somewhat more familiar) dramatic form, thus rendering the play more accessible to English-speaking audiences. But the Calderónian *auto* is, I would argue, both linguistically and thematically more sophisticated than the typical medieval morality, and therefore better served by a translation strategy that does not enforce such an overt and limiting analogy.

Mitchell's other texts (*The Mayor of Zalamea* and *Life's A Dream*) were also created in a collaborative production environment—the excellent Shakespearean director John Barton, in fact, shares co-adaptor credit on *Dream*. They are lively and playable, and if they sacrifice some of Calderón's nuances or alter his structural design, they have served as the occasion for notable productions in the United Kingdom by the National Theatre and the Royal Shakespeare Company.

Choices, Gains, and Losses

Because Barton and Mitchell's version of Calderón's most famous play is, in my view, an excellent text for theatrical production, it bears close scrutiny as an example of the gains and losses involved in the consistent application of a strong stylistic choice by a translator or adaptor. The following excerpt from a famous speech in *Life's A Dream* (as they title it) will serve as a test case.

On the positive side of the ledger, this speech (as is true of the entire translation) displays an inventive, free, and engagingly theatrical response to the original. It is rhythmical without being too dogmatically committed to blank verse; it provides clear emotional access to the character's situation "in the moment" and therefore is highly actable. Here is Segismundo in Act One, thinking through the injustice of his captivity:

A bird is born, a swallow,
Little and damp and shaken,
It grows so bright and dark and feathery,
A spray of flowers on the wing.
It slices through the air so speedily
That it outflies imagining
And leaves its nest forsaken.
Then why can't I
Be like a swallow flying free?

Segismundo goes on, in three subsequent stanzas, to compare his situation—his lack of freedom—with that of "a fish . . . a salmon," "a spring . . . a stream," "a beast . . . a leopard," until he finally erupts:

Born out of rage,
Eaten with rage,
I'm a volcano. Watch me bleed.
Give me a knife—I'll show you surgery
And wrench out, raggedy and raw,
Bits of my heart. Captivity!
So is there some reason or some law
Denies me the one thing I need,
Which God gave swallows and salmon too,
And beasts and leopards: to be free?[10]

Though there is much to admire in this excerpt, a few departures from Calderón's construction of the speech may be called into question. First, Barton and Mitchell have changed the order of Segismundo's comparisons. In the original, the progression is: bird, brute (or beast), fish, stream; the adaptation has: bird, fish, stream, beast. At the end of the speech, Calderón recapitulates the comparisons in reverse order (stream, fish, brute, bird), while the adaptation repeats them in the original progression. Calderón does not name the specific kinds of animals, while Barton and Mitchell make the bird a swallow, the fish a salmon, and the beast a leopard.

Finally, and to my mind most significantly, the translators introduce verbal variety where the original employs strict repetition. Calderón ends each of Segismundo's stanzas with a repeated refrain in which he declares himself superior to the items he has named and ends by asking, with a deep sense of injustice, "And . . . I have less liberty?" (*¿y . . . tengo menos libertad?*). The adaptation, while repeating the word *free* at the end of each stanza, eliminates Segismundo's insistent existential questioning; instead, he simply asks for the same freedoms he observes in the common creatures of his world, and uses verbs descriptive of those creatures to finish his reductive similes ("Then why can't I / Be like a salmon swimming free?"). The net effect, perhaps unintentionally, is the articulation of a smaller idea, less concerned with states of being and more with the immediate problem of freedom of movement in the physical world.

Calderón, by contrast, has given Segismundo a beautifully organic pattern for the development of the four key images in the speech that combines the character's struggle with the idea of captivity with a more capacious notion of the freedom of the whole self. Beginning with the most obvious symbol of freedom, the bird, he progresses through other orders of the animal kingdom and finally reaches the inanimate world of the stream. Each image ends in a specific comparison of "*más*/more" (or in one case "*mejor*/better") and "*menos*/less", as here at the end of the "bird" stanza: "And I, although I have more soul / Have less liberty?" (*¿y teniendo yo más alma / tengo menos libertad?*).

The development of these comparisons through four iterations leads to a rising sense of injury. Comparing himself finally to a *stream*, an inanimate natural object, Segismundo asks: "And I, although I have more life / Have less liberty?" (*¿y teniendo yo más vida / tengo menos libertad?*). The absurdity of this dissonance creates the volcanic eruption, which Barton and Mitchell render beautifully (though with added special effects such as "watch me bleed", "raggedy and raw"), after which Segismundo recapitulates *in reverse* the images that brought him to such an explosive passion. His temporarily disordered mind struggles toward order once again, working his way back image by image to where he started. The adaptors' decision to repeat the images in the same order in which they were first uttered rather than observing Calderón's inversion diminishes this important verbal cue to the shape—what an actor might call the "score"—of the speech.

The presence of significant repetitive patterning, the use of purposefully universal images (bird, not swallow; fish, not salmon), and the somewhat less emotionally raw tonality of Calderón's diction as compared to Barton and Mitchell's give us a less sentimental, more thoughtful picture of the character. Such a Segismundo, I would claim, is more interesting to follow on his journey toward *desengaño* and kingship, as we see his quality of mind from the very first; yet there is no mistaking the drive and theatrical energy of Barton and Mitchell's text, so as in all cases of translation, there is a tradeoff to be negotiated. The sum of all these individually minor changes—even when expressed in language as vigorous and stageworthy as in this adaptation—is a blurring of the character's thought process and dramatic action, which must have consequences in performance, especially as the action progresses and Segismundo's state of mind becomes one of the central themes as well as an engine of the plot. An irony emerges: in the successful pursuit of stageworthy language, the adaptors have, at least in this speech, diminished a deeper sense of stageworthiness, altering or ignoring some of the signifiers through which the actor (and the audience) will build a sense of character and story.

Lest Ye Be Judged . . .

Of course a particular directorial/dramaturgical approach to a given play may require and justify any number of such authorial interventions. The texts in this volume have all been tested in production, and in each one (except the comparatively brief *Great Theater)* I have, in collaboration with directors, dramaturgs, and actors, made some small and, we would claim, judicious cuts in pursuit of clarity and forward motion.

Here is an example of one such strategy: one early passage in *The Phantom Lady* contains a string of topical and classical allusions that elevate the obscurity of the original to the impenetrable; so, preserving the spirit, I have dared to cut a passage or two of elaboration.

A street. Enter DON MANUEL and COSME, who have been traveling.

MANUEL
We missed it by an hour—Madrid's great festival
In honor of the Prince's baptism.

275

COSME

The way things are, an hour late
Is all you have to be.
If Pyramus had shown up an hour earlier,
He wouldn't have found his Thisbe dead.
And Romeo and Juliet—an hour
Might have made the difference for them!
But then of course we wouldn't have
Those famous plays to enjoy,
And that would be a shame . . .

     . . .

The original text contains several less accessible references to illustrate the perils of an hour's tardiness: Pyramus and Thisbe are followed hard upon by Tarquin and Lucretia, and Hero deciding whether to throw herself from her tower, which sends Cosme off on an extended discourse about the playwright Antonio Mira de Amescua, a then-famous but now-obscure older contemporary of Calderón's.[11] Cosme's festival of Golden Age intertextuality continues with a reference to the Moor Abindarráez, who appears in *Don Quixote,* before he returns to his main theme of reaching their lodgings in time to avoid being left out on the street.

I have retained one of the original classical allusions (Pyramus and Thisbe) and, finding the audience in a Shakespearean frame of mind via the connection to *A Midsummer Night's Dream,* for Tarquin and Lucretia I substitute Romeo and Juliet, a more familiar pair of stage lovers for whom timing is also everything. Cosme's subsequent comment about the "famous plays" picks up on the Mira de Amescua reference, allowing preservation of at least a hint of the meta-theatricality in his speech—a characteristic that will recur more vigorously later on—while eliminating references that would be impossible for an American theater audience to understand. And though the speech is quite a few lines shorter in my version, it remains discursive enough to modern ears so that a joke imbedded in the structure can still be realized: one reason to fear they might miss their bed and board is Cosme's prolix chatter.

For such acts of infidelity I seek absolution by association. As translator, editor, and scholar of the Golden Age, Victor F. Dixon, in his essay "Translating Spanish Plays," notes:

> . . . an apt allusion or quotation may pass unnoticed or seem incomprehensible if rendered word for word; we shall serve the author best if we alert our readers or audience to his wit by devising an analogous but comprehensible reference.[12]

In the main, I have tried to preserve the structural intentions and larger rhythms found in Calderón's texts, believing that a play communicates on many levels beyond the denotative meaning. The relative weight, tone, and tempo of the scenes, the patterns of dramatic action (understood both as consequential intentionality and physical manifestations on stage), the variety of intellectual distinction in the characters, and the overall design of the play's dramaturgy all bear directly on the audience's experience of the event. In all four plays in this volume I have condensed an occasional image, usually by omitting an elaboration, in pursuit of two related goals: a closer fit with Calderón's sense of pace (literal English equivalences almost always end up taking longer to speak than their Spanish originals) and clarity of dramatic intention. Where Calderón accelerates the tempo, tells a joke, or turns up the level of metaphor, I have tried to do the same.

In Search of Verse

Following the lead of distinguished pathfinders such as Honig, Mitchell, and Muir/Mackenzie, I rely on a modified blank verse in translating these plays. The dominant line is the pentameter, but I have tried to vary it enough—with frequent use of three-, four-, and six-beat lines—to avoid Round's censure of would-be Shakespeareanism. End rhyme is an infrequent visitor to these translations, but I have found it interesting to employ internal rhyme, assonance, and alliteration in passages where the original strikes my ear as requiring a more elevated, organized, or energetic verbal signature than free verse or pure blank verse might offer.

The following excerpt from Act Two of *The Constant Prince* (the same passage quoted above in the Mac Carthy version) demonstrates this variety of line length and stress pattern, and includes a couple of almost hidden internal rhymes, both "true" and assonantal. In my view, widely separated rhymes provide just enough structure to lift the diction into a higher plane without succumbing to mechanical imitation. And though the passage does not follow Calderón's versification line for line, I believe it accurately conveys the rhythmic and, more importantly, the dramatic intentionalities of the original:

MULEY
I want you to know that in my heart—
In the heart of a Moor—there's loyalty and faith.
I don't know how to begin my story.
I'm not sure I can describe how I've felt
The wild swings of fortune in the world,
The unjust devastation, the inconstant disdain,

The cruel example of the times.
And there's grave risk to me
If I'm seen talking to you here;
Because the King's decree is that no one
Is to treat you with respect. And so, I trust
My pain to speak more clearly than my voice,
And like a slave I come to throw myself
At your feet. I am yours.
I do not come, Infante, to offer you my favor,
But to pay a debt that is now due.
You gave me life; and now I come
To give it back; for doing good
Is a kind of treasure, to be hoarded
Until the need is greatest.

In *The Great Theater of the World,* a similar strategy works to convey the reflective mood of the World as he prepares to greet the "actors" who have finished playing their roles on the stage of life:

Well—the play was awfully short!
But then the play of human life is never long;
The more so when you realize it all comes down
To just an entrance and an exit.
I can report they've left the theater now,
Reduced to their essential matter.
As dust they'll scatter, just as they arrived.
Now as a good stage manager, my job
Is to get back everything I gave them.
I'll station myself right here in this door
To make sure my ghosts have not contrived
To steal any props or little scraps of costume.
As dust they'll scatter, just as they arrived.

Here I have brought the rhymes as far forward as seems possible without shifting into a more recognizable English stanza form. I have prominently repeated a refrain ("As dust they'll scatter, just as they arrived" / *polvo salgan de mí, pues polvo entraron)* in approximately the same structural relationship as in the original.

Above all, when a translator writes for the stage, theatrical reflexes should be brought to bear alongside the linguistic ones that all translators employ.

Nicholas Round frames this notion in a theory of agency, of the text accomplishing specific tasks to advance the action:

> Dramatic language is speakable to the extent that the speech acts achieve their work in context. The translation which proves to be speakable *as the play* may or may not say the things which its source text says, but it must be capable of doing those things which its source-text can do. The strategy must be one of identifying functions—not, in the abstract, meanings—in the source-language and realizing them through the target-language.[13]

While this may seem like an open invitation to adaptation or wholesale revision, I think Round is connecting to a deep sense of the speech act as the primary vehicle (in classical drama at any rate) for the dramatic action. With Lear's admonition to Cordelia that "Nothing can come from nothing. Speak again" Shakespeare renews the immortal metaphor of word as action. A translator must "speak again" the words but more importantly the action, the agency, of the original if the play is to be communicated in theatrical terms. There is, of course, another, more instinctual process also at work, which can be expressed more pointedly. In the theater, one develops a sense of what "speaks" as well as what "reads." The aim of the translations in this volume is toward what speaks.

Cuts That Cut Both Ways

As noted above, there are various small cuts and changes in these texts as printed here. In production, however, I have made or authorized significantly larger cuts than I thought appropriate for a published volume, in the expectation that these translations can also be useful in the classroom and the study. Particularly in *Life Is a Dream* and *The Constant Prince*, the demands of particular production circumstances have required additional excision.

For example, the production of *Prince* that I directed in Pittsburgh omitted entirely the ghostly physical return of Fernando bearing a flaming torch; we thought his unseen voice urging his comrades "To war, to war!" was ghost enough for a contemporary audience, and it allowed the ending to be both swifter and less partisan. But the scene is an important part of Calderón's original vision, and so is included here. We also found it necessary (and possible) to combine some of the functions of Fénix's courtly servants Rosa and Estrella into one character, Zara. Some longer expository speeches early in the play (such as Muley's description of his encounter with the Portuguese fleet) have been thinned carefully. These adaptations are carried over into the published volume, as I believe they do not materially affect the reader's perception of the totality of the work.

Similarly, in *Dream,* the original director's finely calibrated sense of dramatic urgency, and our mutual belief that the seventeenth-century appetite for repetition is lustier than our own, led to a number of significant internal cuts, though in no case was the structure or intention of a scene altered for production. I have retained some of those cuts in this version, but have restored some passages that I believe contain poetic gems or are important for the student of Calderón to encounter.

I cordially invite producers, professors, directors, and dramaturgs to be in contact regarding proposed cuts (or restorations). I have an open mind and a long list of potential suggestions. And my deepest wish for these texts is that they may help bring about more productions of these masterworks on our contemporary stages, as well as assisting a generation of students, scholars, and general readers in their encounter with one of the great voices in the history of theater and drama.

—Rick Davis
Warrenton, Virginia
January, 2008

Notes

1. Mac Carthy's translation appears in Barrett H. Clark, ed., *World Drama, Vol. Two.* This speech is on page 130.
2. Clark, *op cit.,* p. 151.
3. Edward FitzGerald, *Eight Dramas of Calderon,* p. 1.
4. FitzGerald, *op. cit.,* p. 517.
5. See Edwin Honig, *Calderón de la Barca: Six Plays,* p. 343
6. Kenneth Muir and Ann L. Mackenzie, *Three Comedies by Pedro Calderón de la Barca,* p. 75; see also their volume *Four Comedies by Calderón.*
7. Nicholas G. Round, "The Speakable and the Unspeakable," in Louise and Peter Fothergill-Payne, *Prologue to Performance: Spanish Classical Theater Today,* p. 127.
8. The missing characters are the Law of Grace, who functions metatheatrically as Prompter, and Discretion (or Religion), who adds an important voice to the play's constellation of types and serves in particular as a foil (or even a dialectical opposite) to the character of Beauty. See Adrian Mitchell, *Three Plays by Calderón de la Barca.*
9. Mitchell, *op. cit.,* p. 168.
10. Mitchell, *op. cit.,* pp. 95–96.
11. See Melveena McKendrick, *Theatre in Spain 1490–1700,* pp. 129–131
12. Victor F. Dixon, "Translating Spanish Plays," in Fothergill-Payne, *op. cit.,* p. 108.
13. In Fothergill-Payne, *op. cit.,* p. 121.

APPENDIX B
NOTES AND CREDITS ON PREMIERE
PRODUCTIONS OF THESE TRANSLATION

The Phantom Lady

Commissioned and premiered by The Bowman Ensemble, Russell Muth, artistic producer, Matt Ramsay, artistic director. Baltimore, Maryland, July–August, 1992

CAST

DON MANUEL	Bruce R. Nelson
COSME	Ron Bopst
DOÑA ANGELA	Suzy Allison
ISABEL	Johanna Cox
RODRIGO	John Benoit
DON LUIS	Matthew Ramsay
DON JUAN	Joey Scherr
DOÑA BEATRIZ	Shannon Hepburn
CLARA	Zoe Calvert

PRODUCTION STAFF

DIRECTOR	C. Russell Muth
SET DESIGNER	Danila Korogodsky
COSTUMES	Danila Korogodsky, Alisa Mandel
LIGHTING DESIGN	Glenn Stratakes
FIGHT CHOREOGRAPHERS	Paul Gallagher, Dan Curran
STAGE MANAGER	Lisa Klimczack
SET DRESSER	Geoffrey Harris

The Constant Prince

Premiered by Unseam'd Shakespeare Company, Laura Smiley, Artistic Director. Pittsburgh, Pennsylvania, May–June, 2007

CAST

DON FERNANDO, THE CONSTANT PRINCE . . . . . . Joe Domencic
DON ENRIQUE, PRINCE OF PORTUGAL . . . . .Marc Epstein
DON JUAN COUTIÑO . . . . .Brian Czarniecki
DON ALFONSO, LATER KING OF PORTUGAL . . . . . . Marc Epstein
BRITO, *A GRACIOSO* . . . . Evan Endres
KING OF FEZ . . . . .Doug Pona
MULEY, A GENERAL . . . . .Nate Jedrzewski
FÉNIX, INFANTA OF FEZ . . . . .Deanna Brookens
TARUDANTE, LATER KING OF MOROCCO . . . . Parag Gohel
ZARA . . . . Jennifer Koegler
ENSEMBLE . . . . Evan Endres, Parag Gohel, Jennifer Koegler

PRODUCTION STAFF

PRODUCER . . . . Laura Smiley
DIRECTOR . . . . .Rick Davis
SCENIC AND LIGHTING DESIGNER . . . . .Gordon Phetteplace
COSTUME DESIGNER . . . . Marissa Miskanin
SOUND DESIGNER . . . . .Mark Whitehead
STAGE MANAGER . . . . .Stephanie Brauner
PROPERTIES . . . . Louise Phetteplace
PERCUSSIONIST . . . . Bethany Vahabzadeh

Life Is a Dream

First (literal) version commissioned by Voice and Vision Theater, Jean Wagner, artistic director. New York, New York. The present version created for University of Minnesota-Duluth Department of Theatre. February, 2007

CAST

ROSAURA	Brittany Parker
CLARÍN	Brian Kess
SEGISMUNDO	Eric Johnson
CLOTALDO	Tyler Sahnow
ASTOLFO	Leigh Wakeford
ESTRELLA	Jessica Davis
BASILIO	Jed Dixon
CHORUS	Dylan Croeker, Kinsey Diment, Phillip Jents, Scott Mallace, Helen Rogers, Dani Stock

PRODUCTION STAFF

DIRECTOR	Rachel Katz Carey
ASSISTANT DIRECTOR/CHOREOGRAPHER/ VOCAL ARRANGER	Rebecca Katz Harwood
SCENIC DESIGNER	Lauren Meister
LIGHTING DESIGNER	James Eischen
COSTUME DESIGNER	Laura Piotrowski
SOUND DESIGNER	Mark Harvey
MAKEUP DESIGNER	Megan Pelowski
STAGE MANAGER	Samantha Lavell
MUSICIANS	Patrick Carrol, Martha Gagliardi, Nick Gosen, Matt Weyer

Premiere production at George Mason University, Department of Theater, Fairfax, Virginia, February, 2002. First published in *Theater*, vol. 34, no. 1, 2004

CAST

AUTHOR . . . . .Julia Wiedeman
WORLD . . . . .David Burns
KING . . . . .Brandon Mace
DISCRETION . . . . .Bettiann King
LAW OF GRACE . . . . .Erica Wilmore
BEAUTY . . . . .Marisa Davison
RICH MAN . . . . .Robert Winter
WORKER . . . . .Josh McCarthy
BEGGAR . . . . .Maria Rio
CHILD . . . . .Taylor Coffman
VOICES . . . . .Sky Adams, Laura Kozakowski, Kylie Johnston
THE FOUR ELEMENTS* . . . . .Jessica Belan (Fire), Rachel
      Hutchinson (Water), Zach Myers (Earth), Chris Webb (Air)

*The Elements are extra-textual, nonverbal characters used in this production.

PRODUCTION STAFF

DIRECTOR . . . . .Rick Davis
SCENIC DESIGNER . . . . .Eileen Daly
COSTUME DESIGNER . . . . Kathleen McGhee
LIGHTING DESIGNER . . . . .Bethany Thompson
COMPOSER . . . . .Rachel Sarrano
MOVEMENT STYLIST . . . . .Loren Livick
STAGE MANAGER . . . . .Ashleigh Stevens

SELECT BIBLIOGRAPHY

Spanish Texts of Calderón
The translations were prepared primarily from the following texts:

Obras Completas de Calderón de la Barca. Tomo I: Dramas. 5th ed. Ed. Angel
  Valbuena Briones. Madrid: Aguilar, 1966. (for *El príncipe constante*)
Obras Completas de Calderón de la Barca. Tomo II: Comedias. Ed. Angel
  Valbuena Briones. Madrid: Aguilar, 1960. (for *La dama duende*)
La dama duende, e-text, ed. Vern Williamsen. Association for Hispanic
  Classical Theatre. http://www.comedias.org/calderon/Damdue.html
La vida es sueño, edición de Ciriaco Morón. Madrid: Ediciones Cátedra, 1981
La vida es sueño, e-text, ed. Vern Williamsen. Association for Hispanic
  Classical Theatre.
  http://www.coh.arizona.edu/spanish/comedia/calderon/esvidsue.html
Calderón de la Barca: Autos Sacramentales. Ed. Angel Valbuena Prat. Clásicos
  Castellanos, Madrid: Espasa-Calpe, 1967. (for *El gran teatro del mundo*)

Other texts consulted for the translations and the introduction:

The Web site of the Biblioteca Virtual Miguel de Cervantes contains well-
  edited versions of all of the referenced plays in this volume. The URL is:
  http://cervantesvirtual.com/index.shtml

Translations of Calderón

Colford, William. *The Mayor of Zalamea.* Woodbury, NY: Barron's
  Educational Series, 1959.
Cruickshank, Don, and Sean Page. *Love Is No Laughing Matter (No hay burlas
  con el amor).* Bilingual edition. Warminster: Aris & Phillips, Ltd, 1986.
Edwards, Gwynne. *Calderón Plays: One.* London: Methuen, 1991.
FitzGerald, Edward. *Eight Dramas of Calderon.* London, New York:
  Macmillan, 1906.
Honig, Edwin. *Calderón de la Barca: Six Plays.* New York: IASTA Press, 1993.
Mac Carthy, Denis Florence. *The Constant Prince.* In Barrett H. Clark, ed.,
  World Drama, Vol. Two. New York: Dover Publications, 1933.

Mitchell, Adrian. *Three Plays by Calderón de la Barca*. Bristol: Longdunn Press Ltd., 1994.

Muir, Kenneth and Ann L. Mackenzie. *Three Comedies by Pedro Calderón de la Barca*. Lexington: University Press of Kentucky, 1985.

_____. *Four Comedies by Calderón*. Lexington, University Press of Kentucky, 1980.

History, Criticism, and Context

Bentley, Eric, "The Universality of the Comedia." In *Hispanic Review* 38 (1970): 147–62.

Cascardi, Anthony J. *The Limits of Illusion: A Critical Study of Calderón*. New York: Cambridge University Press, 1984.

Cook, Albert. *The Dark Voyage and the Golden Mean: a Philosophy of Comedy*. New York: W. W. Norton, 1966.

Elliott, J. H. *Imperial Spain 1469–1716*. London, New York: Penguin Group, 1990.

Fiore, Robert L. *Drama and Ethos: Natural-Law Ethics in Spanish Golden Age Theater*. Lexington: University Press of Kentucky, 1975.

Fletcher, Richard. *Moorish Spain*. Berkeley: University of California Press, 1992.

Fothergill-Payne, Louise and Peter. *Prologue to Performance: Spanish Classical Theater Today*. London, Toronto: Associated University Presses, 1991.

Frye, Northrop. *Anatomy of Criticism: Four Essays*. Princeton: Princeton University Press, 1957.

_____. *The Secular Scripture: A Study of the Structure of Romance*. Cambridge, MA: Harvard University Press, 1976.

García-Pelayo y Gross, Ramón, ed. *Gran Diccionario Español-Inglés*. Unabridged edition. Mexico City: Larousse, 1993.

Gerstinger, Heinz. *Pedro Calderón de la Barca*. New York: Frederick Ungar, 1973.

Honig, Edwin. *Calderón and the Seizures of Honor*. Cambridge, MA: Harvard University Press, 1972.

Johnston, Brian. *The Ibsen Cycle*. Rev. ed. University Park, PA: Penn State University Press, 1992.

Morales, Manuel Delgado, ed. *The Calderonian Stage: Body and Soul*. Lewisburg: Bucknell University Press, 1997. See especially Marc Vitse, "On the space of La dama duende," pp. 185–207

McCollom, William G. *The Divine Average: A View of Comedy.* Cleveland, Press of Case Western Reserve University, 1971.

McKendrick, Melveena. *Theatre in Spain 1490–1700.* Cambridge: Cambridge University Press, 1989.

Stearns, Peter N., ed. *The Encyclopedia of World History.* Boston, New York: Houghton Mifflin, 2001.

Sypher, Wylie, ed. *Comedy.* Baltimore: Johns Hopkins University Press, 1980.

Varey, J. E. "La Dama Duende de Calderón: símbolos y escenografía." In *Actas del Congreso Internacional Sobre Calderón y el teatro Español del Siglo de Oro.* Madrid, 1981.

Wardropper, Bruce, ed. *Critical Essays on the Theatre of Calderón.* New York: NYU Press, 1965.

Ziomek, Henryk. *A History of Spanish Golden Age Drama.* Lexington: University Press of Kentucky, 1984.

TRANSLATOR BIOGRAPHY

Rick Davis is Artistic Director of Theater of the First Amendment, Associate Provost, and Professor of Theater at George Mason University in Fairfax, Virginia, where he has worked since 1992. In six seasons at Baltimore's Center Stage, he worked as Resident Dramaturg and Associate Artistic Director. He was co-founder and Associate Director of the American Ibsen Theater in Pittsburgh. With Brian Johnston, he has translated five Ibsen plays that have seen productions in many leading regional theaters, colleges, and universities, and that are published by Smith and Kraus. Rick is the librettist for two works with composer Kim D. Sherman: *The Songbird and the Eagle,* an oratorio commissioned and premiered by San José Chamber Orchestra; and *Love's Comedy,* an opera based on the early Ibsen play. Active as a director of theater and opera, Rick has staged dozens of productions for professional companies across the country. His textbook, *Writing About Theatre* (with Christopher Thaiss), is used widely in college drama courses in the United States and Canada. His essays and reviews have appeared in *American Theatre, Theater, The Journal of Social History, Theater Three,* and other publications, and he has contributed to the *Columbia Encyclopedia of Modern Drama* and the *Oxford Encyclopedia of the Modern World.* Rick was educated at Lawrence University (B.A.) and the Yale School of Drama (M.F.A., D.F.A.).